MORDECAI RICHLER'S IMPERFECT
SEARCH FOR MORAL VALUES

Mordecai Richler's Imperfect Search for Moral Values

SHANA ROSENBLATT MAUER

McGill-Queen's University Press

Montreal & Kingston · London · Chicago

© McGill-Queen's University Press 2022

ISBN 978-0-2280-1201-6 (cloth)
ISBN 978-0-2280-1202-3 (paper)
ISBN 978-0-2280-1317-4 (ePDF)
ISBN 978-0-2280-1318-1 (ePUB)

Legal deposit third quarter 2022
Bibliothèque nationale du Québec

Printed in Canada on acid-free paper that is 100% ancient forest free
(100% post-consumer recycled), processed chlorine free

Publication of this book was made possible in part by the financial support of the World
Union of Jewish Studies.

Funded by the   Financé par le
Government   gouvernement
of Canada   du Canada

Canada Council Conseil des arts
for the Arts   du Canada

האיגוד העולמי
למדעי היהדות
WORLD UNION OF
JEWISH STUDIES

We acknowledge the support of the Canada Council for the Arts.

Nous remercions le Conseil des arts du Canada de son soutien.

Library and Archives Canada Cataloguing in Publication

Title: Mordecai Richler's imperfect search for moral values / Shana Rosenblatt Mauer.

Names: Mauer, Shana Rosenblatt, author.

Description: Includes bibliographical references and index.

Identifiers: Canadiana (print) 20220181020 | Canadiana (ebook) 20220181179 |
ISBN 9780228012023 (paper) | ISBN 9780228012016 (cloth) | ISBN 9780228013174
(ePDF) | ISBN 9780228013181 (ePUB)

Subjects: LCSH: Richler, Mordecai, 1931-2001—Criticism and interpretation.

Classification: LCC PS8535.I38 Z73 2022 | DDC C813/.54—dc23

This book was typeset by Marquis Interscript in 10.5/13 Sabon.

Contents

Acknowledgments vii

Introduction 3

1 Ordinary Jewish Values 22

2 Richler's Jewish Hero Figures 47

3 Heroes: Not Just Avengers 77

4 Hero Figures and Special Pleading 97

5 Anti-heroic Canada 131

6 Culture and Moral Values 161

Conclusion 183

Notes 193

Bibliography 203

Index 217

Acknowledgments

I would like to thank Leona Toker of the Hebrew University for her tireless guidance. I was inspired throughout the writing of this work by her meticulous scholarship and generous mentoring. She was and continues to be a model of academic and personal excellence.

Ariela Friedman initially encouraged me to research the novels of Mordecai Richler and I am indebted to her for providing me with insightful feedback on my work. From the outset, Norm Ravvin was an important sounding board for my ideas. I am grateful to him for his judicious reading of large sections of this work and for the support and assistance he has always given unfailingly.

I would like to express gratitude to the late Emily Budick and to Eli Lederhendler for having faith in this project at an early stage and offering important guidance and direction at different junctures.

I have benefited significantly from the support and collegial opportunities that have been provided by the Halbert Centre for Canadian Studies, Hebrew University, the Israel Association for Canadian Studies, and the International Council for Canadian Studies. I am grateful, too, for their assistance.

This work would not have been possible without the early, steadfast vision of my first editor, Mark Abley, who shepherded the preliminary stages of this book with heartening determination. His successor, Richard Ratzlaff, has brought equal wisdom and enthusiasm to this book and his efforts to bring it to fruition have been invaluable. I would also like to thank Kathleen Fraser and Joanne Richardson for seeing the book through to the final stages of production.

My thanks go to my cousin Howard Ehrlich, who died far too prematurely, for his tireless, careful proofreading of this work. I thank my children, Ariel, Adin, Elan, and Yona, for their understanding and good cheer during the long journey that resulted in this book. And, of course, all of this would not have been possible without my husband, Tzvi Mauer, who provided me with back-up of every kind along the way.

MORDECAI RICHLER'S IMPERFECT
SEARCH FOR MORAL VALUES

Introduction

A story about Mordecai Richler is legend in the extended Richler family. More than a few years after he had broken with the extensive Richler clan in Montreal, Richler chose to attend the Sunday morning bar mitzvah luncheon of the son of one of his cousins. Numbered among this sprawling family were several Hasidim, followers of the Lubavitcher Rebbe, who advised his followers to encourage every Jew to perform biblical commandments – in particular to persuade Jewish men to don phylacteries, a ritual item with leather straps that one wraps around the arm and head. As Richler sat there amidst the vast assembly of his relations, typically taciturn, cousins tried to cheer him. He remained stoic. Then one, a Lubavitcher, indeed suggested that Richler put on phylacteries. Richler grimaced. The cousin persisted. Then Richler struck a deal. He would put on phylacteries if the cousin's son would drink a full snifter of scotch. The son, as resolute as his father, readily agreed. The scotch was ingested and phylacteries were donned. Awestruck, the Richlers observed their wayward cousin. As he sat there, leather straps twined around his arm and head, he wept, openly (Wolobromsky).

The anecdote provides no real insights. It does, however, offer a parable for the kind of writer Mordecai Richler was. Caustic, harsh, and ironic one moment, he could instantly shift into poignancy, observing with intelligence and feeling the mechanisms that propel the most intimate of human relationships. He was often belligerent, but never disconnected. His cares ran deep, though he tended to mask them with a display of indifference or even displeasure. He mainly criticized, but sometimes left the perch of the observer and revealed his own frailties. Essentially, the story makes space for the defiance of expectation and a willingness to read texts against the grain of commonplace attitudes. It is just such a space that is necessary to parse Richler's fiction in a way that is not reductive.

– * –

Mordecai Richler, one of Canada's most high-profile and important writers, was a provocative and unsparing novelist from the outset of his career. Already, with his second novel, *Son of a Smaller Hero* (1955), he courted controversy. *MacLean's* magazine awarded the novel its fiction prize but soon after reneged on its commitment to print excerpts. Despite the accolades of critics (George Woodcock, Bill New, Warren Tallman, W.J. Keith) many felt that Richler's second publication, with its portrayal of mercenary, provincial Montreal Jews, was tinged with anti-Semitism. The din of the social outcry almost drowned the plaudits of the reviewers, a phenomenon that would dog much of Richler's publishing career.

Certainly, accusations of anti-Semitism were some of the earliest and most enduring accusations that were made against Richler's fiction, and perhaps they overshadowed his artistic achievements or at least coloured their reception. By the middle of his career, a spate of other criticisms was levelled at his writing. Damning plaints of racism, nihilism, elitism, sexism, homophobia, and anti-Canada sentiments were issued, but they were often general attacks that typically failed to consider Richler's novels in terms of their broader narrative coherence and attempts to construct a moral vision. Thus, it is the goal of this study to perform a close textual analysis of Richler's entire corpus in light of these grievances, granting special attention to the interplay between the novels and the social, historical, and cultural constituents of Richler's on-record comments and environment. The objective is to convey how Richler's fictional texts deal with these issues in a way that possibly justifies these claims or implies alternate readings and understandings.

This methodology, the effort to illuminate a more multi-layered reading of Richler's texts by investigating pertinent inter- and extra-textual elements, resists the principles of Anglo-American New Criticism,[1] which has continued to underscore critical scholarship for more than a century and encourages readers to avoid the inclination to read literature in light of features of an author's biography. A text, according to this school, should be appreciated and considered according to its own narrative constituents and aesthetic composition.

Nevertheless, critics, notably scholars of narrative theory, have since expounded on the importance of the dynamic between a literary work and salient extra-textual matters that enrich, elucidate, and broaden the audience's reading encounter. This approach calls for a careful evaluation of the inner relationships between narrative details – syntactics in narratological terms – that emerge in a close reading, and semantics, a study of the significance of narrative details in terms of their reference to extra-textual realities. Syntactics and semantics are associated with what Benjamin Harshav (1984) calls the internal field of reference (IFR) and the external field of reference (EFR). Harshav's theoretical formula was anticipated by Northrop Frye's earlier concept of the centripetal and centrifugal analysis of literature, which compels the reader to look both inside the text as a closed artistic system and outside it, at the external details, to deepen the understanding of the literary work (1957, 73). According to Frye, the method of "outward" reading is always subordinate to the "inward" examination of verbal patterns, from which spring the aesthetic components of the work, pleasure, beauty, and interest (74). However, Harshav does not emphasize this hierarchy, stressing that a complex understanding of a text depends equally on a study of the IFR as well as the EFR.

Moreover, according to Harshav's model "literary texts create their own IFR while referring to it at the same time" (232). He elaborates, explaining that every literary text "projects at least one Internal Field of Reference (IFR) to which meanings in the text are related. At least some of the referents – personal names, times, places, scenes and episodes – are unique to this text and make no claim for external, factual existence." (235)

In short, a text's specific reality, with all of the content that is particular to it (Harshav gives specific characters and fictional events or situations as examples [233]), forms a set of "referents" that only exist within their IFR. Elements of the text may be based on actual events or historical moments, but in the IFR they refer to each other rather than to external reality. Therefore, when taking only the IFR into consideration, there is no way to go beyond the text "because these referents did not exist outside of it" (233).

By contrast, semantics focuses on the EFR, external referents, information that exists outside of the text: "the real world in time and space, history, a philosophy, ideologies, views of human nature, other texts" (243). Harshav explains that "we need knowledge of the world to make sense of a work of fiction, construct the frames of reference from scattered material, fill in gaps, create the necessary hierarchies, etc." (250). The analysis of both of these fields of references is important, he adds, because meanings of texts are not related exclusively to the texts' specific inner workings.

Richler's novels, which intersect with innumerable elements of his biography and the social, cultural, and religious environments that shaped him as an artist, require assessment according to this dialogue between the internal and external frames of reference. There is a heavily discursive element in Richler's fiction, and taking this interplay into account enables a more nuanced and meaningful reading of Richler's complete oeuvre. Moreover, Richler produced extensive journalistic material, participated in numerous interviews, and wrote a series of thinly fictionalized vignettes in *The Street* (1969), which provide details about his formative years and how they overlap extensively with the histories of his protagonists. It behooves critics to stay alert to this material, especially when it conspicuously intersects with constituents of Richler's fiction.

— ✳ —

While true that some of the most common and vocal gripes were that Richler was anti-Jewish or socially and culturally primitive, before addressing these grievances it is important to first consider the query that rankled many critics of Richler's work, whether his novels only stage an assault on society, culture, and politics or suggest some measure of consolation. Typical was the complaint of M.G. Osachoff: "what [Richler] is *for* is more difficult to discover than what he is *against*" (33). More than a decade later Carol Iannone took Richler to task for insufficient intellectual processing of his material, claiming that his development as a novelist showcased his "decreasing ability to make sense of the experience he nevertheless [felt] compelled to write about again and again" (52). And, writing in *Midstream* in 2005, Josh Lambert, in the same vein, claimed that in Richler's novels "there are no answers at all, only more problems." Yet, when looking at his entire body of fiction writing, his satire, language, narrative patterns, and cultural codes should not be pigeon-holed as a novelistic rendering of unmitigated negativity or existentialist grief. They are not black comedy pitted with social commentary, though Richler admired those very qualities in the 1932 novel *Voyage au bout de la nuit* (Yanofsky, 25) and was influenced by Céline (Kramer 2011, 170).[2] Nor are they as consistently despairing as the writings of Sartre, which also affected

Richler (Kramer 2008, 58, 85, 100), or Camus, which emphasize meaninglessness and question the stability of moral codes. And though they are riddled with outrageous fantasy and surrealism, they do not share any of the grim absurdity of the plays and stories of Beckett or Kafka. Their protagonists never capitulate to nihilism, which suggests a belief that a life governed by moral principles is still possible and that idealism – personal, if not political or social – is attainable. Richler, through his novels, suggests a consistent moral vision. A reading of his fiction allows for a distillation of this vision and shows how positive values are encoded in his writing.

Richler was always adamant that his artistic output was circumscribed by a moral agenda – a search for ethical standards, or what he himself called "values," and the need for a measure of honour and dignity in an age lacking universally accepted norms or moral authority. In her review of *Solomon Gursky*, Francine Prose writes: "What one comes to understand is that for all its gleeful obscenity and dirty dealings, [it] is a moral novel." It is a fitting assessment, and one that could accurately be applied to most of Richler's fictional works.

– ✳ –

Richler's quest for a feasible moral outlook was already evident in his maiden novel, *The Acrobats*. However, it is mainly his "mature" novels that are constructed around a recurring narrative feature, essentially a doubling of the protagonist with a hero figure, which provides a strategy for imbuing the novels with positive values. This pattern creates a space for decency and goodness in a fictional world characterized by a deterioration of such values. It is important to recognize this pattern because rather than the novels always presenting moral and ethical problems that have no answers (Lambert), they propose a narrative scaffolding that, at the very least, suggests moral possibilities.

The hero figures in this configuration are distinct from the novels' protagonists. They are larger-than-life, revered by the protagonist because they lead a fantastical existence governed by heroic ideals rather than legislated or culturally determined values. While the term "hero" evokes the topos of the hero in classical literature – Achilles, Odysseus, Aeneas – Richler's hero figures bear little resemblance to these mythical characters. Instead, they are heroes only of stories-within-stories. Moreover, they are elusive. Having lived colourful lives, they all eventually disappear under suspicious circumstances, lending intrigue and mystery to their histories. Moreover, it is not clear how much of their lives is the stuff of reality or fantasy. On the one hand, the protagonists know them from direct, albeit limited, experience combined with family and community lore. On the other, they function in the novels largely as products of the protagonists' imagination, truly exceptional but elevated by imagined glory. From their memories of these hero figures, and testimonies and eclectic snippets of information about their wanderings and misadventures, the protagonists cobble together an idea of these shadow personalities as unconventional heroes who adhere to a model of lofty morals and personal values. And, as they are mostly *absent*, there is little first-hand evidence to disabuse the protagonists of their images of these men as ideal constructs of authentic human virtue.

Robin Nadel claims that these hero figures, no matter how inspired, do not lend Richler's novels an element of optimism or faith and "fail to compensate Richler's protagonists in any meaningful way" (91). She concedes that they indeed serve as the alter-egos of the protagonists, who perceive these extraordinary men as a connection to imagined power that mitigates their own vulnerability and emasculation (91). However, in her view, they are a psychological crutch that prevents the protagonists from self-actualization. In sum, Richler's novels, according to Nadel, show that hero worship "is a dysfunctional and personally stunting refuge of the cowardly" (102). However, this repeating narrative structure is not mainly a plot device to help the protagonists evolve but, rather, a discursive element that introduces a justification for an ongoing belief in the potential of human decency. In thinking about Richler's novels in relation to notions of "cultural codes" (see Barthes) the divide between the hero figures and the protagonists opens up space for existential insights that show how the protagonists' ordinary values are not just an alternative to the ideological commitments of the hero figures but also a refutation of mid-twentieth-century nihilistic pessimism.

Richler's satire of feminism, Indigenous rights, gender politics, racism, academia, and contemporary culture, in contrast, do not fit into an overall narrative scheme. At times, his attack on what he calls "special pleading," a term almost synonymous with political correctness, is judicious and relevant to debates regarding social attitudes and behaviour; more frequently, however, it seems anachronistic and unbalanced. For the most part, Richler's protagonists tend to view political correctness as anti-heroic. They occasionally find themselves torn between their conservative proclivities and more liberal, progressive thinking, but their overall attitude is that special pleading is at odds with authentic moral fibre.

A problem with Richler's satire on these issues may be that, in contrast to classic satirists, whose satire is framed by "some figure who embodies the author's moral norms and reminds us of his moral purpose" (Spacks, 362), Richler structures his novels in a way that veils moral purpose. A 1970s interview with Richler conducted by Canadian novelist Graeme Gibson illuminates this point. Gibson begins by observing that there is no hope in Richler's novels for the liberals to change. They are sympathetic characters, he adds, but the reader never expects them to do anything about the deterioration of morals and ethics. Richler agrees, but then adds an observation demonstrating his sharp awareness of his audience. "You may not find whatever code of honour I'm groping for as a way to live acceptable, but that's really my obsession" (qtd in Cameron, 124). Richler acknowledges his propensity to antagonize his readers, a price he dutifully paid in exchange for a serious exploration of unconventional ethical commitments.

However, what the interview reveals, most importantly, is how Richler's novels opaquely critique society's predisposition to ascribe admirable human traits to what is popularly considered the mainstream left, presumably the bulwark of "special pleading" sympathies. Almost four decades earlier, George Orwell (whom Richler considered a perspicacious and honest observer of human behaviour [1973a, 7]) had written about the tendency among the middle class, with its liberal inclinations, to pay "lip service" to the troubles of the less privileged, forsaking action while championing a "brand of vague brotherliness" (Breton, 53). Elided in Richler's reply to Gibson is the fact that, *pace* Orwell, in his fiction the proactive champions of moral progress are non-liberals. Embedded in Gibson's line of questioning is the "reader's" assumption that virtuous behaviour is the province of the liberal camp. Richler's novels subvert that conception, which is what makes their moral commitments less readily identifiable. In Richler's fiction, idealism is represented by character types that are rarely associated with virtue-driven aspirations; illiberal renegades function as ethical standard bearers. Richler defies the anticipated reaction of his "target" audience in this respect and requires readers to approach his novels with a willingness to read against normative cultural expectations.

This narrative move illustrates cases wherein "pragmatics," the author's awareness of reader expectations, adds a valuable layer of meaning to the reading of the text, beyond what can be established by addressing the internal and external frames of references alone. The realization that Richler, in his novels, destabilizes the commonplace that liberals are the sentinels of moral vision makes clear that a tripartite approach also enriches the reading of the text. It exposes the writer's consciousness of the target, hurdle, or unexpected readership as well as a consideration of the text and its interface with various audiences (Toker 2005, 92). Moreover, it is a way by which we "may enrich our understanding of the other constituents and the enjoyment of the delicate beauty and the cultural depth of great literary works" (96).

This subversive quality in Richler's satire could seem off-putting to readers and "cold," a kind of criticism aimed at both the deplorable as well as the seemingly virtuous aspects of society (Lewis, 72). The multiplicity of his "special pleading" targets, especially those that could otherwise seem beyond reproach, occasionally neutralize his system of values – a case, at times, of throwing out the baby with the bathwater.

Similarly, critics sometimes allege that Richler privileges entertainment and humour, often sacrificing weighty moral themes for the sake of amusing crudeness. Kerry McSweeney calls Richler's proclivity for base comedy his "deconstructive energy ... which manifests in episodes and emphases that seem tasteless and gratuitous." He notes that many critics have rightly observed "how these and other gross vignettes have weakened the serious satiric, humane and moral concerns of Richler's fiction." In her review of *Solomon Gursky Was Here*, Francine Prose insists that the novel has genuine moral intentions but echoes the claim that its moral positions are frequently undermined by slapstick digressions at the expense, perhaps, of engagement with substantial issues:

> What occasionally blurs the book's moral focus is that Mr. Richler "does" tastelessness and vulgar display so much more damningly, hilariously and with so much more relish than flat-out evil. Consequently, Bernard's self-congratulatory, sloppily sentimental testimonial dinner – a Canadian Football League official presents "Mr. Bernard" with an autographed ball that he then gives to a paraplegic boy in front of 300 cheering guests – and his niece Lucy Gursky's vile, vanity production of "The Diary of Anne Frank" are made to appear more memorably awful than the Ottawa immigration official who scuttles Solomon's efforts to shelter refugees from Hitler before World War II.

At times, then, it seems that the satire almost overtakes the novels' more serious ambitions and that Richler's satiric barbs overreach, blurring the boundaries between social commentary and moral outrage.

Along with "special pleading," Canadian concerns also occupy a pivotal role in Richler's novels. Richler, some have contended, was unkind to Canada in his writing. Yet it figures prominently in his novels. It is, nevertheless, often the butt of satire, depicted as an inconsequential outback and somewhat of a dividing point between the protagonists and hero figures. For the former, Canada is flawed but still home. They are attached to it, despite its disadvantages, and are concerned about its culture, politics, and society. The hero figures, on the other hand, are either unimpressed or dismissive of Canada. This divergence in attitudes is significant since the protagonists rarely have attitudes that contradict their mentors' viewpoints, even passively. In some cases, they are dedicated to values – essentially their "ordinary values" – that are not part of the hero figures' moral outlook. However, they rarely dwell on matters to which the hero figures are indifferent. Thus, the focus on Canada in Richler's novels suggests that the protagonists, despite their self-perception as the hero figures' intellectual protégés, find that their mentors' priorities do not address all of their value commitments. In consequence, in Richler's novels Canada is represented as an unassuming country, decent enough and with notable virtues, but still prone to being underappreciated.

In terms of how Richler's novels deal with the issue of aesthetics and modern culture, Richler again can be seen turning to Orwell in his effort to craft an outlook. Orwell's axiology, a belief in aesthetics underscored by moral purpose, is rehearsed in Richler's worry about the way in which art and artists treat ethical values. For the most part, the protagonists in Richler's novels think of their hero figures as men of taste, culturally sensitive and expert at distinguishing mediocre shlock from great art. This sensibility aligns with the hero figures' moral grounding. It is as though the ability to truly appreciate culture is inextricable from an ethical disposition. However, the hero figure in *Barney's Version*, Boogie Moscovitch, professes a cavalier attitude towards morality and seems to delight in immoral behaviour. This unprecedented breach – a hero figure with a faulty moral constitution – invites speculation about the binary relationship between culture and morals in Richler's earlier novels. It also calls into question the moral positions that are championed throughout Barney's first-person narration because those positions are largely predicated on Barney's faith in Boogie. If Boogie is a fraud, Barney's values, accordingly, are ineluctably misguided. Thus, *Barney's Version* forces a reconsideration of the value scheme that is mostly consistent in Richler's mature novels.

– ✱ –

Regardless of the many reservations in terms of the far-reaching social commentary and artistic shortcomings of Richler's fiction, up until the early 1990s, there had been a steady flow of critical interest in Richler. Already in 1957, Nathan Cohen's article in *Tamarack Review* reflected a fascination with the young Richler and the caustic bellicosity that readers found both intriguing and repellent. But it was once Richler had published *The Apprenticeship of Duddy Kravitz* in 1959 that his status as a major Canadian author began to crystallize. Six years later, in "Mordecai Richler: Craftsman or Artist," Naim Kattan cautioned Richler to resist his penchant for sophomoric excess but also recognized that he was poised to possibly become a major Canadian literary voice. That status was cemented when George Woodcock put out *Mordecai Richler* in 1970 as part of the Canadian Writers series in the New Canadian Library collection on "significant figures on the Canadian literary scene" (Woodcock 1970, 7). In assessing the novels from *The Acrobats* through to *Cocksure*, Woodcock argued that Richler was insufficiently inventive in his writing, which was almost excessively local. Moreover, in anticipating the release of *St Urbain's Horseman*, he wondered whether Richler may have exhausted his imaginative powers, resorting to derivative plots and conceits in his latest novel. Nevertheless, the scope and depth of his study made clear that Richler's stature was uncontested. Not long after, G. David Sheps edited a collection of essays on Richler's work in 1971, mainly by Canadianists, which reflected the breadth of critical reactions being generated in response to Richler's fiction, including a particularly high-profile essay by Leslie Fiedler. In 1983, the first two book-length studies of Richler were released, one by Arnold Davidson and another by Victor J. Ramraj. By the end of the 1980s, two more works on Richler appeared. *Perspectives on Mordecai Richler* (1986), edited by Michael Darling, included essays, such as those by Robert Cluett, Suzanne Ives, and Stephen Bonnycastle, that tackled Richler's texts from a more theoretical vantage point, and Rachel Feldhay Brenner's *Assimilation and Assertion*, a reading of Richler's novels as a response to the Holocaust. At that point though, Richler seemed to fade from the critical landscape. Commenting on this sharp decline in Richler discourse, Sam Sacks, years later, referred to Richler in *Commentary* as "the neglected Canadian-Jewish novelist." It may be that this downturn occurred because Richler, by the late 1980s, was too socially, politically, or even artistically out of step with the currents of social and literary fashion. Still, what is certain is that, aside from various articles and book reviews that continued to appear, no other book-length criticism on his writing was produced beyond 1989. When he died in 2001, it seemed the moment for Richler scholarship had ebbed.

However, in the years soon after a revitalized critical interest in Richler emerged. In 2004, a Richler symposium was hosted at the McGill Institute for the Study of Canada. Meant as an opportunity to refresh the body of existing scholarship, it was also held to redress what organizers viewed as literary critics' neglect of Mordecai Richler (Baum Singer, 11). Six years later, *Canlit* dedicated a special issue to Richler. In the introduction, editors Nathalie Cooke and Norm Ravvin claimed that a new collection of essays on Richler was overdue, and that "[Mordecai Richler] ha[d] been lightly served by the Canadian scholarly community, where equally iconic figures such as Margaret Atwood and Margaret Laurence ha[d] received far more attentive canonization" (Baum Singer, 9).[3] Within a few years of *Canlit*'s Richler issue, more than a dozen Canadian universities[4] listed courses in which at least one of Richler's novels was part of the core curriculum.[5] Similarly, from 2012 to 2017, more SHRCC grants were awarded for Richler projects than had been awarded in the entire decade prior.

During this period, popular interest in Richler followed suit. The media in Canada were rife with tributes to his novels, political commentary, literary observations, as well as his dour demeanour and cynical humour. Subsequently, at least five biographies appeared (Vassanji, Yanofsky, Kramer, Posner, Foran). Charles Foran's *Mordecai: The Life and Times* (2010) won five prestigious Canadian literary awards, including the Governor General's Literary Award for Non-Fiction. At the same time, the long-standing effort to adapt Richler's last novel, *Barney's Version* (1997), to film succeeded in 2010, and the movie had a major release, starring academy award winners Dustin Hoffman and Paul Giamatti, who won a Golden Globe Award for his portrayal of Barney Panofsky. It also engendered an outpouring of praise, interest, and nostalgia for Richler and his politically incorrect, biting fiction, essays, and journalism. "Judged by his profile in the media and entertainment industries," John Barber observed in his 2010 op-ed, "no Canadian author alive or dead is as popular today as Mordecai Richler."

Concurrently, francophone scholars and journalists became more interested in Richler. For decades, Richler had been considered a nemesis of francophone language, culture, and society; eventually, the French Canadian literary community began to reassess his place within the Quebec canon (Cooke and Ravvin, 7). In 2007, Boréal Press published, *Un certain sens du ridicule*, a collection of Richler essays translated into French, which discuss Richler's childhood and his understanding of the writer's calling. Québécois critic Yan Hammel argues that a reconsideration of Richler's novels is required because it is too simplistic to dismiss him on anti-francophone grounds. As one of Quebec's most gifted writers, he adds, there must be engagement with Richler even if his politics provoke knee-jerk rage among the French Québécois community, especially the nationalists (58–9). Plus, at least twenty-eight articles as well as some translations of English essays and reviews on Richler have appeared in French-language peer-reviewed journals since 2012.

Indeed, it seems the tide has turned in terms of critical inquiry into Richler's work. Accordingly, it seems a particularly apt moment to introduce a study that evaluates the discourse in his fiction in relation to his entire oeuvre.

– * –

With the publication of *The Apprenticeship of Duddy Kravitz* (1959), Richler seemed to have broken new ground. The book ushered in a sea-change in Canadian literature, expanding the parameters of the novel, its ideas, and language (Woodcock 1990, 16–17). It is still arguably Richler's best-known title and the work that most likely fomented his reputation as the Canadian Philip Roth, a writer unafraid to expose the dark underbelly of the Jewish community. In fact, Roth's breakout works, the novella *Goodbye, Columbus* and its accompanying short stories, were published the same year.

In their fiction, both Roth and Richler continually revisit the neighbourhoods and communities of their youth. Just as Roth frequently dramatizes the hum and timbre of post-Second World War Newark, Richler's works depict time and again the Montreal of his early years and Quebec's Eastern Townships. Richler's Montreal is not sentimental. The evolution of the city's Anglo-French divide permeates his novels, dramatizing the political and social tensions that were ever-present during his career. And Richler is especially acidic in his treatment of the provincial language policies that favoured French and the francophone separatist movement. Moreover, Richler's Montreal is a city with a sinister legacy of anti-Semitism. The novels, notably *St Urbain's Horseman*, make much of the anti-Jewish attitudes and violence that emanated from the city's French quarters. English Montreal, though, is also guilty of anti-Semitic feelings in much of Richler's fiction. And Montreal, like New York, is also a big city, with the kind of corruption and political shenanigans that are to be expected. Yet the vitality with which Richler evokes Montreal, the cold-water flats, coffee shops, and pool halls of Mile End; the middle-class pretension of Queen Mary Boulevard; the suburban excess of Cote St Luc; and the engaging thrum of the city's downtown is compelling. When Ted Kotcheff's film, *The Apprenticeship of Duddy Kravitz*, came out in 1974, and *Lies My Father Told Me*, based on Ted Allan's 1949 short story, was released the following year, Jewish Montreal already had a mythic quality thanks to Richler's work.

Richler was candid about his deliberate effort to reconstruct the Jewish world of his youth in his novels.[6] With the completion of *The Apprenticeship of Duddy Kravitz* in 1959, he wrote to his friend, novelist Brian Moore, about his ambitious agenda: "I'm staking out a claim to Montreal Jew-ville in the tradition of H. de Balzac and Big Bill Faulkner" (qtd in Weintrub, 230). More than two decades later, in an article that originally appeared in the *New York Times*, Richler explained that his raison d'être as a writer had not changed since the start of his career. "I'm stuck with my original notion," he wrote, "which is to be an honest witness to my time, my place and to write at least one novel that will last, that will make me remembered after my death" (1990, 6).

However, the differences between the two writers are significant and shed light on the ways in which Richler is distinct with terms of being a twentieth-century Jewish novelist. First, unlike Roth, Richler is not an ironic writer. His novels are saturated with irony, true. But at their core is an earnest attempt to grapple with the most basic questions regarding decency and human dignity. Roth is a much more postmodern writer who prods and provokes but makes no pretense of any quest for existential answers. His novels do not suggest a belief in an endgame or faith in any moral commitments. The main exception might be *The Plot against America* (2004), an allohistory that implies a certain faith in the underlying vigour of American democracy and the fail-safes that have made the United States an unprecedentedly secure Diaspora for its Jewish citizens. But, in the bulk of Roth's work, there are no heroes or villains, only individuals, flawed to various degrees, their one avenue to redemption being a scathing level of self-awareness. His novels dislocate moral, social, and cultural conventions without any recourse.

Second, as is the case in *The Plot Against America*, Roth's intellectual and ethical investments are deeply bound to his position as an American in the modern era. His identity as a Jew leads him to subjects and themes that touch on Jewish life, but his attention to these topics is typically ambivalent. Roth's novels never celebrate any aspect of Jewish life or participate in a continuum of Jewish literature or culture. Even when considering many of his most "Jewish" works, the eponymous novella and short stories in *Goodbye, Columbus* (1959), *The Ghost Writer* (1979), *The Counterlife* (1986), *Operation Shylock* (1993), and *The Plot against America*, his Jewish commitments, whether cultural, religious, or ideological, are shallow, parochial, or incidental. Even in these novels there is a pervasive ambiguity surrounding Jewish identity, and it is usually unclear whether his Jewish characters "owe any allegiance" to their Jewish roots (Wisse 2000, 318).

Richler's fiction, in opposition, seems to enact a feverish impulse to piece together a kind of moral coherence despite a growing sense of moral fragmentation. This does not mean that Richler's work is free of postmodern elements. For example, in *Solomon Gursky Was Here* (1989), as Barbara Korte observes, "the borderline between fact and fiction appears confusingly permeable" and "particularly pertinent in relation to the core piece of Richler's revisionist historiography," the disaster of the legendary Franklin expedition. With this fictive thread, "Richler himself becomes a most artful manipulator of evidence and documents" (498). In this kind of postmodern storytelling, Korte, in referencing Linda Hutcheon, notes that that there develops an "indeterminacy about the referent of historiography" (500). In the case of *Solomon Gursky*, this means insisting that Jews are as Canadian as their French and Anglo countrymen, even if an imaginative subplot about Jewish survivors of the Franklin expedition has to be enlisted to make this understood.

Still, this knotty weave of fact and fiction in *Solomon Gursky* does not impinge upon the broader argument for Jewish dignity and ethical principles, which is essential to Richler's mature novels. It is complex but does not preclude the possibility of a moral life. Therefore, while postmodern elements in Roth's novels underscore the fragility of moral positions, these qualities in Richler's texts are more targeted.

While addressing specific issues relating to Richler's recurring themes, they do not override the more pressing question regarding the problem of morality and decency in an age with no moral consensus.

It is important to also consider Richler in relation to earlier Canadian Jewish writers. First, Richler is a direct heir of Montreal writer A.M. Klein. The brutal lampoon of Klein in *Solomon Gursky Was Here*, where he is reimagined as the pompous minor poet L.B. Berger, suggests that Richler had only scorn for the older writer. Indeed, in his essay, "Mr. Sam," Richler reflects on Klein's position as Sam Bronfman's in-house writer, describing a fawning sycophant who compromised taste and dignity for the opportunity to hobnob with Canada's most affluent Jewish family and enjoy a miniscule fraction of the family spoils (Richler 1998, 26–7). Moreover, Richler's writing is in no way reminiscent of Klein's dense prose, laden with cultural allusions of immeasurable scope. Nevertheless, Klein was an immensely important figure for Richler, and the title of Reinhold Kramer's essay, "Richler, Son of Klein," does not overstate the case. Klein's classic novel, *The Second Scroll* (1951), which follows the quest of an unnamed Montreal journalist to explore the rebirth of the Hebrew language in the newly created Jewish state, is the blueprint for the better part of Richler's fictional output.[7] The historical, religious, and cultural reach of Klein's slight novel is immense, burnishing a Jewish legacy without reducing it to sanctimonious cliché. Richler borrowed both structure and sweep from Klein, and added a new Canadian Jewish voice to the field of Canadian literature. Klein's work is intimately in conversation with Jewish intellectual history, the major tomes of classic Jewish texts, and the pivotal events that have shaped the Jewish people as both a Diasporic nation and one awash in the complexities of nationhood. Richler's fiction is not as rich in this regard. Still, woven into his fiction is a decided nod to Klein and a serious commitment to ideas, motifs, and narratives that are threaded throughout Jewish history and literature. For example, references in his novels to Rabbi Akiva, the first-century scholar who helped create the Mishnah, the text that gave legal, intellectual, and spiritual form to Judaism, or the twelfth-century scholar Maimonides, the paramount Jewish scholar of the Middle Ages, are part of the mandate in Richler's fiction to champion Jewish culture's intellectual tradition. With allusions to Jewish writers, such as Isaac Babel, Richler's fiction participates in Babel's tradition of reframing Jewish stereotypes and also pays tribute to the richness of the Jewish literary legacy. These are qualities that play a significant role in Richler's induction into the ranks of modern Jewish writers in a way that marks a wide chasm between him and Roth.

The way Richler integrates the Golem myth into his novels is a compelling example of how he commandeers Jewish tradition for his own purposes and fuses his writing to a chain of modern Jewish story-telling with religious, cultural, and mythical overtones. Specifically, Richler's hero figures – namely, in *St Urbain's Horseman* and *Solomon Gursky*, but in other novels as well – can be seen as linked to stories of the Golem, a non-human, sometimes monstrous creature. Mythologized in the modern era as a being created out of clay by Rabbi Judah Loew ben Bezalel, the Maharal, in the 1600s, the Golem has been popularly depicted as a giant originally designed to protect the Jews of the Prague ghetto. As a Jewish literary trope, the image has been drawn upon by many writers. Richler's grandfather, Rabbi Yudel Rosenberg, famously wrote a controversial tale about the Golem, "Wonders of the Maharal" (1909), which enjoyed wide distribution (Leiman, 28). He wrote the tale as if based on a lost manuscript by the Maharal's son-in-law, Rabbi Isaac ben Samson Katz, which was ostensibly recovered from the Royal Library of Metz (33). Though it was soon exposed as a "modern forgery" (32), Rosenberg's version helped disseminate the Golem myth to a wide audience and made this figure popular in Jewish folklore (Vassanji, 25). For example, in H. Leivik's 1921 poetic drama *The Golem*, the Maharal's creation is a monstrous being who defies his creator and actually endangers the Jews when he becomes an uncontrollable renegade (Wisse 2000, 154). I.B. Singer's 1969 novel *The Golem* is likewise inspired by the legend wherein the Maharal infuses life into the soulless creature, as are Cynthia Ozick's *Puttermesser Papers* (1997), with its female Golem, and the 2000 Pulitzer Prize-winning *The Adventures of Kavalier and Clay* by Michael Chabon. Richler's hero figures, though not monstrous fabulations, have this mythic quality. Furthermore, as they are products, to a certain extent, of the protagonist's imagination and charged, not unproblematically, with the defence of the Jewish community, they inscribe his novels in the Golem tradition, albeit in a less fantastical context.

– ✳ –

In terms of Canadian Jewish literature, Richler is part of the quartet of the celebrated Montreal writers, which includes Klein, the poet Irving Layton, and writer/musician Leonard Cohen. However,

Richler's work is only really in dialogue with Klein's corpus. Regardless, the foursome represent the golden age of Canadian Jewish writing and are often classified as a united cohort. Outside of this group, Richler's works are not much in unison with other Canadian Jewish writers. That may be because Canadian Jewish writing, as Norm Ravvin argues in *Not Quite Mainstream*, lacks a geographic centre and recurring themes (16). Ravvin also contends that among Canadian Jewish writers there is no real "kingpin" (16). Yet, when taking stock, it is hard to name any Canadian Jewish writer who has garnered more critical and popular attention, or cast a larger shadow, than Richler. Of course there have been a number of other successful Jewish writers, not least Adele Wiseman, Matt Cohen, Norman Levine, Chava Rosenfarb, and Anne Michaels; and, more recently, Nancy Richler and David Bezmozgis. But it would be inaccurate to suggest that Richler is not the first name that springs to mind when those inside, as well as outside, critical circles discuss Canadian Jewish writing.

Returning to the matter of pragmatics, another factor that has made Richler such a presence in Canadian literature is the fact that he wrote with a keen awareness of potential readers' reactions. For instance, he knew that *Son of a Smaller Hero* was going to enrage Montreal's Jewish community. In correspondence with his friend William Weintraub, he confessed that his soon-to-be-released novel was likely to be labelled anti-Semitic. *MacLean's* decision to backtrack on its publishing commitment could not have been a surprise. But he was ready to respond, telling Weintrub that the accusations were irrelevant. The novel, he explained, was not a Jewish-problem book because, in his mind (at that time), "there [was] no such thing as a Jewish outlook or a Jewish Problem or Jewish Spokesman" (qtd in Posner, 87). Whether or not he fully believed this disclaimer, he was not insensitive to the anticipated audience backlash and fronted the novel with an emphatic warning: "Any readers approaching this book in a search for 'real people' is completely on the wrong track and what's more, has misunderstood my whole purpose. *Son of a Smaller Hero* is a novel, not an autobiography" (i). Joel Yanofsky comments: "It was not the usual wink to the reader, who, if he even bothers to read it, takes it with a grain of salt. Instead, Richler isn't winking; he's waving both arms in the air like a man trying to prevent a train wreck" (64). With this author's warning, Richler was almost

confessing his guilt for having over-shared the intimacies of Montreal
Jewry. At the same time, he was practically instigating controversy,
knowingly transforming his work from a literary achievement into a
social issue sensation.

Likewise, several years later, while working on his 1960 novel
Cocksure, Richler wrote to his publisher confessing that his new
book was "getting very dirty" and might be too lewd for him to read
yet alone publish (Yanofsky, 153). Indeed, the book was banned from
the W.H. Smith chain in Britain and totally outlawed in Ireland,
Australia, New Zealand, and South Africa. Reinhold Kramer (2008,
190) argues that, in writing the titillating book, Richler was overly
concerned with seeming hip, "too much indebted to the times,
and so came across (not completely against his intention) as a tem-
porizer." Again, part of Richler's prominence had to do with his
understanding of the times and what kind of storytelling would spark
cultural conversations.

Then again, with the upcoming release of *Solomon Gursky Was
Here* in 1989, Richler understood that he would be provoking the
wrath of Canada's most prestigious Jewish family, the Bronfmans, and
those within its extensive sphere of influence. He foresaw the potential
of a libel suit, if not from the Bronfmans then from Senator Leo Kolber,
spoofed in the novel as the obsequious Bronfman consigliore Harvey
Schwartz (Kramer 2008, 311).[8] By this time, however, Richler, had no
cause to be anxious about the greater Jewish community finding his
parody of the Bronfmans threatening. In the late 1980s and early
1990s Richler's journalistic crusade against French separatism in
Quebec had won him favour with the Montreal Jewish community,
or at least created a détente that led to a softer judgment of his earlier
novelistic sins. This was especially true after the release of his controversial 1991 article in the *New Yorker*, "Oh Canada! Oh Quebec!"
(Yanofsky, 236). Moreover, a younger generation of Canadian Jews was
less reactive to Richler's satire of Jews and Jewish life (Vassanji, 224).
At a remove from Montreal's Jewish ghetto and less troubled by Jewish
stereotypes than their parents and grandparents, this generation was
more forbearing in relation to the novels' Jewish elements. Thus,
Jewish readers were unbothered by the novel's satire, and critics,
journalists, and pundits felt no need to take Richler to task for his
comedic hijinks.

— ✳ —

At this juncture, Richler scholarship is still somewhat embryonic. There is much work to be done. Because of Richler's subjects and themes, his novels are thick with material that demands theoretical inquiry from different quarters. This work by no means exhausts the relevant approaches to his novels. It does, however, investigate many of the major claims and assumptions about Richler's fiction and tests them according to a close reading of the novels as individual works and as part of a complete oeuvre.

1

Ordinary Jewish Values

Rather than being identified as Jewish writers, Saul Bellow, Philip Roth, and Bernard Malamud preferred to be known as American writers, heirs of an American literary tradition whose works emanate from their Jewish experience. In 1974, Bellow wrote (qtd in Rubin, 5):

> I am often described as a Jewish writer; in much the same way one might be called a Samoan astronomer or an Eskimo cellist or a Zulu Gainsborough expert. There is some oddity about it. I am a Jew, and I have written some books. I have tried to fit my soul into the Jewish-writer category, but it does not feel comfortably accommodated there. I wonder, now and then, whether Philip Roth and Bernard Malamud and I have not become the Hart Schaffner and Marx of our trade. We have made it in the field of culture as Bernard Baruch made it on a park bench, as Polly Adler made it in prostitution, as Two Gun Cohen the personal bodyguard of Sun Yat-Sen, made it in China. My joke is not broad enough to cover the contempt I feel for the opportunists, wise guys, and career types who impose such labels and trade upon them.

Bellow wished to register that his early influences sprang from classic American sources: "I did not go to the public library to read the Talmud but the novels and poems of Sherwood Anderson, Theodore Dreiser, Edgar Lee Masters, and Vachel Lindsay" (5). Similarly, Grace Paley (2005, 14–15) describes herself as a student of the great authors, recalling a passion for literature that began, not with Sholem Aleichem and Y.L. Peretz, but with Longfellow and that stretched all the way to Joyce, Proust, and Gertrude Stein.

Early in his career, Mordecai Richler espoused similar views. "I don't consider myself a Jewish or a Canadian writer. I am a writer" (qtd in Posner, 87). At the dawn of his career, he was self-conscious about his Jewish identity; his first novel, *The Acrobats* (1954), displays few Jewish associations or concerns. But Richler faced a far different critical arena than the one that confronted Bellow and his contemporaries, and he was not in jeopardy of being considered an ethnic rather than a Canadian writer. When he started writing fiction, Canadian literary output had been relatively modest and the national culture doyens were eager to identify new Canadian talent. Therefore, they embraced Richler, and the prevalent Jewish themes in his subsequent novels seemed to be a natural expression of Canada's culturally diverse identity rather than the focus of a niche writer. Moreover, with his urban settings and cosmopolitan outlook, he was credited with transforming Canadian literature, helping it evolve from a rural genre, provincial in subject matter and old-fashioned in style, to a modern literature, urbane and sophisticated. According to George Woodcock, in particular, *The Apprenticeship of Duddy Kravitz* was largely responsible for bringing "an end to that subjection to outdated conventions of taste which had held Canadian writing for too long in colonial stagnation" (1991, 19). Thus, there was no cause for Richler to doubt his status as an important Canadian writer. In later years, he described himself as a "big city Canadian – an urban Jew" (Woodcock 1970, 9). Apparently he had resigned himself to his identity as a Canadian and a Jew and ceased to resist these categorizations.

As Richler was a confessed "Jewish" writer, it is not surprising, then, that the hero figures in his novels are, without exception, Jews – Ashkenazi Jewish men who exhibit integrity and live by an honest, if not perfect, moral posture. They are the children of immigrants whose forbearers originate from Eastern Europe and Russia. Moreover, they are post- but not anti-Orthodox, almost all native to Montreal's Jewish ghetto, and still bear traces of the Old World that had produced their grandparents and great-grandparents, despite their world travels and cosmopolitan ways. The protagonists too (not unlike Richler himself, it is worth noting) are consistently Montreal-bred Jewish men. But, unlike the lives of the "heroes," theirs are bound to the constraints of the quotidian. They are intelligent family men who are tethered to bourgeois demands but appreciate renegades, mavericks, and politically incorrect rabble-rousers. They themselves do not flout the law, yet they revere reckless idealists with the wherewithal – or perceived where-withal – to live according to their own moral compass and pursue justice with Mosaic aplomb.

Richler positioned his protagonists as the living examples of a value system that is grounded in the limitations of reality, and the hero figures as the embodiment of moral imperatives that are instinctual absolutes of right and wrong. By including the hero figures in the novels' storylines, and making them the moral icons that the protagonists revere, Richler produced a distinct moral vision that is, in many ways, a counterbalance to much of modern life's moral relativism; it is also a criticism of the Jewish anomie that is depicted in the novels – banal Jewish life that is a result of a vacuous tradition drained of its moral and spiritual power in the modern era.

While Richler's hero figures are committed to an uncompromising moral outlook, it is the doubling of protagonists with hero figures in the novels that provides a legitimate value scheme for a twentieth-century Jew who has forsaken traditional Jewish beliefs but still clings to faith in a moral existence. The protagonists' Jewish values, while not necessarily in concert with traditional Jewish ideals, form a basic moral code. In essence, they are values that are congruous with ordinary life: for the purposes of this study they are referred to as ordinary Jewish values. In theorizing the typology of the hero figures, in contrast, it is useful to consider the concept of supererogation, a term borne of Roman Catholic religious dogma but reconsidered anew within the study of ethics beginning in the mid-twentieth century with James Urmson's groundbreaking work, *Saints and Heroes* (1958). Supererogation is a useful construct because it addresses the nexus between ideas of morality and notions of how these ideas should be acted upon. On the one hand, it is "ideal morality, the morality of love, virtue, and aspirations, which is not formulated in universalizable principles" (Heyd, 180), and the kind of larger-than-life moral stance that pervades the hero figures' lives. On the other, supererogation emphasizes duty, and the hero figures are men who consistently enact their beliefs. The protagonists do not perform outsized moral gestures. They navigate their lives according to a moral system that is expected of decent people generally, the kind of normative behaviour that is "not too far beyond the capacity of ordinary men on ordinary occasions" (Urmson, 212). However, the hero figures have an ethical posture that leads them to conduct their lives in a way that goes well beyond the call of duty and aligns closely to Urmson's outline of supererogation characterized by heroism that is genuinely selfless activism (200–6). At the same time, it must be acknowledged that Urmson's view of supererogation, grounded in the norms of social morality or the commonly perceived understanding of universal good (see Heyd, 180), does not always fit the deeds and motivations of the hero figures. At times, they are merciless, blurring the divide between vengeance and justice, which taints the moral integrity of their actions. Thus, it might be more accurate to view them not as models of supererogation but as compelled by supererogatory impulses, such as disregard for personal risk and a propensity for doing far more than anybody has a right to expect of them or what the vast majority aspires to achieve. In the context of Richler's novels, I call this phenomenon "Jewish heroics."

In these novels, the value systems of the protagonists and hero figures are presented as distinct yet complementary, each one comprised of an amalgam of moral positions and attitudes that, when combined, form a just and plausible Jewish outlook for the twentieth century. This composite serves as a moral platform and alternative to the complacent, socially acceptable, and often hypocritical Jewish code of living depicted in the novels. It is a counter for what Richler represents as the Jewish establishment's platitudinal inertia. But, most important, in terms of the novels' thematic emphases, it is a corrective to timid, law-abiding Jewish compliance and is expressed through dignified yet ordinary values and fantastical heroics.

The *ordinary* Jewish values that are expressed through the consciousness of Richler's protagonists can be difficult to identify because they are seldom articulated directly. Instead, they are realized by these characters in the way they live their lives – through their oblique observations, ever-present existential preoccupations, and psychological obsessions with the people they consider worthy of reverence. While Richler's novels have often been attacked for their lack of moral coherence, the values espoused by his protagonists are in line with those that belong to Jews whom Irving Howe once described as non-believers with the "wish to be within the bounds of the culture or among the adherents of the community" (Howe, 10). The persona of such a Jew, Howe argues, is a matter of "fragmentary identification" based upon: "(1) [T]he remembered power of the immigrant experience … the pressures of childhood and adolescence ... (2) [The belief that] there is a body of ethical values within or derived from Jewish tradition. (3) [A moral obligation] to keep alive the memory of the Holocaust. (4) ... [Support for] the State of Israel as it provides focus within history for Jewish life" (10). Richler's protagonists may not have a comprehensive moral vision, but they closely resemble a generation that, according to Howe, tried to synthesize a moral outlook when faith no longer sufficed as a foundation for values. In terms of Richler's protagonists, integral to this moral vision are loyalty to one's wider family, filial obligations, faith in the traditional "family man," and respect for Old World Judaism when it is sincere but not self-righteous.

Since the publication of *Son of a Smaller Hero* in 1955, Richler's novels have, in fact, reiterated a fairly consistent and well-defined set of ordinary Jewish values, which are conducive to people living normative lives in ordinary circumstances – moral duty in its most basic sense (Urmson, 198). In part, they are championed in the novels by the narrative voice and the protagonists' actions and views. It is important to note that, in Richler's novels, narrative authority and characterization are heavily weighted, often being the instruments of value construction. This may partially explain readers' frequent oversight of the novels' value schemes. Richler, rather than describing characters directly, invariably resorts to "indirect presentation" in describing them, wherein the narrator "does not mention the trait but displays and exemplifies it in various ways, leaving to the reader the task of inferring the quality they imply" (Rimmon-Kenan, 61). Indirect presentation, accordingly, requires the reader to be alert to nuance, innuendo, and allusion when encountering characters and how they correspond to the ideas, values, themes, and conflicts within the novel.

The most pervasive of the ordinary Jewish values in Richler's novels is family loyalty, and *The Apprenticeship of Duddy Kravitz* presents one of the clearest examples of how Richler's novels privilege the valorization of family commitments. Duddy Kravitz is a character with few scruples. Instances of his scheming riddle the novel, and he emerges as a coarse young man who easily rationalizes his own moral, ethical, or legal misdemeanours. The people most injured by Duddy are Yvette Durelle and Virgil Roseboro, ironically the only two people who provide him with disinterested loyalty and friendship. Duddy does not reciprocate their fealty. His loyalties are almost tribal in nature, and the only untouchable bond in Duddy's life is his allegiance to his family and, by extension, to other Jews. Duddy is not bigoted on principle, but he operates according to instinct and unexamined emotion. He is reconciled to his family's shortcomings and spares no effort when they are in need. Thus, he accepts the fact that his father moonlights as a pimp; he sacrifices his interests for his brother Lennie and travels to New York to persuade his estranged Aunt Ida to come back to be at the bedside of his dying uncle. None of these attitudes and actions are easy for Duddy, but he feels a compulsion to "do the right thing" for his family. It is not a matter of volition but a set of primal reactions.

In contrast, Duddy exploits Yvette's access to Catholic French Canadian landowners in the countryside north of Montreal and then treats her with careless disregard. After he has "made love to her quickly," Yvette asks him, "Do you like me? A little, even?" Duddy only replies, "Sure. Sure thing" (Richler 1995, 110). Yvette herself knows that she is an outsider in Duddy's world. After she takes Duddy to the lakeside property that becomes his obsession, and he offers her fifty dollars to keep the property a secret, Yvette responds, "You wouldn't be ashamed if you had come here with Linda," referring to the daughter of Duddy's Jewish employer. "You'd never offer her money, either" (110). Regardless of Yvette's love and constancy, she cannot be co-opted into his clan (Pollock 1986, 128). Duddy is certain that he will never marry her, yet he allows her to feel as though she is part of his future, included in his dream. When the character of Duddy Kravitz appears in *St Urbain's Horseman* (1971), he has, in fact, married a Jewish woman, Marlene Tyler, "née Malke Tannenbaum" (Richler 1991b, 208). Following his nuptials, he is interviewed by the media about his recent marriage and explains, "there was never any doubt in my mind that I would marry one of our own brethren. I've seen too many mixed marriages. It just can't work" (209).

Similarly, Duddy takes advantage of Virgil. He allows him to drive his delivery truck though he knows that Virgil's epilepsy makes the work potentially life threatening. He takes little responsibility when Virgil eventually becomes a paraplegic as a result of a truck accident, and he later steals from Virgil's trust fund to finance the payment on his waterfront property. Duddy never acts so viciously towards his family or community. It is immaterial that Max Kravitz regularly belittles Duddy and that his Uncle Benjy habitually insults him. He feels an inherent sense of responsibility towards them that is essential to his identity.

In examining the business-friendship triangle that links Duddy, Yvette, and Virgil, it is important to note that Duddy is an English Canadian, Yvette a French Québécoise, and Virgil an American. By treating his relationship with Yvette as a dalliance and exploiting her access to Quebec landowners, Duddy may be seen as enacting Montreal Jewry's revenge fantasy against the historically anti-Semitic French Québécois community. From the end of the nineteenth century, when European Jews began immigrating to Canada in significant numbers, they mainly settled in Montreal, where anti-Semitism was pervasive among both English Protestants and French Catholics (Troper, 8). However, it was French Catholic politicians and religious leaders who made hardline anti-Semitism a foundation of their political agenda. In particular, the two-time premier of Quebec Maurice Duplessis, from his early career in the mid-1930s until his death in 1959, consistently riled his constituents against Quebec's Jews (57). Quebec's francophone population resented the Jewish community's integration into English-speaking Canada. It was the French Catholic leadership, however, that refused to accept Jewish students and forced the English Protestant educational board – amidst much reluctance – to accept them. The policy was made law in the Provincial Education Act of 1903 and was largely responsible for the English Canadian orientation of Quebec's Jewish population (48–9). Duddy's readiness to dupe Yvette is not vindicated by this historical backdrop, but it is contextualized and hints at a communal impulse towards defiance in response to widespread discrimination essentially against Jews but also against English Canada.

By overworking and thereby endangering Virgil and stealing from him, Duddy, as a Jew, may be read as abusing the friendship of an unsuspecting Christian. However, just as relevant, or even more so, is the fact that Virgil is an American. Since the early 1800s, anti-Americanism has been "a central buttress" of Canadian national identity" (Granatstein and Hillmer, 4). It is a prejudice rooted in "a distaste and fear" of American military, political, cultural, and economic might, combined with "a snippet – and sometimes more – of envy at the greatness, wealth and power of the Republic and its citizens" (4). Historically, Canadians have felt overshadowed by their southern neighbours and tended to relish instances when the US has been humbled on the international stage. Jack Granatstein recalls an incident that illustrates the Canadian penchant to celebrate American disgrace:

In the months after the Soviet Union put up Sputnik, the first
satellite launched into an earth orbit, the [theatre] newsreels
featured the United States' effort to develop the huge missiles
necessary to duplicate the Russians' feat. The American missiles,
however, blew up with amazing frequency, collapsing back to
earth in showers of smoke, flames, and explosions ... The
newsreels of these disasters played in Canadian movie houses
to a startling response. When huge missiles strained off their
launch pads only to collapse in ruination, audiences all across
Canada ... clapped, laughed, and cheered, reveling in the
Americans' humiliation and failure. (122)

Duddy's treatment of Virgil is despicable but, in this historical context,
is also emblematic of a comeuppance of American bravado at the
hands of a Canadian underdog.

Indeed, Duddy is as much an English Canadian as a Jew when dealing with Yvette and Virgil. Because his wily tactics and quest for wealth
are constant with standard anti-Semitic views of Jewish behaviour, it
seems as though he is cast as a contemporary Shylock. Duddy takes
advantage of Yvette and manipulates Québécois landholders because
their bias against Jews leaves him with few options if he is to acquire
the lakefront property that he desires: as a Jewish English Canadian
he is hardly an ideal buyer for French farmers, who are generally
reluctant to release their properties to non-Québécois outsiders, above
all Jews. In contrast, Duddy's betrayal of Virgil is staged, at least partially, as a reversal of traditional roles: it is not an American who cons
a Canadian naïf but the other way round. This is not a morally sound
inversion of roles but one that reflects Canadians' recorded gratifica-
tion at American failure or weakness.

During the period in which the novel is set, the late 1940s, Jews
had scant access to the higher echelons of Montreal's (and generally
Quebec's) educational, political, and corporate leadership
(Troper, 42). It is historically accurate that a character such as Duddy
would have experienced few opportunities to empathize with those
outside of his narrowly circumscribed world. Still, his willingness to
exploit and betray Gentiles specifically seems to justify the anti-
Semitic conception of the Jew as insular and self-interested. In the
novel, however, his loyalty is presented as a positive value, within
limits. It indicates an idealistic commitment that is preferable to sheer
money-lust without any principles, serves as redress for French

Canadian anti-Semitism, and underscores Canadians' drive to outshine their American neighbours.

The Apprenticeship of Duddy Kravitz was not Richler's first work about an underprivileged schemer who is keen to penetrate the moneyed class. As the uncredited script doctor of one of the best-received feature films of 1959, *Room at the Top*, Richler had helped bring the hero of John Braine's novel, Joe Lampton, to life on the screen (Kramer 2008, 137). Not nearly as inventive or colourful as Duddy, Joe seduces the daughter of a wealthy businessman in order to climb the socio-economic ladder of an English town. He has none of the moral misgivings that trail Duddy, does not wallow in self-loathing, reflect upon his avaricious motives, or try to disentangle himself from his fraudulent courtship. He is portrayed as a class underdog but is quite ready to sacrifice his older lover, Alice Aisgill, and young fiancée, Susan Brown, in order to get the life he covets, which includes a trophy wife and enough wealth to quell the condescension of the town's elite.

Despite accusations that Richler mainly libelled Jews, especially in *Duddy Kravitz*, it was the script of *Room at the Top* that was his first work about a selfish upstart with a tendency to abuse his friends' and lovers' loyalty for the sake of money. In this light, Duddy Kravitz is not so much Richler's modern Shylock as a Jewish adaptation of a mid-twentieth-century English swindler. He behaves immorally but nurses a sense of remorse. Unlike Joe Lampton, he has a personal code of values and regrets the misfortune he brings upon Yvette and Virgil.

Duddy Kravitz has often been compared to Sammy Glick in Budd Schulberg's 1941 novel *What Makes Sammy Run?* (see Kattan; Wisse 2000). In both works, the protagonists are driven, crass Jewish boys with immigrant roots who wish to get ahead at any cost. In the *Modern Jewish Canon*, Ruth Wisse accuses Richler and Schulberg of vilifying Jewish success. She claims that "they turn[ed] ambition into a particularly Jewish form of corruption" (2000, 276). However, the analogy is not entirely legitimate. Sammy Glick craves power, wealth, and glamour. He has no other value system. His hunger for success is blamed partly on his deprived childhood, but he has only the faintest loyalty to his roots, expressed in a small allowance he sends his family once he acquires a fortune. Duddy's motivations are different. Underlying his drive for land is his Zeyda Simcha's mantra that "a man without land is nothing." To own land and develop it would make him a success according to the wisdom of his religiously observant grandfather, the one person who has shown him life-long affection. Moreover, Duddy is indifferent to money for the sake of sheer wealth. He wants his land to serve as a form of redemption: an opportunity to show his father and other non-believers that he could be a success, a comeuppance to Montreal's Gentile aristocracy with its bigoted attitudes and restricted summer resorts, and a means of realizing his grandfather's dream.

Some critics have labelled Schulberg's novel anti-Semitic, suggesting that it is a condemnation of Jewish power in the film industry during the 1940s and the materialistic culture that it inspired. Schulberg's introduction to the novel insists that he simply tried "to throw some light on one of the less glamorous but not insignificant phases of Hollywood life" (vii) and that Sammy was a "victim" of his poverty, historical moment, and character weakness (xviii). *The Apprenticeship of Duddy Kravitz* has also been described as an anti-Semitic book. However, the Duddy Kravitz character is complicated; he is not simply a Jewish reprobate. His allegiance to his family may not parallel a general sense of universal values contingent upon moral duty, but for Duddy the Montreal Jewish ghetto is its own universe with its particular cultural codes and the only value scheme he can imagine. One may call this insularity, yet it may also be rootedness of a special kind, one that Duddy wants to literalize by purchasing his own plot of land.

While Wisse views Duddy as a soulless and rapacious villain, his more idealistic qualities are recognized by Zailig Pollock (1986, 124): "Duddy is ferociously single-minded in his pursuit of the values of St. Urbain Street – totally, uncynically, even, in its way, idealistic." These values, Pollock continues, include "taking care of one's own" (128) and never forgetting one's roots. For Duddy, unlike Sammy, they are a critical part of being a success. Josh Lambert similarly recognizes Duddy's idealism and believes that the novel is about "patriotism, land ownership and identity." In particular, Lambert views Duddy's hunger for land as a reinterpretation of a Zionist commitment and evidence that Richler deliberately imbued the novel with the spirit of Jewish nationalism. Lambert's claim regarding Zionism is not especially convincing, but what is noteworthy is his willingness to see Duddy as a character driven by more than just the prospect of a swollen bank account and an upper-class front. It is true, as Lambert notes, that Richler wrote engagingly about his youthful escapades in the ultra-Zionistic, leftist youth group HaShomer HaTzair (see Richler 1994) and made Israel an important issue in *St Urbain's Horseman*. But Duddy's loyalties are simpler than

Zion (Woodcock 1991, 67). Everything he holds sacred emanates from his devotion to family (67).

For Duddy, family commitments are, as noted above, an involuntary reflex, innate and indestructible. Most of Richler's other protagonists also consider family loyalty an undisputable value, though not one that they always manage to uphold. Consequently, they suffer guilt, angst, and injury to their self-worth because of their inconsistent or inadequate fidelity to their families or their families' value systems and cultural codes. The earliest novel to seriously explore this breach in family values is *Son of a Smaller Hero*, a semi-autobiographical work that, despite the paratextual disclaimer, mirrors much of Richler's childhood life and path into young adulthood. The novel's protagonist, Noah Adler, is conflicted. Because he cannot tolerate hypocrisy and self-righteousness, he turns his back on his grandfather, his Zeyde Melech, and his Orthodox ways. Though his grandfather's business transactions are less reprehensible than they seem, Noah's indictment of Melech Adler launches his flight from the social and cultural confines of Montreal's Jewish ghetto. He then begins a journey of self-exploration that leads him into the arms of a Gentile woman and eventually across the Atlantic. Noah suffers for the distance he puts between himself and his community, but the narrative makes it clear that his family's world, mainstream Jewish Montreal, is not only void of meaningful values and compelling religious sentiment but a repugnant caricature of social climbing and avarice. Success in this cultural environment is symbolized by a move from the humble world of St Lawrence Boulevard, popularly referred to as "The Main," to the upscale neighbourhood of Outremont, epitomized by its main thoroughfare, Queen Mary Road:

> The Queen Mary Jews walked like prosperity, grinning a
> flabby grin which said money in the bank. Notaries, lawyers,
> businessmen, doctors. They wore their wives like signposts of
> their success and dressed them accordingly. The children were
> big and little proofs, depending on the size of their achievements.
> (Richler 1989b, 13)

Nevertheless, Noah is pained when he moves into his own apartment, leaving his parents to face the disapproval of the Adler clan in the wake of his departure from the family and its traditional Jewish lifestyle. He imagines his mother "lonely in her kitchen chair, lonely even on a crowded streetcar, sit[ting] among them defiantly, her white, chapped hands folded on her lap and her swollen eyes outstaring them" (22). He understands that he has left his mother to bear the brunt of the Adler wrath against him, a once favourite scion who has squelched every hope his family harboured regarding his future. Noah, still, is able to forgive himself. *"It is necessary, at times to hurt others. But I'm hurting her very much. I'd better be right"* (22, emphasis in original). This type of clichéd philosophizing is common in Richler's earlier works, but the underlying preoccupation with moral autonomy does contribute to the novel's overall complexity.

When producing novels that dramatized Montreal Jewish life, Richler anticipated a fierce backlash – the kind represented in Philip Roth's *The Ghost Writer* (1979) – especially from his family, relatives, and old acquaintances. In terms of *Son of a Smaller Hero*, with characters and scenes that parallel large portions of Richler's early life, Richler observed: "there was a violent reaction and I expected that and I expected people to be hurt" (qtd in Cohen 1971a, 32). In an essay entitled, "My Father's Life," he recalls having, like Noah, suffered pangs of conscience for the pain he caused his parents by charting an independent life – a life apart from his family, bearing little resemblance to the aspirations, commitments, and sorrows of his aunts, uncles, cousins, and various relatives far and near. He gives the following account of his grandfather's response:

> Before a court composed of just about the entire family, he denounced me as a violator of the Sabbath ... My grandfather grabbed me by the ear, beat me about the face, and literally threw me out of the house. I lingered across the street, waiting for my father to seek me out, but when he finally appeared, having endured a bruising lecture of his own, all he said was, "You deserved what you got." (Richler 1984, 65)

This recollection illustrates the consequences Richler faced for having rejected his family's traditions. Hence, it is not surprising that in creating a semi-autobiographical novel with a protagonist who renounces his own family's ways, Richler expected a severe and vocal reaction.

While distancing oneself physically from one's family is always an option for Richler's Jewish protagonists, ignoring one's conscience is impossible. Just before departing for Europe, Noah tells his grandfather, Melech Adler, "I am going and I'm not going. I can no more leave you, my mother, or my father's memory, than I can renounce myself" (Richler 1989b, 199). Commitment to family stays with one even in rebellion, and this principle is repeatedly reinforced in Richler's corpus of fiction and his autobiographical writing.[1] In a sense, Richler's personal writings signal to readers that, despite his satiric attacks on Montreal's Jewish world, the author experienced remorse for the heartache he could not help but inflict. Richler knew people would be hurt by the autobiographical content of *Son of a Smaller Hero*, but he believed that he had "written a serious book" and justified the pain as the cost of that level of achievement (qtd in Cohen 1971a, 32).

Most of Richler's subsequent novels deal more specifically with issues of filial responsibility, even when their protagonists fail to act as dutiful sons. In *St Urbain's Horseman*, Jake Hersh winces thinking of his disloyal feelings towards his mother. He recognizes her love and good intentions but cannot extricate them from her manipulative behaviour and Jewish chauvinism. Much as he would like to be a devoted son, he is unable to overcome his antipathy towards her. When his mother arrives in England to help the family through Jake's sordid sex-scandal trial, he ricochets "between icy cruelty to his mother and what she, understandably, came to cherish as acts of filial kindness" (Richler 1991b, 32). In relation to his father, Jake suffers even further heartache. Upon attending his father's funeral he is torn between mourning his father and lamenting his selfish disappointment with a man who was an inadequate husband to his mother, a failed provider, and a poor role model. Kerry McSweeney argues that, in *St Urbain's Horseman*, the chapters set in Montreal are amusing but of little narrative or thematic importance. This view overlooks the way in which these chapters are instrumental in portraying the importance of family among Montreal Jews – how, for instance, the values of the Hersh family are integrated into Jake's personal system of incontrovertible principles. The Hersh family is close-knit and Jake, despite having struck out on his own, is still very attached to them. This is evident in his frequent reminisces of his Montreal youth and his reaction to his father's passing:

Sitting with the Hershes, day and night, a bottle of Remy Martin parked between his feet, such was Jake's astonishment, commingled with pleasure, in their responses, that he could not properly mourn for his father. He felt cradled, not deprived.

He also felt like Rip Van Winkle returned to an innocent and ordered world he had mistakenly believed long extinct. Where God watched over all, doing His sums. Where everything fit. (Richler 1991b, 391–2)

Moreover, Jake has built his own life according to these principles, though he has reframed them. Family is the cornerstone of his life, a choice that is not accidental. It is possibly the most enduring vestige of the value system that was impressed upon him throughout his early life.

Another sphere in which the importance of family is evident in Richler's novels is the representation of the protagonist as a family man. In *St Urbain's Horseman* Jake has a troubled conscience because of the emotional torment he causes his wife Nancy as a result of his friendship with Harry Stein, a repugnant Jewish bookkeeper who ensnares him in a bizarre sexual-harassment imbroglio. The narrative does not probe Jake's troubled conscience or relate Jake's profound apologies to his wife. Instead, his remorse is revealed through one poignant moment. "Oh Nancy, Jake thought," overcome by his wife's suffering, "and began to sob. Without control. Without dignity" (Richler 1991b, 38). The importance of being a good husband is likewise obvious in *Joshua Then and Now* (1980), where Joshua Shapiro believes himself responsible in no small measure for his wife Pauline's nervous breakdown, consequent depression, and disappearance. Much like Duddy Kravitz, the one value Joshua holds dear is family. It is "family which supplies the meaning in his life" (Bonnycastle, 176), and he is devastated by his failure to abide by his own code of family commitment. He knows that without his wife and children his life has no significance and no moral centre.

In *Barney's Version*, too, the protagonist, Barney Panofsky, suffers after he undermines his happy third marriage. He has a one-night stand with an extra from one of his television programs, infidelity being the one misdemeanour he knows that his wife, Miriam, will not forgive. He then experiences daily regret for the remainder of his life. The break with Miriam is especially significant as Miriam Greenberg is the only likeable Jewish spouse of any of Richler's protagonists. Many critics repeatedly faulted Richler for the thinness of his female characters in general, and Richler himself admitted in an early 1970s interview with Graeme Gibson that he had failed to create multi-dimensional woman characters (287). The portrayal of Miriam, self-willed, with the gumption to leave Barney, suggests that Richler was attempting to redress his tendency to draw lead women as compliant fantasy figures, Gentile beauties, often uniformly intelligent, attractive, domestic, and obliging.

By making Miriam Jewish, Richler was also defying detractors who claimed it was beyond his reach to imagine a Jewish woman who was not a tragic cliché of over-indulgence or a caricature of a manipulative shrew. However, it is Barney Panofsky's earlier marriage to Clara Charnofsky that has an even stronger Jewish resonance. In the novel, Barney demonstrates a penchant for conventional values when, as a young man living in Paris, he agrees to marry his girlfriend Clara because he believes that she is carrying his child. Again, for Richler's protagonists, there is no shirking essential family responsibilities. Clara is unruly, crass; she regularly humiliates Barney, referring to him as Shylock and Prince Charmingbaum. Nevertheless, Barney refuses to abandon her or his unborn child. The irony is that Clara is later revealed to be filled with contradictions. Her anti-Semitic slurs acquire a new meaning when she turns out to be the daughter of devout Orthodox Jewish parents. The baby she is carrying is not Barney's but the outcome of Clara's affair with Cedric Richardson, a black man and Barney's close friend. And, regardless of her verbal harassment and unfaithfulness, she needs Barney's love and heavily relies upon him.

Barney, like many of Richler's protagonists, does not easily extricate himself from situations that touch upon his belief in being a devoted Jewish son, husband, and father. The world that he comes from is almost identical to that of Noah Adler, filled with men who stand by their families, remain loyal to their wives, and support their children:

> They had known each other for years, and most of them
> were related in one way or another. They, the sons, were still
> orthodox. The synagogue was a habit and a meeting place for
> them. The *Goyim*, a mystery. Something to talk about. They
> were substantial men. Extremely good to their wives and
> enormously fond of their children. (Richler 1989b, 106)

These kinds of men were Barney's formative role models, making it impossible for him to abandon Clara even when his friends insist that it is an obvious mistake for him to link his future to hers.[2] Miriam may represent a concession to those who were unimpressed with Richler's ability to render female characters, especially sympathetic

Jewish ones, but Clara is a complex character too and, despite her malicious taunts and repellent behaviour, is painted in a sympathetic light as a woman with undeniable appeal. In contrast, the novel's other prominent female character, Barney's second wife, referred to only as the Second Mrs P., is relentlessly satirized. She represents every over-indulged, academically successful but intellectually dim Jewish woman bred within the confines of the Jewish establishment and is portrayed as lacking any vestige of redeeming charm. She is, as Reinhold Kramer writes, Richler's "revenge against the Jewish yenta" (356).

Identification with Old World Jewish culture and values is another important way in which Richler's protagonists structure their value system. In his novels, Richler sought to reproduce the Jewish world of his childhood, a world where Jewish life was the norm and the lives of non-Jews were alien and incomprehensible (1973b, 10). It was a world in which stolid Jewish Orthodoxy was the automatic spiritual default. The foundation of its mores and cultural tastes were based on what members of the Canadian-born generation of Montreal Jews had inherited from their Polish- and Russian-born parents. In some ways, this is evident simply through their preference for Jewish fare – spicy salami and chopped liver with onions. Yet, for Richler, Old World Jewish culture represents authenticity and is often juxtaposed with newly fashionable Jewish ways – social, spiritual, or cultural. For example, in *Son of a Smaller Hero*, after Melech Adler understands that Noah partly loathes him because he is a shady businessman, he muses, "Noah would have respected me if I'd been a scribe" (Richler 1989b, 52). Even though Noah has no great regard for Jewish Orthodoxy, Melech Adler has a visceral understanding of Noah's appreciation of idealism and its labours, even if it takes the form of religious devotion. And, in *The Apprenticeship of Duddy Kravitz*, Duddy's uncle Benjy, a theoretical, if not practising, communist, articulates the importance of traditional Jewish forms in a paradoxical manner:

> There used to be … some dignity in being against the synagogue. With a severe orthodox rabbi there were things to quarrel about. There was some pleasure. But this cream-puff of a synagogue, this religious drugstore, you might as well spend your life being against *The Reader's Digest*. They've taken all the mystery out of religion. (Richler 1995, 166–7)

The hallmark of this "religious drugstore" Judaism is the novel's parody of the bar mitzvah film that Duddy produces for the Cohen family with the help of the feckless director, Peter John Friar. The movie is a bizarre pastiche: shots of a preening rabbi, a cliché bar mitzvah ceremony, African tribal dances, a gift table laden with subscriptions to *National Geographic*, a season's hockey tickets, phylacteries, and "a pile of fifty silver dollars in a velvet-lined box" (182). Richler satirizes this kind of film by having one character justify it, pretentiously suggesting that it is an example of comparative religion, something that the unnamed speaker studied at Montreal's McGill University. "Comparative *what*? I'll give you such a schoss" (175) is the matter-of-fact reply, the counter-voice in the tension between Old World ideas of Jewishness and Jewish kitsch masquerading as cultural sophistication. While watching the film, Mr Cohen asks his father if he is "all right" (177), only half-joking that the film seems to have triggered a stroke in the elder patriarch. The question implies that the film is an insult to traditional, meaningful Jewish life and, as such, has left the elder Cohen visibly distressed.

The narrative then records Mr Cohen's own reaction to the movie and how it reflects the way in which this world of upwardly mobile Jews has become inured to a maudlin, vapid version of Jewish life:

> it's worth it, every last cent or what's money for, it's cheap at any price to have captured my family and friends and foolish rabbi. He reached for Gertie's hand and thought I'd better not kiss Bernie. It would embarrass him. (185)

Mr Cohen is one of a cadre of men in Richler's novels whose allegiance to family is unshakeable. But the narrative makes it clear that he is also highly concerned with cost effectiveness and insufficiently critical of newfangled Judaism. He is part of the novel's critique of a Jewish world that treats Judaism as a commodity and a constituent of an environment heavy with Jewish sentimentality but lacking authentic traditions and customs deemed incompatible with modern, middle-class sensibilities.

The novel's assault on modernized Judaism is in keeping with Richler's own on-record views. Describing his *cheder* studies as a young boy and the earnest efforts of his teacher to impart the wonder of Judaism through mystical tales, he wrote:

All the same, we certainly preferred Mr. Feinberg's Chasidic
lore to the logical platitudes of Young Israel's new "modern"
rabbi, who was such a big hit with the ladies' auxiliary, if
not with the men, who, on Sundays, were expected to attend
father-and-son breakfasts featuring reviews of books by
Sholem Asch or Budd Schulberg, who wrote filth about our
people. The twinkly Rabbi Bloom ... made a pitch for what
he called "the kids." Instead of a Sadie Hawkins Day Dance,
like *they* were having, how about a Queen Esther Ball ...
He also attempted to appeal to our reason. Pork, he said, was
forbidden because it would have spoiled in the heat of Canaan,
the children of Israel were enjoined to wear hats to protect
them against sunstroke, etc. Suddenly all the magic was gone.
(Richler 1987, 53)

For Richler, as for Duddy, Judaism sanitized for the twentieth century
was trivial. He may not have accepted the truth of traditional teach-
ings, but he appreciated the esoteric sense of wonder that was part of
old-fashioned belief.

This view of Judaism may explain Richler's inclination to create
truly God-fearing Orthodox characters who, though ineffectual, are
endearing. In *Solomon Gursky Was Here*, one of the most earnest,
appealing and eccentric characters is Henry Gursky, an heir of his
family's liquor fortune who chooses Hasidic Judaism and Canada's
arctic North over the high-society opulence of Montreal's Westmount
neighbourhood. A sure sign that Henry is meant to be likeable is the
fact that he is a cherished friend of the protagonist, Moses Berger. On
the one hand, rarely is characterization "direct" in Richler's novels. The
narrative typically traffics in ambiguity. However, "direct presentation"
occurs when an opinion is expressed "by the most authoritative voice
in the text" (Rimmon Kennan, 63). In Richler's novels, the protagonist's admiration of another character, even if uneven, is usually an
indication that the latter represents some aspect of the text's sacred
values. Another example illustrating this point involves the character
of Norman Charnofsky, Clara's mitzvoth-observant uncle in *Barney's
Version*, who is portrayed charitably. He gains Barney's good opinion
and proves to be candid, intelligent, and tragically self-destructive – the
last attribute a clue that, for Richler, pious Orthodoxy may be noble,
but also impractical and naive.

In light of Richler's own precocious rejection of Jewish ritual observance at the age of thirteen (Foran, 63), it is significant that his novels evoke a sympathetic rather than satiric image of sincere religiosity. Richler sardonically attributed his break with Orthodoxy to the lure of the pool hall and baseball games on the Sabbath. Yet his alienation from Judaism was also, or perhaps mainly, a result of the tyrannical reign of religious observance enforced by Shmarya Richler upon his children and grandchildren, which sometimes included corporal punishment (Kramer 2008, 37–9). Whatever the impetus, it is unquestionable that, from his early teens, Richler was not committed to Orthodox beliefs or practices. Nevertheless, there is evidence that he was somewhat wistful about his early *cheder* studies with Eastern European rebbes and the tradition that he had all but abandoned. In 1987, in his contribution to a book of modern popular biblical exegesis, he wrote:

> My children ... had a different upbringing. Foolishly, we
> spared the *cheder*, short-changing them with a liberal education.
> I'm okay, you're okay; no hang-ups, but no magic, either;
> too bad. But now, when they sit down with my wife and me to
> the Passover table, there are many things they want to know.
> They ask more than four questions. After all these years,
> I have become their Mr. Feinberg. (Richler 1987, 55)

Another bow to Old World Judaism is evident in *Joshua Then and Now* where Joshua Shapiro's father, Reuben, a small-time wrong-side-of-the-tracks gangster, becomes an unconventional Bible scholar, in awe of God and respectful of the synagogue. Reuben is the type of character that Richler's novels most often portray in a positive light because, despite his rough edges, he has a straightforward sense of right and wrong and admits his mistakes and weaknesses rather than play the hypocrite.

When Joshua is a teenager, Reuben explains to him that the Bible is full of sound wisdom and historical precedents. When dramatizing the entrapment of the Israelites in Egypt, Reuben exclaims, "They were working like niggers and they were not being paid a dime" (Richler 2001, 89). The irony is that Reuben is not speaking with racist intent. The comparison, in his mind, suggests historical camaraderie that is emphasized by gauche language. Later, when explaining God's mercy, Reuben assures Joshua that the commandments are like questions on a test: one does not have to achieve a perfect score to do well. He elaborates that, in any case, it is possible to mollify God regardless of biblical transgressions. "Like these are the Days of Awe and all you got to do is repent, even adultery, *sincerely*, but ... God doesn't keep a sheet on you" (89–90). Reuben is one of the few people whom Joshua admires unconditionally, and his admiration extends to his father's biblical sense of the world and his conception of how to be the right kind of man. The reader, too, is charmed by this rudimentary theology, and Reuben's character is responsible for much of the novel's comic relief.

Reuben also resorts to the Bible in justifying his tendency to favour underdogs, an attitude that is held by most of Richler's positively drawn characters, and another of Richler's personal beliefs that suffuses his novels. Richler viewed the writer as "a kind of loser's advocate, as a witness to injustices in this world ... speak[ing] for those people who are not getting a fair share of the sun" (qtd in Gibson, 271). Reuben, like Jake Hersh, Barney Panofsky, and Moses Berger in *Solomon Gursky Was Here*, identifies with the disadvantaged. Contrary to traditional Jewish interpretations, in retelling the story of the patriarch Isaac's sons, Reuben sympathizes with Esau rather than his younger brother Jacob. He describes Jacob as a "cunning little bastard, a momma's boy, a jealous type" and, more accusingly, "a real Outremont kid, always looking for angles." Esau, conversely, is a "fine fella, a hunter," who knows how to please his father (Richler 2001, 95). He then tells Joshua that Jacob stole the blessing of the firstborn from Esau and, with it, the credentials to become a biblical patriarch. But he also makes it clear that when it comes to divine plans, there is no second-guessing the Bible. "But, what the hell, Jacob is one of our holy fathers ... and he's tricked in turn by this guy, Laban, a real con, when he comes sniffing around, looking for a wife" (95).

Reuben's sense of justice, indeed, has biblical overtones. He equates justice with honour and the fulfilment of promises and commitments (even when those promises pertain to illicit matters) rather than with obedience to the law. For example, when his long-time mentor Sonny Colucci is owed money for a gambling debt by a highly respected Outremont dentist, Dr Orbach, Reuben has no qualms about exercising his loyalty to his old friend and exacting justice – a kind of straightforward talion. Reuben is not the kind of fearless hero that Richler's characters worship, but he is of a similar ilk. When he visits Orbach to pressure him to repay his loan, the dentist chastises

Reuben: "A Bible reading-Jew collecting for *goyishe* mobsters. Shame on you, Shapiro" (92). Of course, the real shame is that a professional, prominent in Montreal's affluent Jewish community, has accrued an $11,000 gambling debt to an underworld figure, and the double standard is not lost on Reuben. When he explains his career choice, telling Orbach that his own opportunities had been limited due to his lack of education, Orbach counters that such problems did not stymie Bernard Gursky. Reuben's rejoinder is that he, too, would have "liked to make millions out of bootlegging" (92). In other words, Reuben may be the lackey of a small-time Mafioso, but he is true to his values, straight from the Pentateuch, and will not tolerate name-calling. He is no worse than a bootlegging tycoon and, at the very least, tries to be the kind of Jew who sports a clear notion of right and wrong. His task is to punish men who fail to uphold their commitment to contractual agreements, and for him there is nothing morally equivocal about this job description.

The kind of communal hypocrisy that emerges in the episode with Dr Orbach is yet another example of factors that led to young Richler's conclusion that flagrantly public displays of piety are often hypocritical or, at best, meaningless. As a boy, Richler was disillusioned when he learned that the men in his synagogue regularly overbid for the honour of blessing the Torah during the Shabbat service, "acting as shills trying to embarrass nonmembers, prodding them into paying heavily for a piece of the Torah action" but paying "only half of their declared bid" themselves (1987, 52). This uncompromising intolerance for dishonesty may have run in Richler's family. In a short story told from the perspective of the mythical Sabbath Queen, Richler's maternal grandfather Reb Yudel Rosenberg chided Montreal Jewry a generation earlier for its attitude towards the bidding process for the honour of blessing the Torah during Shabbat and the High Holidays services. In particular, he criticized those Jews who no longer observed the Sabbath but eagerly performed conspicuous displays of piety:

> When they have *yortseit* or on Rosh ha-Shana/Yom Kippur
> they come into a synagogue and buy a "fat" *aliya*. The *gabbai*
> together with the president delight in such a fine guest and
> beckon to the *shammes* to seat him in a good place ... is this
> not a desecration of God's name and a disgrace for the Torah?
> (Robinson et al., 108)

This is the type of critical attitude that Richler appreciated and incorporated into his novels. He tended to satirize the proud, self-satisfaction of men who had amassed a fortune, achieved little else, but still comported themselves as paragons of respectability worthy of accolades. In *Joshua Then and Now*, as in most of his novels, pompous self-righteousness is always associated with the materialism of Jewish life in the New World, while Richler's Old World Jews are usually free of vulgar pretension and conspicuous displays of affluence (Bell, 70).

Joshua Then and Now is often used as an example when critics accuse Richler of writing novels with a "lack of felt direction" (Iannone). Stephen Bonnycastle posits that this novel's moral unity is undercut by the fragmented narrative, with constant shifts in time and setting, which pre-empt any meaningful thematic or character development (69). Possibly, one reason *Joshua Then and Now* seems morally uncentred is that it is the only mature novel (see Ramraj) in which Richler did not insert the hero figure. Reuben Shapiro performs that narrative function only to a limited extent: he lacks the all-knowing panache of the heroes in Richler's other novels, heroes who are more mysterious and seemingly more savvy, courageous, and ambitious. Moreover, Richler's fully realized hero figures are wholly committed to their independent vision of moral idealism. Returning to supererogation and how it often encompasses a moral vision that extends well beyond mainstream social morality (Heyd, 182), Reuben Shapiro may not be heroic, but he is in fact very loyal to moral conventions, a confluence of Old World biblical fairness and underworld justice.

Distinct from the privileging of Old World Jewish attitudes in Richler's works is the overt condemnation of the philistinism and social-climbing impulse of the Jewish nouveau riche, especially when upwardly mobile Jews strive for acceptance in Gentile social circles. In this regard, Richler does not riddle his novels with appeals to Jews to hone aesthetic sensibilities or adopt behaviours that suggest sophistication and grace. Instead, he chastises moneyed Jews and lampoons their vulgar ways through satire, creating dialogue and scenarios that reveal them as déclassé with a pathetic insatiable drive to be accepted by non-Jews.

In *Solomon Gursky*, Richler's version of the respectable Jewish businessman who has amassed wealth but lacks the sense to use it in a dignified, meaningful way, is Harvey Schwartz. He is a lawyer who functions as counsel for the Gursky family, loosely based on the

Canadian liquor barons, the Bronfmans. He is portrayed as a syco-phant, forever ingratiating himself to the official head of the empire, Bernard Gursky. He has a boorish wife, the author of the maudlin memoir *Pain, Hugs and Chocolate Chip Cookies*, who mistakes wealth for taste and excess for aestheticism. To prove his worth and social status, he lives in a mansion in Westmount – the apex of Montreal's elite W A S P neighbourhoods.

The exaggerated self-importance cultivated by a character such as Harvey Schwartz is sharply satirized by Richler in *St Urbain's Horseman* when Duddy Kravitz makes an appearance as the publisher of *The Canadian Jewish Who's Who*, "an epoch-making compendium that was destined to become part and parcel of our incomparable Jewish heritage" (Richler 1991b, 170). This is yet another of Duddy's profit-making scams designed to relieve successful Jewish professionals and businessmen – men similar to Harvey Schwartz – of a small sum for the honour of appearing in a self-congratulatory directory of moderate success stories. It is evident that Duddy's target clientele is not reticent – a crowd eager to be toasted for its substantial, but hardly historic, achievements. Preying on this uncensored vanity, he clears $50,000 "in legitimate profit" (170–1).[3] Richler loathed this kind of provincial triumphalism; in the words of Margaret Atwood, he "had a horror of being pompous" (qtd in Posner, 311) and could not tolerate gratuitous self-promotion in others.

The related issue of Jewish success validated by privileged non-Jews was first given serious attention in two novels that predate *Solomon Gursky*. In *Son of a Smaller Hero*, Noah Adler imagines that the non-Jewish academic social circles in downtown Montreal are an oasis of taste and culture. But when he infiltrates that world he finds people whom he comes to see as impostors. They have read important books and learned to appreciate fine music but are unsure of their world, beliefs, and vision for their futures. Noah decides that it is not worth trading Montreal's Jewish ghetto for these intellectuals, who seem to be just as stagnant in their lives as he feels he is in his. In *Duddy Kravitz*, Duddy's brother Lennie befriends a group of wealthy Gentile students at McGill and almost abandons his medical studies for the sake of their camaraderie. However, he discovers that he is nothing more than their tolerated minion, an updated "court Jew" – a realiza-tion that brings him back into the fold of his native St Urbain Street. In both of these instances, the narrative treats these characters sym-pathetically because they eventually recognize that there is no hidden magic among the Gentiles. They forsake their effort to assimilate and the aspiration to be refined and sophisticated. By contrast, Harvey Schwartz never has such a moment of reckoning.

In terms of the vulgar materialism of the post-immigration generation, the Second Mrs P. in *Barney's Version* has no rival. *Son of a Smaller Hero* mocks the economic success of the Adler brothers. The decadence of Joshua Shapiro's childhood friends, Irving Pinsky, Jonathan Cole né Yosel Kugelman, and Eli Seligson, is a minor subplot in *Joshua Then and Now*. And, in *Solomon Gursky Was Here*, the character L.B. Berger develops into a base and craven man who compromises intellectual integrity for the sake of lucre and his ego. Still, the Second Mrs P. is Richler's harshest portrayal of nouveau riche exhibitionism. The nameless second wife spends much of her early romance with Barney planning the renovation of his home with the help of an interior designer, reads the *New York Times* mainly to identify books that would likely be discussed at dinner parties, and cannot stand "nobodies": "Yes, the Second Mrs. Panofsky was an exemplar of that much-maligned phenomenon, the Jewish-American Princess" (Richler 1998a, 164), the diametrical opposite of Barney's first wife, Clara. In the pièce de résistance that portrays her brash tastes and manner, Richler creates her side of a farcical phone conversation during which she also proves incomparably bratty, crass, cruel, and vacuous.

It would seem that, according to the ordinary Jewish values in Richler's novels, the Second Mrs P. has a redeeming quality – her pronounced commitment to family. When speaking to her mother on the phone, she appears to be a loyal daughter, attuned to her mother's anxieties and paranoia. However, ideal wives in Richler's novels mainly reserve their love and affection for their husbands and children. Only male protagonists are blamelessly dedicated to other family members. Exacerbating the problem of the Second Mrs P's family connection is the unworthiness of her parents as recipients of her devotion. Her father is parodied in the novel, christened "the ultimate mock Wasp Jew" and portrayed as a self-righteous vulgarian with a pathetic tendency to speak in lofty prose. His wife is also a model of social pretension, wearing a pince-nez, jiggling a tiny bell to beckon the serving staff at dinner, and admonishing Barney for his table manners at their first meeting. Richler's protagonists are men who feel an affinity to unpolished, street-wise, hardworking fathers, and the novels treat them as appropriately dedicated offspring. Conversely, the Second Mrs P. is implicitly criticized for dividing her loyalty between Barney and her superficial, self-congratulatory parents. Moreover, she appears repugnant for having failed to recognize and reject her parents' uninspired materialism and gauche self-importance the way Noah Adler rejected his family's insular world and narrow values.

Thus, Richler's protagonists, though they do not always abide by them, represent *ordinary* Jewish values: family loyalty, the reaffirmation of the "family man," and an appreciation of Old World Jewish tradition. Partly because of the failure of their good intentions, these characters overlap with the tradition of what Ruth Wisse describes as the American schlemiel. In the modern context, the Jewish literary hero, Wisse's schlemiel, is transformed from a fool who softens reality with a deliberate misinterpretation of life's hardships to a Jewish everyman who experiences the world with "a full heart" (Wisse 1980, 82). The contemporary schlemiel is defined by "committed emotional involvement" and is a counter-statement to the American literary hero, modelled on the "stoical containment" of Hemingway's protagonists (82). In Richler's mature novels characters are seldom described as stoical or reserved. Almost unanimously, critics have found Richler's work steeped in emotion, so much so that the urgency of feelings seems to blur the line between narrator and author (Sheps 1971, xiv). This abundance of emotional energy is often channelled into satire that decries much of Jewish life, but it is also used to celebrate ordinary Jewish values that the narratives scrutinize yet ultimately reaffirm.

Richler's Jewish Hero Figures

Heroic Jewish values, as opposed to ordinary ones, come to light in Richler's novels through the lives of hero figures. These values are not necessarily unified or coherent, but they are usually based upon an idealized sense of justice, Jewish empowerment, rightful vengeance, a libidinous spirit, and an unapologetic quest for pleasure that is far removed from rabbinic stringency and Talmudic wariness.[1]

Previously, it was argued that Richler's hero figures do not neatly fit into the category of supererogation because they are too indifferent to social morality. Their actions, although often beyond the call of duty, are not necessarily a contribution to the common good or even the good of the Other. Nevertheless, they are heroic in J.O. Urmson's terms: these characters choose valiant activism when the majority is inclined towards basic duty. Notably, they insist on standards of justice that are beyond the norms of everyday life as experienced by ordinary men. They do not follow a circumscribed code that is "formulable in rules of manageable complexity" but rely upon their individual conception of moral ideals. Finally, they act heroically out of their own volition, regardless of social pressure and cultural expectations, underlying motivation being essential to the definition of supererogation (Urmson, 211–13).

Richler's protagonists, in contrast, live, or try to live, by ordinary values, but they treasure heroic values. The code of honour and principles of the hero figures – sometimes evident in their lives but just as often surmised by the protagonists – are the values that the novels ultimately idealize. However, this formulation of Jewish heroics constitutes an unrealistic baseline of liveable codes and cannot be upheld by ordinary people in normative circumstances. Thus, the novels present heroic values as an ideal but reaffirm ordinary values as a plausible way to live one's life with honour and dignity. Victor Ramraj's description of Jake Hersh in *St Urbain's Horseman* is a useful illustration of the contrast between these two value categories and how they intersect in the protagonist's mind. Jake, he writes, is reasonable and socialized, but he "yearns for heroic confrontation and challenge, symbolized by the Horseman in the novel" (Ramra,j 9). Jake, like other protagonists, cherishes the fantasy of the moral avenger, or Jewish force of justice. However, he knows that the Horseman fantasy must remain just that, a fantasy, in order to be preserved since real life curbs unrestrained heroism, moral or otherwise, or reveals it as altogether flawed.

Heroic values not only distinguish Richler's protagonists from *their* heroes but also add an element of redemption and hope to his works, tempering the apparent nihilism for which they have been criticized (e.g., in Darling 1986 and Sheps 1971). Richler himself often went on record refuting such criticism and insisting that his novels were largely efforts to fashion a viable moral code and expressions of his continual search for "values with which in this time a man can live with honor" (qtd in Cohen 1971a, 38). Indeed, the novels' Jewish heroics are a part of Richler's attempt to fashion a workable paradigm of moral values. They are not simply "a reformulation of tedious polemics" fitted into novelistic structure – a tactic that could reduce novels to stories that "one might pick up to enjoy, be moved by, and perhaps learn something from" but not consider in terms of intellectual possibilities (Harrison, 71). Rather, they form a system of values that prove Richler both a product and an observer of his age, one who is able to evoke his era but also transcend its dominant cultural and intellectual conventions.

The prototype of Richler's hero figure is Jerry Dingleman, the Boy Wonder in *The Apprenticeship of Duddy Kravitz* (1959). Dingleman is described early in the book as possessing many of the traits that become the hallmarks of the hero figures who stand for the most exalted ideals in Richler's fiction. According to the Boy Wonder's most ardent admirer, Duddy's father Max, he is brilliantly enterprising, a crackerjack gambler, fearless, unlike "mere mortals" (Richler 1995, 22), undaunted by non-Jews, a lady's man, loyal to his community, and "no atheist" (65). For Duddy, raised on Max's legend of the St Urbain Street urchin who became the neighbourhood's greatest, and possibly most notorious, success, the Boy Wonder is a mythical creature. Adding to his mystique is the fact that, despite Duddy's requests to meet with Jerry Dingleman and present him with some of his business ideas, Max always proffers the same reply: "Not yet. Next year maybe. When you're ready" (65). The delay heightens Duddy's curiosity about the magical figure and makes the latter seem even more impressive, powerful, and almost messianic in his ability to model a better future. Duddy is so enraptured with this image that he fantasizes how "point for point he was a lot like the Boy Wonder before he had made his name" (65).

Nevertheless, there are early indications that the Boy Wonder is a false hero. A debonair appearance and conspicuous virility are basic features of Richler's heroes, but Jerry Dingleman is afflicted with polio as an adult, leaving him disfigured. Moreover, his sexual prowess is in question. More important, his underworld activities are mere money-making schemes, not idealistic ventures or humanitarian feats, as is the case with Richler's more fully realized hero figures. This is a critical failing. Duddy imagines Jerry Dingleman as a man of noble character, wise and awe-inspiring. Instead, he discovers a hackneyed mobster who can be charitable but also sadistic, insisting on humiliating his petitioners by having them appear at his ramshackle office on "Schnorrer's Day" (152). Dingleman also engages in drug trafficking; he dupes Duddy into smuggling heroin across the American border. Richler's real heroes only skirt the law in order to achieve some higher purpose, but Dingleman's narcotics dealings are tawdry: he is a low-life operator rather than a St Urbain hero.

It is clear by the end of the novel that Dingleman lacks all scruples. He has tried to purchase waterfront land in the Quebec countryside that Duddy, an underprivileged boy from his own childhood haunt, has already begun to acquire. It is especially cruel as he knows that the land is Duddy's economic and emotional stake. Still, more than any of these attributes, it is the way in which Dingleman functions in the novel that renders him a failed hero. Initially, the Boy Wonder is presented as a legend, the fodder for Max Kravitz's dramatic rags-to-riches rhapsodizing. But, when Duddy has his first personal encounter with him, immediately the myth of greatness is deflated. He recognizes a man who is indifferent to the values of the world that nourished his success.

In subsequent novels, the protagonists, and readers, too, have little if any direct access to the hero figures. They know them primarily through family lore and community gossip. They are never in a position to become reasonably well acquainted with the men who are the larger-than-life heroes of their minds' eye. The physical absence of the hero figures is a plot-construction strategy that is essential to Richler's novels because it allows the protagonists to imagine these men, legends of uncertain ethical standing, as hero figures who are beyond moral reproach. They are unknowable, too mysterious to be subject to direct scrutiny, and can, therefore, represent a set of heroic values that are super-human. Ensconced in shadows, they are known by reputation and significant acts of valour but remain enigmatic, unreachable, and therefore unassailable.

Richler's writing, by his own admission, is saturated with critiques of human foibles. His early tendency to be disparaging and unsympathetic, in fiction and in life, was the basis for the widespread charge that his novels, weakened by misanthropic hopelessness, "lacked a coherent moral vision" (Darling, 1). In his early novels, all characters are exposed to censure, with the "hardness" that was his admitted style of concerned observation.[2] But the inclusion of the hero figure character, a narrative strategy that emerged as Richler matured as a novelist, added a positive subtext that was previously absent. Because these characters are elusive, but not imaginary, the protagonists are able to conceive of them as men of virtue who are unsullied by the grit of daily life while unequivocally committed to a code of heroic values.

Recounting Richler's personal disappointment in the former baseball player Kermit Kitman (Richler 1969), Joel Yanofsky remarks that Richler's tendency to be disenchanted "shouldn't be surprising – no pedestal was strong enough to hold [his] heroes for long" (252). For Richler, Kitman was a disappointment because he proved too real. A talented Jewish baseball player who had not lived up to his early promise, he was susceptible to the pitfalls of flesh-and-blood existence and this, for Richler, led to his fall from grace. In the controlled world of fiction, Richler's ephemeral hero figures exist outside the bounds of ordinary life and are not constrained by reality's limitations. Accordingly, they are never disappointments because they are known almost exclusively by remarkable deeds.

At the same time, the hero figures are tolerable because they are not saintly do-gooders without vices or faults. They are egotistical rogues with independent dispositions that make them engaging literary characters. They are not rigidly ideological like the heroes of Gorky's socialist realism. Nor are they robotically valiant, like Ari Ben Canaan in Leon Uris's novel *Exodus* (1958), a monolithic hero, emboldened by specious Zionist rhetoric, "super powers and steely determination" (Furman, 47). In terms of credibility, Richler's hero figures may be no more plausible than Uris's arch-Zionist, but their larger-than-life personas are not one-dimensional portrayals of naive martyrdom. Consequently, they add layers of complexity to the novels and dramatize a compelling, if not always compassionate, moral outlook.

As Carol Iannone notes, almost every Richler protagonist, like Richler himself, "suffers from the double remove from the wellsprings of heroism and power" (51). Richler himself wrote that "to be a Jew and a Canadian is to emerge from the ghetto twice" (1968, 8). Poised as a response to this reality, Richler's hero figures redress the Jewish propensity towards vulnerability and disempowerment. They are commanding individuals who know how to get what they want. They have an instinctual ability to garner power, hold sway over others, and make their opponents shrink with a sense of helplessness.

Jewish empowerment is one of the recurrent themes in Richler's work. In his essay "The Great Comic Book Heroes," initially published in 1967, Richler explains the appeal of comic book heroes for men of his generation: "They were invulnerable, all-conquering, whereas we were puny, miserable, and defeated" (1978, 128). Thus, it is not surprising that Richler was inclined to create characters that shared some of the strength and power of his childhood icons.

The earliest Richler character who fully represents the empowered Jewish hero is Joey Hersh in *St Urbain's Horseman*, a man who stands for dignity, self-respect, self-assertion, and moral justice, especially in the eyes of the protagonist, Jake Hersh. A substantial amount of critical attention has been devoted to the character of Joey Hersh as an expression of a response to the Holocaust. Thomas E. Tausky suggests that Joey is modelled on Simon Wiesenthal – indeed, sections of the novel dealing with the experiments of Josef Mengele are based on Wiesenthal's memoirs (78). Rachel Feldhay Brenner writes that Joey mainly serves as the avenger for extreme persecution. And, for Jake Hersh, according to Norm Ravvin, Joey's pursuit of Mengele is "a self-validating link between his own comfortable life and the suffering of the Holocaust" (1994, 125). It is undeniable that the novel's attitude towards the Holocaust is largely expressed through Jake's fantasy of Joey as an enforcer of post-Holocaust justice, which is an important part of the novel. However, Joey Hersh's character also represents the value of Jewish empowerment in a more generalized sense and is a blueprint for future Richler hero figures.

Joey Hersh amazes Montreal's Jews: "the neighbors were astonished to learn that not only could Joey ride horses but he had a commercial pilot's license" (Richler 1991b, 137). The former skill is referred to in the novel's title and is a central motif throughout the book; it is also an allusion to Isaac Babel's play *Sunset* (1926), which Richler had adapted for television in 1963 (Foran, 305), where the central character, the Odessa mobster Benya Krik, distinct from mainstream Jewish literary heroes, "rode a horse boldly, and so had stopped being a quaint, harmless member of the Hebrew faith" (Foran, 344). *St Urbain's Horseman* presents Joey as brash and dangerous: the Jew here need not be a proverbial victim.

Joey's refusal to play the role of the submissive Jew is underscored by the way in which he taunts his old community when local acts of anti-Semitism are perpetrated. "What are you going to do about it?" he asks after vandals deface businesses and a synagogue in the Jewish ghetto. It is a refrain that recurs throughout the book. While the Jewish community is inclined to keep a low profile in response to anti-Jewish provocation, Joey insists on resistance rather than conciliation (Ravvin 1994, 127). When an old friend offers Joey cash to maintain a low profile and avoid retaliation, Joey, like some Dostoevskian character, "reached for his cigarette lighter, lit the envelope ... and did not drop it until the money was engulfed in flames" (Richler 1991b, 134). Trying to battle the rising anti-Jewish sentiment, establishment Jews, such as Joey's Uncle Abe, meet with local politicians who respond with trite public statements. But Joey is uninterested in petitioning. He galvanizes a squad of vigilantes who retaliate, matching violence with violence. The episode results in Joey mysteriously leaving Montreal.

Word of his subsequent whereabouts trickles back to Montreal, but for Jake Hersh the residual image of Joey becomes a life-long symbol of Jewish empowerment, dignity, and quest for justice. And, because that symbol is based only on a childhood memory, it remains unadulterated. The novel's other characters, even the sympathetic and likeable ones, are prone to actions that breach Jake's sense of heroic values. But Joey, indefinitely in abstentia, can always be recalled as an emblem of Jewish heroism. In his case, there is no physical presence or compromising actions to tarnish Jake's memory of greatness. Richler writes that comic-book super heroes were reassuring because they were "infinitely more reliable than real-life champions" (1978, 128). For Jake, Joey is a hero for much the same reason. He is not a pure fabrication of Joey's imagination but a legend that is unconstrained by the limitations of real life.

It is no coincidence, argues Robin Nadel, that *St Urban's Horseman* is set in 1967, the year Israel achieved victory over Syria, Jordan, and Egypt in the Six Day War. As Richler's first novel to feature an empowered, physically imposing Jewish hero, she believes it is one of the many "tough Jewish novels" that appeared in the wake of the war. Based on the idea that Israel's military finesse had paved the way for the new Jew, "suntanned, battle-hardened, muscular and tall," this American Jewish genre is defined by ultra-masculine Jewish protagonists and the physical resilience of post-Holocaust Jewry.

However, in emphasizing Joey's commitment to Jewish self-defence, Richler situates *St Urban's Horseman* within a broader tradition of twentieth-century Jewish writing that valorizes resistance and sometimes controversially casts Jewish passivity as a form of complicity in anti-Semitic aggression. One of the widely known earlier examples of such works is the poem "The City of Slaughter" by Hayim Nahman Bialik. Written in the aftermath of the 1903 Kishinev pogrom, it sarcastically berates the local Jews, "the sons of the Maccabees," for timorously enduring anti-Semitic attacks, which had been frequent occurrences since 1880:

> Come, now, and I will bring thee to their lairs
> The privies, jakes and pigpens where the heirs
> Of Hasmoneans lay, with trembling knees,
> Concealed and cowering – the sons of the Maccabees!
> The seed of saints, the scions of the lions!
> Who, crammed by scores in all the sanctuaries of their shame,
> So sanctified My name!
> It was the flight of mice they fled,
> The scurrying of roaches was their flight;
> They died like dogs, and they were dead![3]

Lucy Dawidowicz writes that the "spirit of defiance" in Bialik's poem became popular during the Holocaust and "remained alive in the ghettoes" (329). Certainly it is echoed in the 1 January 1942 proclamation that Abba Kovner delivered to a gathering of 150 Jews in the Vilna ghetto, which famously begins, "Let us not be led like sheep to the slaughter" (qtd in Dawidowicz, 334). This plea for self-defence resonates in *St Urban's Horseman*, as well as in *Joshua Then and Now* and *Solomon Gursky Was Here*, and defines an important aspect of Richler's model of Jewish heroics. Kovner was not deluded when he urged Vilna's Jews to resist the Nazis. He understood that they were doomed but was determined "to exact vengeance from the Germans and to die fighting, to die ... 'with honor'" (330). Jewish dignity based on such a conception of resistance is important in Richler's work. More than celebrating the post-1967 Jewish man as conceived by Paul Breines in *Tough Jews*, it underlies a long-standing idea that Jews do not have to apologize for who they are or resign themselves to mistreatment.

Jews such as Kovner (Bauer, 341) and Bialik eventually came to view a return to Palestine and the fight for national independence as the only viable form of resistance and Jewish dignity. As a youth, Richler, too, harboured this vision of the Jewish nation and, as a rank-and-file member of the Habonim youth movement, became "a zealot for Zion" (1994, 32). But he later grew disillusioned with Israel and disenchanted when the struggle to build the new state turned into a morally complex Jewish-Arab struggle – one that had been already predicted in the late 1800s by the founding exponent of cultural Zionism, Ahad Ha'am, and was later anticipated by Albert Einstein (36). After visiting Dheisheh, a Palestinian refugee camp in Bethlehem in the early 1990s, Richler expresses his mixed feelings regarding Israel and Jewish power.

> I was grateful that, for once in our history, we were the ones with the guns and they were the ones with the stones. But, taking it a step further, I also found myself hoping that if Jerry, Hershey, Myer, and I had been born and bred in the squalor of Dheisheh rather than the warmth of St. Urbain, we would have had the courage to be among the stone-throwers. (1994, 222)

Richler was also circumspect vis-à-vis the Jewish state because of what he perceived as "Israeli contempt for Diaspora Jews" and the idea that Jewish pride was a specifically Israeli commodity (252).[4] Richler recounts an episode from his 1962 visit to Israel: a local bartender boasts how one patron, a wealthy Spaniard and former anti-Semite, said to him, "But you're not Jews; you're different. You've fought for your land, you've spilled blood for it, and you have pride. The Jews in Spain only fight for their families and their businesses" (253). Richler is incensed by this slight of Diaspora Jews, which is reworked as an incident in *St Urbain's Horseman*: Jake Hersh responds indignantly to such an anecdote by explaining that plenty of Canadian Jews have fought for their country, or, like his cousin Joey, for Spain as well (254).

On a more visceral level, Richler takes Israel to task for its fundraising energies and self-portrayal as a refuge for potential victims of lurking anti-Semitism. He parodies Israel as the twentieth-century incarnation of the money-grabbing Jew, constantly trying to extract funds from Diaspora brethren. Compounding this image is the portrayal of Israelis in *St Urbain's Horseman* as ungrateful and condescending to sentimental Jewish tourists who come to Jerusalem to alleviate Zionist guilt with lavish spending (252). In addition, Richler claims that, despite its reliance on Jewish financial generosity worldwide, Israel exploits the slightest anti-Semitic provocation as a tool to draw Jews from New York and Los Angeles to Jerusalem and Tel Aviv. "Israelis schooled in realpolitik ... welcome every such incident as proof that Diaspora Jews live in 'rented rooms,'" he claims sardonically, "and an excuse to pressure Diaspora Jews from the West to make haste and immigrate to the Jewish State" (249).

Thus, Richler's Jewish heroics include the value of resistance but specifically in relation to anti-Jewish aggression in the Diaspora because, as he sees it, Israel and its citizens espouse a nationalist piety, which is distasteful to him. One of the unforgivable qualities of any character in Richler's novels is self-righteousness, and his Israeli characters, such as Colonel Elan in *St Urbain's Horseman,* are usually prone (much like Ari Ben Canaan in *Exodus*) to sanctimonious self-assurance. In *This Year in Jerusalem* (1994) there are some more nuanced portrayals of Israelis, mainly Richler's cousins who immigrated to Israel from Canada. Yet even they appear somewhat smug, as if they were superior for having left the comforts of Montreal for the challenges of life in the Jewish homeland. It is this perceived "Israeli contempt for Diaspora Jews" that Richler cannot tolerate; he condemns this attitude by recollecting one more bar room story he once heard:

> There was a sweet, elderly lady ahead of me in line, and she asked the teller something in Yiddish. The teller, an unpleasant young woman, actually yelled at her. "We don't speak Yiddish here. That's the language of the ghetto." To this day, I wake up some time in the middle of the night, furious with myself, because I didn't reach over the cage and slap that arrogant, mindless little bitch hard. (1994, 254)

The bank teller's reaction to Yiddish infuriates Richler on two counts. It reflects a common attitude of Israelis in the nascent Jewish state towards Diaspora Jews as well as a certain strain of early Zionist rhetoric in which Jews outside of Israel are second-rate, having contributed nothing of value to life in Israel or elsewhere.[5]

— ✳ —

Solomon Gursky in *Solomon Gursky Was Here* also represents the novels' commitment to Jewish empowerment. Like Joey Hersh, he, too, is a formidable equestrian, a pilot – he returned from the First World War "wearing a flying officer's uniform" (Richler 1990b, 271) – and a Jew undaunted by Gentiles. At the age of seventeen, he acquired the seed of the family's fortune by trouncing five local businessmen in a game of high-stakes poker, beating them out of the deed to a general store, a hotel, a blacksmith's shop, and "more money than the Gurskys had ever seen at one time" (268). He bore no resemblance to his father, Aaron Gursky, whom the locals considered a "jumpy Jew" (261) and a harmless fool.

As in Joey's case, Solomon's concerns touch on the Holocaust and the issue of resistance. In 1933, Solomon's planned business trip to Scotland turned into an unexplained European tour of "Berlin and Munich and London and Cambridge and finally Moscow" (278). Upon return, Solomon moved into his office with a cot and shortwave radio; and "unsavory, shifty-eyed little strangers, wearing funny European-style suits, dribbling cigarette ash everywhere, met with him there and left with their pockets bulging with cash" (279). Solomon is not only heroic in terms of his actions but also in relation to his vision. He has an uncanny ability to identify impending danger to the Jews, and his reactions are swift, strong, and unqualified. He does not just quibble with government functionaries about the Jewish condition in Europe or rely primarily on legal recourse. He seeks out the most expedient way to address the predicament of European Jews and takes decisive steps.[6]

Solomon is not as mysterious as Joey Hersh, but he is similarly unknowable. He never reveals his thoughts, his motivations and suspicions. In some ways he is, as John Leonard noted in *The Nation* in 1990, reminiscent of Zelig in Woody Allen's eponymous film: "a tourist among the traumas of the century: with Mao on the Long March; on hand for the plot to kill Hitler; running guns, like his grandfather, except to the nascent State of Israel; placing the last telephone call to

Marilyn Monroe; helping to plan the raid on Entebbe; sitting beside Maureen Dean at the Watergate hearings." Then, after Solomon is ostensibly killed in an airplane crash, he truly becomes a heroic phantom figure. A trail of evidence implies that he is alive, posing as the affluent Sir Hyman Kaplansky or as the eccentric businessman Mr Cuervo. Moses follows the trail of Solomon in these guises, and, through research, hearsay, and speculation, develops an image of Solomon as a man whose acts of Jewish self-assertion were not just heroism but an ineluctable way of life.

It is significant that in these novels Jewish power is not only a value but an obsession. The heroes' focus on empowerment becomes a heroic value when it is privileged above other concerns and, in terms of Urmson's conception of heroism, takes precedence over fear and self-interest. Solomon chooses to focus his attention on Europe's Jews just as Prohibition is coming to an end in the United States. For the Gursky brothers, the change in legislation is a harbinger of immense opportunity for their liquor business. But Solomon is unmoved. Compelled to investigate the Jewish predicament in Europe in 1933, he misses an opportunity to align his family with powerful liquor barons in Scotland, remaining indifferent to his brother Bernard's inept efforts to merge the Gurskys with well-respected whisky-brewing establishments.

Joey Hersh's money-making prospects are not as clear as Solomon's. He has a glamorous past as a professional baseball player and Hollywood actor, but Uncle Abe insists that he has mainly been a gigolo, adept at swindling gullible women out of large sums of money. He does not neglect a business empire for the sake of his heroic compulsion. Nevertheless, his commitment to Jewish power has a selfless quality. The narrative makes it clear that this selflessness is largely imagined by Jake Hersh, but elements of it do seem true. The Jewish power represented by Solomon and Joey is inextricable from an ethic of altruism; their interest in wealth is consonant with their desire to wield power for the sake of their unselfish values. While Joey's Uncle Abe and his peers try to protect their community with quiet appeals to the government, and Bernard Gursky strives to make himself untouchable through his high-profile philanthropy, Richler's hero figures eschew establishment channels of power. They prefer direct responses to anti-Jewish sentiments and action that have more to do with immediate and true justice than law, circles of polite influence, or general policies of appeasement.

A significant part of Solomon's heroism is also connected to his retaliatory provocations in the face of latent anti-Semitism. Despite the diversity of personas he assumes during his life, he always poses as a Jew and an easy target for the anti-Jewish aggression of royalty, socialites, and parliamentarians. In 1953, deceptively sanguine about his Gentile acquaintances' anti-Semitic inclinations, Solomon, in the guise of Sir Hyman Kaplansky, invites thirteen non-Jews to his Passover Seder. "The precise number gathered at the most famous of all Passover noshes," he informs his guests. But the Seder turns out to be a ruse. After ironically thanking his guests for attending since he understood "how prejudiced they were against *some* of his kind ... especially those sprung from Eastern Europe ... [who] were insufferably pushy and did in fact drive a hard bargain" (375), Sir Hyman serves matzah filled with "warm, red sticky stuff" (377). The Seder is not an ingratiating offer of hospitality but an act of retribution, with the traditional blood libel transformed into a form of Jewish revenge. It is an elaborate stunt to show this cross-section of upper-class men and women that the Jew will not be a laughingstock, and it leaves Solomon at the end of the night "happy as a Jew at a fire sale, having himself a proper fit of giggles" (379).

To represent Solomon as a man of his times, and his heroic impulses as keeping pace with the events shaping the destiny of the Jews, the narrative intimates that he was involved in the creation of the fledgling Jewish state and somehow orchestrated the Israeli raid on Entebbe. Maintaining the alias of Mr Cuervo, Solomon, it is clear, is involved in handling the weapons cache required for the mission and the rescue operation that became legendary. When the operation is complete and the Israeli planes have returned to Israel, Mr Cuervo likewise disappears from Nairobi, a hint that his presence there was not a matter of leisure. Richler's fantasy positions Solomon as a hero in the face of anti-Jewish terror and, at the same time, turns the table on self-admiring Israelis by crediting a Diaspora Jew with the success of the operation.

While Jewish empowerment is a value championed by Richler's hero figures, obedience to the law is not. It is, indeed, mainly disregard for the legal system that places the hero figures outside the parameters of supererogation, which encompasses not only "opportunities to act beyond duty and to exercise the individual freedom in virtuous ways" but also "conscientiousness, responsibility, obedience to the law, and fairness"

(Heyd, 182). Thus, the hero figures are, indeed, only partially spurred by supererogatory drives, and lawlessness, combined with a self-styled kind of magnanimity, emerges as central to the novels' heroics.

In many cases, Richler's novels celebrate lawlessness as a kind of mobster ethic that seems to express Richler's own long-standing fascination with Jewish gangsters. In particular, Richler believed that the line between sanctioned and illicit business practices is often artificial and that hard-working businessmen, due to formal legalities, are maligned as criminals when, in fact, they are no worse than a great many respectable hoteliers, bankers, stockbrokers, and land developers. Richler probably best expresses this attitude in the article "Lansky" (1998), a tribute to one of the most infamous Jews in the history of organized crime. Richler admired Lansky's rebuttals to opponents of gambling: "If Socrates and Plato had trouble defining what morality was, how can people come along, just like that, and lay down that gambling is immoral" (1998b, 49). Richler, too, seemed to believe that gambling was not among the most pernicious of sins. He quoted Lansky as he was comforting Frank Costello, who was worried that society would always conflate gamblers with gangsters: "Look at history. Look at the Astors and Vanderbilts, all those big society people. They were the worst thieves. Now look at them. It's just a matter of time" (49). Like Richler himself, Lansky had recoiled from his pious origins but never downplayed his Jewish identity, and he had a high regard for the life of the mind. He had little use for Mosaic law and rabbinic scholarship but enjoyed matzah and gave money to Israel during the War of Independence. He was also famously bookish. An FBI operation once yielded little information about Lansky's life of crime but did reveal that he was in the midst of reading a history book, a grammar, and a book of French quotations (50). And, in his own way, Lansky was committed to values based on integrity:

> Other gangsters welcomed partnerships with Lansky because he was not greedy and had never been known to hoodwink an associate. Lansky was proud of the fact that knowledgeable gamblers had never doubted the integrity of the tables in either his Florida or his Cuban casino. (50)

Richler overlooked the murderous and viciously criminal aspects of Lansky's career, which Robert Rockaway chronicled in *But He Was Good to His Mother* (22–4). Yet it is this sentimental portrait that inspires the romantic vision of the gangster that informs several of his hero figures. In several instances, gangster activity enhances the heroism of these men as long as bloodshed is kept to a minimum, legal violations are those that might be easily committed by any large-scale corporation, profit earnings are partially motivated by some noble values – not only avarice – and those values include the proper Jewish concerns: retaliation against anti-Semitism, support of Israel when it is under attack, and an ever-ready willingness to defend Jewish dignity.

Of all of Richler's novels, *Joshua Then and Now* presents the best example of an impressive, small-time gangster who upholds heroic values. While Reuben Shapiro is not one of Richler's mysterious hero figures and does not embody the protagonist's idea of ultimate wisdom, he does have many of the hero figure's features, including confidence in his own moral compass rather than legal axioms. When young Joshua asks his father whether he had been in the liquor business, Reuben is evasive, but not dishonest: "You could say I was in deliveries … sort of" (Richler 2001, 64). With his interest in biblical justice, he does not view the transportation of liquor as a disgrace: it may be illegal but hardly sinful. Likewise, when Reuben helps his life-long mentor Sonny Colucci provide clients with arson services, his professional activities are described by an apt euphemism: he had simply "drifted into the insurance business" (69). His sense of extra-legal equity suggests that he is a solid, reasonable man with a well-cultivated ability to differentiate between real wrongdoing and legal formalities: a lawbreaker, but not a criminal. Therefore, when reporters approach Joshua's vacation home in the Quebec countryside to pester Joshua about his sexual indecency trial, Reuben has no qualms about chasing them away in a threatening manner. "He unzipped his windbreaker to show that he was wearing a gun. 'If you don't turn around right now,' he said, 'I'm going to shoot out your tires. Ping ping ping'" (7). Reuben is not only a mouthpiece for one of the novel's moral perspectives; he is also a jokester and, as noted above, one of the book's primary sources of humour. Thus, the right to defend his family with threatened violence, especially if it enables him to amuse himself at the expense of jaded reporters, does not present a moral dilemma for him: it is one of the foundations of his moral outlook, which does not necessarily include legalities.

Joshua's Canadian father-in-law, Senator Stephen Andrew Hornby, who, paradoxically, has "a little of Colucci in his soul," easily befriends Reuben Shapiro. Joshua, more impressed than his father by the prestige of social status, believes that the senator, with inherited advantages and polished manners, is an aristocratic. He "measures his own moral lapses against what he took to be the senator's uncompromising standards." Eventually, however, Joshua discovers that his father-in-law is not a paragon of moral conduct but "the sum of old alliances, with political connections he could redeem at his convenience" (381). Despite these privileges, the senator proves disarmingly unpretentious and, even more saliently, aware that sound moral judgment and lawful conduct do not necessarily coincide. As a legislator himself, he knows full well that the law, on many occasions, is broadly understood to accommodate all sorts of large- and small-scale power-brokering, and admittedly enjoys the ample and legally suspect benefits of influence and power. Thus, in his eyes, Reuben's underworld propensities in no way tarnish, or even contradict, his biblical acumen, good sense, natural intelligence, fatherly instincts, and family loyalty.

Besides their shared scepticism of jurisprudence, the two men come to enjoy a true friendship. To a certain extent, the senator is enamoured with Reuben. He is childishly giddy at the opportunity to rebel against his establishment persona and fraternize with a former boxer from the wrong side of the tracks who has significant connections to a mid-level Mafioso. It is not as if the senator does not know how to sidestep legal encumbrances. When a local policeman, Orville Moon, questions Reuben and the senator about their suspicious nocturnal adventure to collect "nightcrawlers" (388), the senator does not hesitate to rebuff the officer and remind him of the favours he has done him in the past. Though the two men are in possession of bootleg alcohol and a firearm, the senator feels no compunction. It is clear that he once used a liberal interpretation of the law to help Moon secure his pension and oblige him in other ways, and sees no reason why this incident should not be assessed with equal flexibility. But his nerve is also reinforced by his association with Reuben and the exhilaration of being the nighttime expedition's "wheelman." He aligns himself with Reuben and emulates his moral confidence. In fact, the senator's moral courage is a version of instinctive justice in contrast to Reuben's well-reasoned creed. Ironically, the senator, a man who has spent the better part of his career as part of Canada's legislature, ends up as Reuben's sidekick, taking his moral and legal cues from a man who may revere biblical wisdom but has spent much of his life skirting the law. The novel reiterates basic typology. Reuben, the Jew, with his quirky, biblically inspired sense of morality, is the stern law-keeper in the tradition of

Moses, and the senator, the Christian, is inspired by Reuben but proves more fluid in his moral judgment, an agent of the spirit of that law rather than the law itself.

An interesting context for the gangster element in Richler's hero figures' lives can be found in the works of American-Jewish writer Daniel Fuchs, particularly *Summer in Williamsburg* (1934). Fuchs's novels, like Richler's, depict an immigrant Jewish milieu rife with tensions between Old World and New World values. They also focus on the author's childhood neighbourhood, its residents, families, local feuds, and secret romances. Fuchs devotes much attention to the role of the gangster in that milieu. In part, Fuchs's use of gangsters is political: it is a socialist diatribe on the socio-economic distress of the Depression era. His characters have to choose between the "virtue and powerlessness" of an honest life with few economic prospects or "corruption and success" as the surest path to a life of material comfort (Krafchick, 30). While Richler's use of gangsters does not resonate with political rhetoric, his novels do bear a similarity to Fuchs's in that they focus on the gangster as a symbol of the unstable divide between business and crime, suggesting "a continuum between the businessman and the criminal" (22). This link first emerges in a scene from *Son of a Smaller Hero* when Richler's Melech Adler swindles an Irish scrap supplier. In the eyes of his grandson, who is not aware that the supplier was in the habit of likewise deceiving his business associates, the family patriarch is transformed from a businessman into a thief (1989b, 14–15).

Richler was also sensitive to the reverse problem: the denigration of businessmen whose entrepreneurial ventures were illegal, even though they were a no greater threat to society than respectable corporate establishments. Recalling the famous bootlegging legacy of the Bronfman family, Richler says:

[The Bronfmans] have remained unaccountably ashamed.
Too bad. [They] sinned far less against the common weal
than J.P. Morgan, John D. Rockefeller, or other robber barons.
They did not put the lives of immigrants at risk, paying them a
pittance to descend into extremely dangerous mine pits. They
did not manipulate the stock market, wasting small investors,
and neither did they hire goons to break strikes in their
factories. (1998b, 25)

This view partly accounts for Richler's hero figures' participation in organized crime. When resorting to gangster antics to achieve idealistic goals, according to this view, their "business" practices are no more unethical than the commercial affairs of respected tycoons. For Fuchs, gangsters are economic victims. They are human, with the capacity to behave generously, but their world offers no solutions for their economic and social aspirations (Krafchick, 30). Nevertheless, their involvement in underworld activity is never presented as a viable alternative to life's cruelties and hardships. In Richler's work, in contrast, gangsterism is commonly part of a moral fantasy, and the hero figure's underworld dealings are often depicted as acts of valour.

– * –

While breaking the law is not always a disgrace in the moral code constructed in Richler's fiction, it is shown to be so when it becomes a way to exploit the innocent and vulnerable. In Richler's novels, gambling is a good example of unlawful activity with the power to reveal a character either as a despicable rogue or an intrepid hero. In *Son of a Smaller Hero*, Noah Adler's cousin Shloime evolves from a pool hall regular to a common hoodlum who takes part in the battery and assault of a Jewish ghetto favourite, Mr Panofsky. Shloime is not a gangster, only a neighbourhood gambler who is driven by excitement and hopes of a quick income. His gambling is not attributed to a higher purpose and does not signify strength of character. He is a nervous gambler, "excited" (Richler 1989b, 54) when playing pool in the presence of a renowned neighbourhood thug. He does not have the steadfast character of a real risk-taker. In *The Apprenticeship of Duddy Kravitz*, another unlikable character, Irwin Schubert, ensnares Duddy in a fixed game of roulette, a similar instance in which gambling reveals not a character's admirable backbone but his degenerate personality and propensity to prey on the vulnerable.

In contrast, the gambling of Richler's hero figures signifies risk-taking, a penchant for adventure, and an admirable level of confidence. During a childhood blackjack game, Joey Hersh beats Jake and his childhood friends. The boys expect their elder to have mercy and return their money. He does not. "Gambling is gambling" (Richler 1991b, 134) is his instructive explanation. Joey knows how to win but also understands the power of the game. Solomon Gursky wins a fortune in an annual town poker game when he is seventeen through cunning and self-assurance. He is not new to gambling; he brings two hundred dollars to his first game – "his poolroom earnings" (Richler 1990b, 264). However, his win is due not to ingenuity but to his unshakeable character. And, as Solomon matures, his nerve becomes even more steadfast. He keeps company "with Dutch Schultz and Abbadabba Berman" and has business dealings with Jacob "Greasy Thumb" Guzik, Solly "Cutcher-Head-Off" Weissman, Boo-Boo Hoff, Nig Rosen, and Moe Dalitz (340) – figures whose names are synonymous with organized crime in the 1930s. Essentially, Solomon's daring as a gambler evolves into the courage and bravado to deal with some of the most dangerous men of his times.

– * –

Along with the values of Jewish empowerment and extra-legal justice, living a life of pleasure is another central feature of Richler's hero figures. These men almost personify anti-Semitic stereotypes: they are lusty and lascivious, with an insatiable appetite for women, good food, fine liquor, and myriad luxuries. Yet this hunger represents the characters' vitality, their endless ability to engage in life and not repulsive gluttony. They are not self-effacing Jews who are content to live in peace. Instead, they are prepossessing renegades with a Dionysian joie de vivre. It is as if Richler appropriates the image and makes his hero figures masters of pleasure rather than licentious consumers of bawdy excess.

This play on a racial stereotype is reminiscent of the tactics used by Dr Bledsoe, a character in Ralph Ellison's *Invisible Man* (1952). The nameless protagonist is shocked when he witnesses Dr Bledsoe's fawning over the university's white donors and trustees. He is no longer the imposing director but a cliché of the black, submissive servant, ever ready to act the gracious inferior. When questioned, Dr Bledsoe replies that playing the role ironically places him in a position of power. In order to be heard and effectively manipulate his "superiors," he dons the expected façade of the genteel lackey. Ostensibly submissive, he has actually reversed the role distribution implied in the stereotype:

I say "Yes, suh" as loudly as any burr-head when it's convenient, but I'm still the king down here. I don't care how much it appears otherwise. Power doesn't have to show off. Power is confident, self-assuring, self-starting and self-stopping, self-warming and self-justifying. When you have it, you know it. (Ellison, 119)

Bledsoe believes that when he assumes a traditional role, the white community is at ease and thereby prone to manipulation. The stereotype is his tool in a power game.

Richler's hero figures also treat stereotypes as a game, but their objective is the deflation of traditional images of Jews rather than acquisition of social and political power. They arrogate the role of pleasure connoisseurs to achieve three goals: to taunt anti-Semites – preferring to have something to show for it if they are, anyway, to be accused of debauchery; to contest the anti-Jewish chauvinism of the wealthy, self-satisfied elites in their pleasure pursuits; and to relish enjoyments that are often considered beyond the taste and discernment of solid Jewish citizens, often believed to be too provincial and unrefined to appreciate such pleasure.

In *Cocksure* (1960), Ziggy Spicehandler is an early, yet only partially realized, model of the libidinous hero figure. Though Ziggy is larger than life, somewhat legendary, and idolized by the protagonist, Mortimer Griffin, he is not a hero figure because he does not represent any type of idealism or any version of Jewish dignity. However, he is the novel's most unapologetic hedonist, living for his own enjoyment without reservation. Ziggy is described as the stereotype of the physically repulsive Jew,

> short, hirsute, barrel-chested. His hooky nose had been twice broken and he had a thick neck and waxy tangled hairs protruded from his jug ears. His fingernails were black, there were warts on his broad square hands and you could tell, just looking at him, that in other people's houses he filled his pockets with cigarettes and peed without lifting the seat. (Richler 1968, 30)

Nevertheless, women find Ziggy "exciting" (30). And he responds enthusiastically. Only minutes after arriving at Mortimer's house after an absence of several years, Ziggy seduces Mortimer's wife, Joyce. When he returns to town, he "giv[es] London another whirl" (46). *Cocksure* is a heavily satiric novel not meant to be read as realistic, and Ziggy is, to some extent, a caricature. He is improbably irreverent and unscrupulous. But his character is a nexus in Richler's overall moral paradigm because it signals the emergence of a specifically Jewish celebration of hedonistic tendencies. If Ziggy Spicehandler is a "Jewish satyr" (Woodcock 1970, 50), this is an identity he embraces. Rather than deny his lusty image, he revels in it. Born Gerald Spencer, he had an expensive middle-class education, knew stage classics, Latin and Greek, and spoke like a gentleman (118). Therefore, becoming Ziggy, reclaiming his family's former surname and becoming an emblem of indulgence, is a deliberate strategy of Jewish self-reinvention.

Solomon Gursky closely resembles Ziggy though he is a far more complex character who epitomizes Richler's hero figure as a man of prodigious appetites and desires. Solomon, unlike Ziggy, is not parodied. He is ironic and fantastical but not satirized. He lives with a hunger for pleasure but fully understands the cost of his quest. As a young man, he is often trailed by a "flutter of society girls, seducing one of them into submitting to outrageous sexual acts and then sending her back to her mountainside mansion, himself avenged but also, he would complain ... diminished" (Richler 1990b, 120): Solomon does not hesitate to strike back at the privileged elite through sexual degradation. Yet he understands that in turning an anti-Semitic stereotype into an instrument of revenge he also demeans himself.

Solomon is described by an old friend, Tom Callaghan, as "this notorious thundering Jew, who will not be denied" (299). And his one love, Diana McClure, recalls their first meeting: "he charged with such audacity and appetite and, above all, rage" (299). In living his life according to his every yearning and whim, Solomon is uncompromising and "indifferent to the damage" (297) he causes. In the guise of Hyman Kaplansky he is a cavalier womanizer with an endless store of ploys to seduce socialites. After bemoaning his (false) homosexual tendencies, he allows one woman to become his mistress in an effort, as it were, to cultivate his stymied heterosexuality. In another instance, there is a hint that he has become the lover of Princess Diana. His escapades with another woman are unexplained except for her diary entry rating Sir Hyman's sexual prowess as "ALPHA-PLUS followed by four exclamation points" (381–2). But his earlier conquest of Clara Teitelbaum most clearly demonstrates his indifference towards the aftermath of his victories. Still known as Solomon Gursky, he seduces a young Jewish girl, a virgin he finds physically irresistible but infantile and vapid. Later, in an effort to rid himself of her, he tries to persuade his youngest brother, Morrie, to marry her. After Morrie declines, Solomon ends up leaving town. He does return six months later to marry Clara, but she is already his victim. "She was six months pregnant at the time, living in seclusion in the Victory Hotel, her parents having disowned her" (348). Her life has been irrevocably altered, and Solomon returns not to fill the post of loyal spouse but "merely to give the child a name" (348).

Less of an imperious sexual predator than Solomon but even more a
Jewish playboy than Ziggy is the hero figure of Bernard "Boogie"
Moscovitch of *Barney's Version*. In self-deprecating fashion,
Boogie tells his friends, "I've got all the faults of Tolstoy, Dostoevsky,
and Hemingway rolled into one. I will fuck just about any peasant
girl who will have me. I'm an obsessive gambler. A drunk. Hey, just
like Freddy D., I'm even an anti-Semite, but maybe that doesn't count
in my case as I'm Jewish myself" (Richler 1998a, 8). The addendum
to the comment, Boogie's insistence on his Jewish identity, is not random. The son of assimilated Jews, Boogie, born Bernard Morrow,
"was counted on to infiltrate the family deep into the WASP hive" (9).
Instead, he reclaims his family's original surname and deliberately
reinvents himself as a Jew. In the novel, Boogie is revered by the protagonist Barney Panofsky largely because of his Renaissance Man
persona. But Boogie's identity as a specifically Jewish glutton
for sensual pleasure is central to his character. After disappearing for
weeks at a time – when it was rumoured he was visiting a yeshiva in
Mea Shearim or possibly a monastery in Tuscany – he would surface
in Paris "accompanied by a gorgeous Spanish duchess or an Italian
contessa" (10). By availing himself of adventures – intellectual, sensual,
and other – while revelling in his Jewish identity, Boogie subverts
conventions of Jewish identity by becoming a pleasure connoisseur.

In addition to being sexually voracious, Richler's hero figures have
an appetite for extravagance. As Sir Hyman, Solomon Gursky throws
large parties that attract "politicians, film and theater people, men 'who
were something in the City,' art dealers, journalists, and any American
of consequence who happened to be in London" (Richler 1990b, 368).
Two days following one of these soirées, Sir Hyman disappears, presumed drowned during a morning swim in rough water. To Moses
Berger it is clear that Solomon has, once again, staged a vanishing act
only to reincarnate himself again as another operator in another place.
The suggestion is that his palatial home and priceless possessions are
meaningless to him. He has the ability to amass wealth and live a lavish
life but mainly uses conspicuous consumption as a means to cultivate
the persona of Sir Hyman and hide from the legal and personal imbro-
glios that have become too entangling for him to overcome.

Opulence is an important part of Joey Hersh's deliberate image as
well. After fleeing Montreal as a boy, he returns as a man in "his fire
engine red MG" (Richler 1991b, 132). To Jake Hersh, the car is not
just a display of wealth. It "could have been a magnificent stallion

and Cousin Joey a knight returned from a foreign crusade" (132). In clothing, Joey also exudes Old World luxurious decorum:

> The next morning Joey went shopping and then the parcels began to come. Exquisite white shirts and black silk socks from the Saville Rowe Shoppe on Sherbrooke Street. A sterling silver cigarette case from Birks. A suit not from Morrie Gold&Son, with padded shoulders, a two-button roll, and slightly zoot trousers, but from a tailor with an authentic British accent. (133)

Over and above granting him pleasure, cultivated taste is Joey's means of attaining distinction. He does not just keep company with beautiful women but associates with "high quality girls who sipped martinis, their legs crossed delicately" (135). His possessions and lifestyle are not merely expensive, they are the foundation of his image as a different kind of Jew, one who has not only means but the acumen to use them discerningly in the process of defining himself.

Though Richler's novels tended to sell well, received awards, and increasingly met with critical praise (see Kramer 2008), they were often attacked for their treatment of Jews. One Canadian Jewish newspaper compared *Son of a Smaller Hero* to the anti-Jewish propaganda in the Nazi *Der Stürmer* (Yanofsky, 100). In the late 1960s, an audience member at a public reading informed Richler that an instructor at a local university had assigned students a term paper on the topic whether or not Mordecai Richler is an anti-Semite (Posner, 211). Many audience members made it clear that they believed the answer was affirmative: they accused Richler of Jewish self-hatred (199, 201). And, in a published collection of letters, author Margaret Laurence writes of Richler as a friend and colleague yet regrets his lack of compassion, noting that his treatment of Jewish characters and community "makes [her] feel like vomitting [sic]" (Lennox and Panofsky, 92).

Richler insisted that he found such accusations beneath his consideration (Posner, 201). However, there is evidence in his novels, especially in relation to some of the hero figures, that he was not indifferent to the claims that his writings ignored Jews' genuine social, economic, and political vulnerability. The most poignant example of a problem with the values of the hero figure involves an exchange between Jake Hersh and his Uncle Abe in *St Urbain's Horseman*. Jake blames Uncle Abe for Joey's disappearance and insinuates that the community behaved in a cowardly way when Joey took it upon himself to defend Montreal's Jews with force. Uncle Abe is unmoved by Jake's accusation and argues that Joey's interpretation of empowerment was dangerous and possibly motivated by reckless egoism more than sentiments regarding Jewish dignity. He starts by explaining the predicament of Montreal Jews at the time:

> You have no idea how close we were to a race riot here ...
> Those days they were painting *À bas les juifs* on the highway,
> the young men were hiding in the woods, they weren't going
> to fight the Jews' war. We could all be shoveled into a furnace,
> as far as they were concerned ... Your *zeyda*, my father, came
> here steerage to be a peddler. He couldn't speak English and
> trod in fear of the *goyim*. I was an exception, one of the first
> of my generation to go to McGill, and it was no pleasure to be
> a Jew-boy on campus in my time ... In my time, we were afraid
> too, you know. We couldn't buy property in the town of Mount
> Royal, we smelled bad. Hotels were restricted, country clubs,
> and there were quotas on the Jews in universities. I can
> remember to this day driving to the mountains, Sophie, she was
> four months pregnant ... I got a flat tire on the road and walked
> two miles to a hotel to phone a garage. No Jews. No dogs,
> it said on the fence. (1991b, 404)

Uncle Abe tries to prove to Jake that Joey's violent self-defence tactics could have compounded the Montreal Jews' predicament and made their status even more precarious. When Joey returned to his family as a young man, he had long been absent from Montreal and was unfamiliar with the community's past, its struggle for security and sense of tenuousness. Jake admires Joey for his instinctual drive for vengeance, but Uncle Abe's comments undermine the idealization of that kind of response and cast proud vigilantism as imprudence. They allude to the complications associated with resistance, the likelihood of its ineffectiveness and the possible threat of retaliatory collective punishment (cf. Bauer, 248).

Richler was well aware of the history of anti-Semitism in Quebec as well as Canada in general. He grew up when the local patron saint of Québécois nationalism was the "virulent anti-Semite" Abbé

Lionel Groulx and Maurice Duplessis was premier of Quebec (1936–39/1944–59), a leader whose government, on the whole, was "sickeningly anti-Semitic (Richler 1992, 79). He recalls the Quebec countryside highways vandalized during his youth with swastikas and associated graffiti. And in writing about the Quebec separatist movement's origins, he reminds his readers of a 1942 rally organized by francophone politicians to protest Canada's participation in the Second World War, a rally "which ended with a mob charging down The Main, smashing the plate-glass windows of Jewish shops, yelling, 'Kill them! Kill Them!'" (90). Thus, Uncle Abe's views, grounded in the real peril faced by Quebec Jews in the mid-twentieth century, may be Richler's attempt to infuse his novels with a consciousness regarding the position of the Jewish community during that era and its reluctance to further weaken its status with rash, violent behaviour. Ramraj goes one step further, positing that Uncle Abe is a mouthpiece for Richler, a character whose observations "appear to have authorial sanction" (Ramraj, 95). It is as if the author recognizes a certain prudence in mainstream Jewish communal attitudes expressed through the voice of Jewish experience and seniority.

In contrast to *St Urbain's Horseman*, with its clues that Richler is not blind to the problems of Jewish self-defence and the conflicts inherent in the novel's value system, both *Solomon Gursky Was Here* and *Barney's Version* seem to condemn Jewish establishment values and represent Jewish heroics as uncontested ideals. In *Solomon Gursky* the analogy between the Gurskys and the Bronfman family is unambiguous, and already, before publication, Richler was "rehearsing a disclaimer about any Gursky/Bronfman linkages that he would repeat over and over when the book appeared" (Foran, 535). As respectable, philanthropic, high-profile, and powerful community leaders, the Bronfmans in many ways epitomized Canada's Jewish establishment. However, Solomon Gursky, who does not actually bear a biographical resemblance to any specific member of the Bronfman family, is a repudiation of virtually everything the family represents. The values expressed through his character as a hero figure are not thrown into question at any point in the novel. There is no caviler, such as Uncle Abe of *St Urbain's Horseman*, with the ability to undermine his identity as a brilliant maverick who stands for cosmic justice and truth. Moreover, the novel's protagonist Moses Berger is never disabused of his fantasy of Solomon as a super-human rebel, alternately saintly and mischievous. Solomon's image is not subject to any meaningful scrutiny that would partially redeem the values of the Gurskys or the Jewish milieu that celebrates them as exemplary Canadian Jews.

The one person who would be expected to offer a more sober account of Solomon's life is his older brother Bernard, a character modelled on the real-life figure, Samuel Bronfman, known better as Mr Sam (see Newman). But Bernard is such a pathetic, despicable man that any of his recollections are likely to be immediately dismissed. As one of Richler's most vulgar characters, "Mr. Bernard is in a class by himself, self-serving and manipulative on a grand scale (Yanofsky, 221). Thus, the novel's apparent endorsement of Solomon's value system is never destabilized: the main witness to Solomon's various improprieties does not have the moral status to undercut Solomon in any way. Solomon's values always appear superior, despite the way in which they are continually contrasted with a mainstream social code that casts Bernard – who is personally repulsive – as a secular saint, an impeccable businessman, faithful husband, doting father, commanding leader, and model citizen.

While Richler's novels tend to privilege Jews of the Diaspora over Israelis, the Jewish state is another issue that features in Richler's novels, treated alternately as a crowning achievement of Jewish history as well as a troubling locus of Jewish sentimentality. In *This Year in Jerusalem*, Richler writes that, as a teenager, he was enthralled with the State of Israel. His youthful participation in the Habonim youth movement led him to develop a "Jewish warrior fantasy" (Richler 1994, 21). In his early novels, Israel often symbolizes sincere Jewish idealism. It is the one profound value of Wolf Adler in *Son of a Smaller Hero*, who paints his father's office "blue for the first six feet and white the rest of the way up. An Israeli flag [hangs] behind the desk" (Richler 1998b, 57). And in *Duddy Kravitz* it is the redemptive focus for Lennie Kravitz after he overcomes the disgrace he has suffered at the hands of his non-Jewish classmates at McGill. When Duddy shows his family the land he has purchased, Lennie says, "I wouldn't want a lake here if they gave it to me on a silver platter. Why develop things for them? Now Israel, that's something else" (Richler 1995, 367). These references to Israel reflect a quixotic vision of Israel that was part of Richler's early life and was still evident in *St Urbain's Horseman*. It is a romanticism that the Canadian Jewish author A.M. Klein, often considered the founder of Canadian Jewish writing (see Pollock 1994), had explored in *The Second Scroll*. Klein's seminal novel, the first important benchmark of Canadian Jewish fiction, depicts Israel as a monument to historical justice that eliminates the Jews' need for vengeful violence (Brenner 1989a, 73). Richler's early writing does not go so far as to suggest that the creation of the Jewish state precludes the demand for historical restitution. Still, in the early part of Richler's career, Israel stood for a romantic ideal approached with a degree of reverence.

By the time Richler was writing *Solomon Gursky Was Here* and *Barney's Version* he had a more complex view of Israel. Personally, he had become disappointed in its increasing religiosity and overall dealings with the Palestinians (Foran, 587). Moreover, whereas Israel's swift, ingenious defensive capabilities are celebrated in Richler's novels, the Canadian Jewish community's indiscriminate support of Israel, its politics, social practices, and culture is an object of satiric condescension.

Solomon Gursky's involvement in the raid on Entebbe is, according to the novel, positive and justified. It is an instance of heroism for an Israeli cause that is morally sound. The positive handling of the issue in the book is consistent with popular attitudes towards the military mission, which is commonly viewed as an example of Israel's ingenious defensive prowess in response to unprovoked aggression. Yet when Moses Berger catches a segment on Israel on the news six years after the Entebbe mission, he waits for his friend, newscaster Sam Burns, to communicate his abhorrence of a different Israel. He expects Sam to appear "disgusted by the massacre of the Palestinians in Sabra and Shatila" – a 1982 raid perpetrated by Lebanese Phalangists against Palestinians refugees in southern Lebanon. Instead, the broadcast cuts to "an interview with the self-satisfied thug himself, defense minister Arik Sharon" (Richler 1990b, 409). Moses expresses the widespread outrage against Israel that was prevalent after the massacre (though it was not an Israeli operation and had been neither planned nor executed by Defence Minister Ariel Sharon – facts that were confirmed by the Kahan Commission of Inquiry overseen by Israel's Supreme Court [see "104 Report of the Commission of Inquiry"]). Nevertheless, as the narrative is focalized through Moses, his reactions become the novel's perspective, further reiterated when Moses consoles himself with the knowledge that his good friend and Gursky scion Henry Gursky had died ignorant of Israel's infamy: "Happily, Henry [Gursky] hadn't lived to learn of the raids on the refugee camps, winked at by the party in power in the country that was to be a beacon unto the nations" (409). There is no indication at this point in the novel that Solomon has ceased his cooperation with Israel following the Uganda raid; but neither is there evidence that he has any association with the Israeli government headed by Menachem Begin so loathed by Moses.

This murkiness is important as Solomon would collapse as a hero figure if Moses discovered that his hero had been in cahoots with a morally repugnant political leadership. Thus, the novel suggests that, despite Moses's discomfort with a Jewish state that is no longer a de facto underdog, a facile position on Israel is not possible. The narrative vacillates between Zionist romanticism and disillusionment, respectively. It is a tension that Richler's writing shares with *Operation Shylock* (1993), a book that Philip Roth insisted, despite readers' scepticism, was a "confession" rather than a work of fiction. Roth, however, goes much further than Richler in questioning Israeli politics, society, and identity, setting up a discourse that asks whether it would be better for the Jews if Israel did not exist. In this work, the proposition is advocated by a man who has assumed the identity of the Jewish American author Philip Roth, a bizarre character whose outlandish antics undermine his authority. Nevertheless, the idea is articulated, staged as a possibility no matter how radical. None of Richler's novels go so far as to suggest that the condition of the Jews would be improved by the dismantling of the Jewish state. The expectations and criticisms of that state might be severe, but they do not call for a return to pre-1948 circumstances.

In *Barney's Version*, it is not Israel the country that is satirized but the Jewish community's attachment to Israel. Following the death of Clara, Barney resolves to prove himself "a straight arrow" in order to attract "Mrs. Right" (Richler 1998a, 161). It is his attempt to reconstruct his identity and create distance from the world of Boogie Moscovitch, the novel's hero figure who had betrayed him. To achieve this goal, he "infiltrates" what he sees as "the Jewish establishment" and becomes a fundraiser for the United Jewish Appeal. This act of self-promoting volunteerism creates a narrative opportunity to depict the Jewish community's self-satisfaction and its paradoxical relationship to Israel as a rallying point rather than a value in itself. It is also an attitude that is antithetical to the novel's heroic values, which are distinct from bourgeois priorities and the trap of stereotypical Jewish destiny. Boogie succumbs to fatal character flaws, but he is a paragon of counterculture cynicism. As such, his influence over Barney, as well as the novel's moral tone, casts a denigrating shadow over the narrative's articulation of mainstream Jewish life, which includes attitudes towards Israel.

Richler was long a critic of the self-congratulatory traditions in the community, such as honorary dinners, award events, and plaque ceremonies. In *Barney's Version*, the character Irv Nussbaum, Barney's fundraising handler, is a parody of that phenomenon, with his prominently displayed Man-of-the-Year plaque and photographs of Golda Meir and Mr Bernard Gursky receiving a doctor of letters on behalf of the Friends of Ben-Gurion University of the Negev (161). Irv also voices the cynical way in which community leaders tap into the wellspring of sentimentality that Jews feel towards Israel in order to boost their fundraising dividends:

> Don't get me wrong. I'm against anti-Semitism. But every time some asshole daubs a swastika on a synagogue wall or knocks over a stone in one of our cemeteries, our guys get so nervous they phone me with pledges. So, things being how they are this year, what you've got to do is slamdunk your target about the Holocaust. Shove Auschwitz at him. Buchenwald. War criminals thriving in Canada to this day. Tell him, "Can you be sure it won't happen again, even here, and then where will you go?" Israel is your insurance policy, you say. (162)

This motivational talk loosely translates into a pro-Israel rendering of "the means justifying the ends," with a rationalization of the psychological manipulation that, despite the speaker's disclaimers, is almost anti-Semitic. Even more cynical, however, is the novel's approach to Israel-advocacy in any form. Irv Nussbaum may resort to cynical tactics, but his objective is sincere. Nevertheless, the novel's depiction of Nussbaum is merciless, totally dismissive of his good intentions and based upon an underlying cynicism with regard to any suggestion that Diaspora Jews "need" Israel.

In his non-fiction writing, Richler voiced similar views. He accused the pro-Israel fundraising apparatus of welcoming anti-Semitic acts "as a prod to both big donors and much-sought-after 'Anglo-Saxon' aliyah" (Richler 1994, 249), and he considers contemporary anti-Semitic views and antics in Canada as the province of "freaks ... and other nutters ... on the fringe" (249). He portrays anti-Semites as marginal outsiders; unlike the reams of successful Jews who have entered the highest echelons of power and influence.

In this context, too, it is worth referencing Philip Roth and his 1969 article in *Commentary*, "Writing about Jews," in which he similarly minimizes the relevance of anti-Semitic threats in the United States. Expressing confidence in the place of Jews in American society, he says: "If the barrier between prejudice and persecution collapsed in Germany, this is hardly reason to contend that no such barrier exits in our country" (2005, 57). He adds that, for Jews in the modern era, "there are courses to prevent it from ever being 1933 again that are more direct, reasonable, and dignified than beginning to act as though it already is 1933 – *or as though it always is*" (59). Yet in 2004 Roth released *The Plot against America*, an allohistory that can be read as a possible admission that his rejection of Jewish paranoia may have been too absolute – that it is within the bounds of reason to at least imagine the United States as a society that could conceivably fall under the control of a fascist, anti-Jewish leadership. It validates the impression of the United States as vulnerable to a paradigm shift in national identification: Roth seems to be revoking his injunction against visions of a different kind of American reality.

None of Richler's novels stage any similar shift. They never champion a Jewish viewpoint – one that would have been in keeping with conventional Jewish positions – regarding anti-Jewish incitement. His fiction remains true to the notion that anti-Semitism, at least in Canada, has greatly receded and that casting Israel as a Jewish safety net is dishonest.

It seems that some critics (Laurence, Wisse) and readers have been too dismissive of Richler, seeing him as wholly antagonistic to Jewish values. It is fair, indeed, to concede that his works do not always reaffirm the values of the Jewish establishment in the twentieth century. Yet, in a limited way, traditional values are upheld in his novels by the protagonists, who believe in a code of ordinary Jewish ethics by which they earnestly try to govern their lives. Through his hero figures, however, Richler imbues his works with a less conventional set of values that force a reinterpretation of what it means to be an ideal Jew in the modern era. Whereas Jews are historically known as keepers of the law, heroism in these works is more often than not pitted against formal legal codes. And, if Jewish self-restraint is the converse of Western hedonism, the hero figures circumvent this binary, living as Jews but indulging in sensual experiences – not simply as gluttons or lechers but also as knowing, even deserving, connoisseurs of Dionysian revelry. Most important, however, in place of cautious compliance, Richler's hero figures prefer valiant action and romanticize the notion of resistance stripped of its potential hazards.

Heroes:
Not Just Avengers

With the publication of *St Urbain's Horseman* it was plain that Richler shared his grandfather Yudel Rosenberg's interest in the character of the Golem, a mythical creature who, in Jewish folklore, is a powerful "servant of man's needs," a monster-like version of a Jewish saviour or messiah (Scholem, 338). But, what was less evident is that motifs of messianism in a much broader sense have been a pervasive element in his writing since the publication of his earliest works. Richler does not rely upon a coherent or unified form of these messianic elements but, rather, borrows from an array of Jewish and Christian concepts that have had varying levels of prominence and popularity throughout history. This eclectic version of messianism is transformed in his books into an optimistic impulse that is mainly focused on messianic hero figures invested with the power to cure the physical and existential ills endemic in Jewish life in particular and in the modern world in general.

Michael Greenstein and Rachel Feldhay Brenner claim that Canadian Jewish writers (A.M. Klein, Henry Kreisel, Adele Wiseman, Leonard Cohen, Irving Layton, Eli Mandel, and Richler) struggle to repossess a European past and "rediscover themselves in their parents' old world" (Brenner 1998, 285). Early Canadian Jewish writing often conflates a messianic search with a longing to reclaim European roots. By contrast, the messianic motif in Richler's novels is not a device for recovering a cultural heritage; rather, it is a way of keeping an optimistic balance between the novels' sharp satire and Nietzschean cynicism on the one hand and hope for a modicum of sanity and moral clarity on the other.

Messianic allusions are already evident in *Son of a Smaller Hero*. The first name of the family patriarch, Melech Adler, is Hebrew for "king" – the basic messianic faith asserting that "a king from the House of David will arise who will preside over a peaceful, prosperous, monotheistic world with the Temple rebuilt and the Jewish people – including at some point its resurrection – returned to its land" (Berger, 18). As a child, the novel's protagonist Noah Adler adores his grandfather, "allowing no other to carry his prayer shawl" (14) on the way to synagogue. But, after watching his *zeyde* conduct a crooked business deal – a transaction in which dishonesty is actually an accepted practice by both parties – he is disillusioned. Melech, like many other Richler characters, proves a false hero, a corrupt king, too proud to stoop to explain his seemingly underhanded business tactics to his grandson and perhaps even long unaware of the need for such an explanation.

The first of Richler's characters to be widely recognized as a messianic presence is Joey Hersh in *St Urbain's Horseman*.[1] Early in the novel, Jake Hersh notes that the Hersh family is descended from "the House of David" (Richler 1991b, 94), suggesting that Joey, in particular, is an heir of a messianic legacy that is expected to emerge from King David's lineage. Fashioned by Richler as a tireless Nazi-hunter with "sheer energy and vivid maleness that makes hapless Anglo-Saxon rivals pale into the woodwork" (Iannone, 52), he is a character laden with overtly messianic symbolism. Most conspicuously, the name Joey alludes to the "Messiah ben Joseph," the son of Joseph, or one who springs from Joseph's stock, a messianic figure who is discussed in the Midrash as a preliminary saviour, presaging the arrival of the ultimate messiah born of the Davidic line (Patai, 165). The messianic overtones in his portrayal also link him with the Jewish warrior, Bar Kochba, who was regarded by Jewish sages, notably Rabbi Akiva, as a "warrior messiah." The era of this messiah – like the period of Roman rule in Judea experienced by Bar Kochba and the years of the Holocaust into which Joey is born – is expected to be plagued by catastrophe, war, famine, and even transgressions of the natural laws established by God at creation (Werblowsky, 42).

Yudel Rosenberg's frequently anthologized short story, "How the Maharal of Prague, with the Aid of the Golem, Foiled a Plot by the Evil Priest Tadisch to Convert a Beautiful Jewish Girl to Christianity," is included in Richler's 1994 memoir, *This Year in Jerusalem* (187–200). In the story, the Golem is a "man" named Yossele, a Yiddish diminutive for Joseph, who can be summoned by human forces, in this case the plea of the Maharal.[2] This aspect of

Rosenberg's tale seems a conspicuous parallel to Jake Hersh's efforts to summon Joey, who, he believes, has the power to avenge not only Nazi crimes but all anti-Semitic acts and most other barbarism. Further supporting the idea that Joey is a messianic figure is his tendency to assume the alias Jesse Hope. While "hope" is quintessential to messianic belief, the name Jesse echoes an oft-quoted reference in the Book of Isaiah to a future messiah from "the stock of Jesse"; Jesse also being the name of King David's father. Thus, Joey Hersh is associated with the messianic tradition of the biblical prophets, the folkloristic Golem motif found in classical Jewish texts, and Yudel Rosenberg's Golem stories, "which exercised a profound influence on Jewish and European literature of the twentieth century" (Robinson et al., 105).

In *Solomon Gursky Was Here* several pseudo-messianic characters are involved in fraudulent messianism, foolhardy messianic beliefs, and messianic entitlement. The novel's most outrageous character, Ephraim Gursky, marks his arrival in nineteenth-century Canada by assuming the role of self-styled deity among the Inuit in the far north.[3] Positioning himself as a preacher-God, he begins his leadership by outlining his laws:

> "Thou shalt not bow down to Narssuk, whose prick I have
> shriveled, or to any other gods, you ignorant little fuckers. For
> the Lord thy God is a jealous God, visiting the iniquity of the
> fathers upon the children unto the third and fourth generation
> of them that hate me." He enjoined them not to steal or kill, unless
> ordered to do so by Ephraim, and instructed them not to take his
> name in vain. "Six days shalt thou hunt, providing meat for me
> and Izzy, and on the evening of the sixth day thou shalt wash thy
> women and bring them to me, an offering." (Richler 1990b, 327)

Years later, having travelled south in search of gold, Ephraim establishes the Church of the Millenarians, persuades his rural disciples to sign over "their livestock and the deeds to their properties to the Millenarian Trust Company" (132), and devises a ruse to require the community's young women to frequent his log cabin. To initially attract followers, Ephraim distributes a pamphlet entitled *Evidence from the Scriptures of the Second Coming of Christ in the Eastern Townships about the year 1851*. The scam endures for two years until the suicide of one of the followers. Then Ephraim absconds, taking the land deeds with him.

Also embroiled in messianic fantasy is Ephraim's grandson, Henry Gursky, a Jewish convert to the world of Lubavitch, a Hasidic group originating in Europe but transplanted to New York that places singular emphasis on messianism.[4] At one point in the novel, Ephraim Gursky, assuming the role of God of the Eskimos, promises his disciples that "he would send them a Messiah in another generation. The Messiah, a descendant of Ephraim, would return their ancestors to them and make the seal and caribou so plentiful that nobody would starve again" (328). Then, in a serendipitous turn of fate, Henry joins Lubavitch, moves north, and, in fact, proves just such a saviour. Abiding by Ephraim's dictates regarding Yom Kippur, including fasting, many Inuit who had settled "too far north" found that the Day of Atonement lasted months rather the usual twenty-four hours. As a result, many starved, "dying devout, unless Henry, that good shepherd found them, and hurried them south to the sun and deliverance" (328). Thus, Henry is cast as an actual Jesus figure tending to his flock and an accidental Jewish saviour.

Richler resorts to caricature in drawing both Ephraim and Henry. The former revels in extreme burlesque, the latter in cringeworthy pathos. Still, they are important constituents in the novel's construction of a messianic continuum. The rabbinic exegesis in the Midrash refers to the messiah in several instances as the Messiah son of Ephraim (Patai, 165), and in a bizarre fashion, Henry, the grandson of Ephraim, comically fulfills his destiny.

Important in terms of the role of Solomon Gursky, and generally in Richler's novels, is the extent to which Christian and Jewish symbols are intertwined. Repeatedly, the idea that long-assumed dead messiah figures will be resurrected resonates with the motif of the Second Coming. In *Cocksure*, the return of Ziggy Spicehandler to London is mockingly referred to as his "second coming" (Richler 1968a, 116), and when Solomon Gursky's brother Bernard dies, his body "[lies] in state for two days in the lobby of the Bernard Gursky Tower and, as he fail[s] to rise on the third, he [is] duly buried" (188).

However, Solomon's messianic attributes are portrayed in a more substantial fashion. On one hand, he is presented in the Jewish "messiah-king" tradition. This tradition identifies the messiah by many names and symbols, but one of its mainstays is that the messiah will follow in the footsteps of the biblical sons of Aaron, high priests who were "anointed" with oil upon induction into the holiest level of service in the Tabernacle. It is a ritual that was later used as Jewish kings assumed their reign and biblical prophets became leaders (Patai, xxi–ii). Richler draws on much of this material in creating Solomon Gursky. He is his grandfather "Ephraim's anointed one" (Richler 1990b, 167) and literally a son of Aaron (albeit Gursky). He is named Solomon, like King David's son, the wisest, most successful and powerful king in the history of Israel.

At the same time, Solomon is portrayed in Christian messianic terms. Despite evidence that suggests his demise, Moses expects Solomon to resurface among the living. In 1934, Solomon flies north in treacherous weather conditions, in a private plane, to escape trial as a bootlegging outlaw. Days later, charred pieces of his Gypsy Moth aircraft are discovered across a large swath of the Arctic, along with an attaché case adorned with the initials SG. The Gursky family accepts the evidence of death (especially Bernard, as it appears that he orchestrated Solomon's crash) and immediately begins to mourn their lost brother. But Moses is unconvinced that Solomon has perished. Likewise, some years later, when Moses discovers that Solomon is in fact the eccentric British socialite Sir Hyman Kaplansky, he refuses to accept the report that Sir Hyman drowned while swimming one morning in rough seas. Having traced the activities of Sir Hyman, he is convinced that Solomon Gursky has wilfully disappeared, intending to surface in another guise, embark upon another mission, and respond to aggression against Jews in Canada, England, Europe, or even Israel, if need be. He is certain that Solomon has outsmarted death and remains on the lookout for signs of his resurrection.

Similarly, Barney Panofsky in *Barney's Version* spends the better part of his adult life waiting for his friend Boogie Moscovitch to return despite the circumstantial evidence indicating that Boogie is dead and the prevailing suspicions that Barney murdered him. In all of Richler's novels featuring a messianic hero figure, the reader, along with the protagonist, is meant to anticipate the return of these characters – even if this anticipation is mixed with scepticism. They are, to some extent, Jesus figures who, the narrative insinuates, may cast a larger shadow when presumed dead than when undoubtedly alive. In these works, the conceit of the anticipated Second Coming is critical because it propels the protagonists' ceaseless search to uncover a moral mandate based on justice and viable values. Feldhay Brenner's argument that "Richler's recurrent affirmation of unequivocal commitment to moral values seems to contradict the hopelessness of his world picture" (1998, 72) overlooks this quest. Yet it is this hopeful quest that under-cuts the novels' pessimism and moral outrage. It allows for faith in moral progress at least at some point in the future.

– * –

While Richler draws extensively on messianic material from diverse traditions, his works are most heavily indebted to Jewish ideas. Messianism has long been a socially, culturally, and theologically loaded phenomenon, "a permanent and ever-present feature, at times latent, at times manifest, of Jewish history" (Werblowsky, 43). Richler employs a mélange of messiah-related images and themes, of which the most prominent are the immediate antecedents to the arrival of the messiah, the attributes of the messianic age, and the qualities of the messiah figure.

Since notions of Jewish messianism have evolved over centuries, and have been adjusted to the historical, spiritual, and religious milieu of each generation, they do not form a consistent theological outlook. Still, there are a few broad conceptions of Jewish messianic faith that have been constant. For example, it is believed that the preamble to the messianic era will be characterized by universal evil, idolatry, arrogance, and a particularly harsh persecution of the Jews; evil will prevail in distinct contravention of God's will; an inspired individual will emerge with the ability to read the signs of redemption in the horror and destruction of his age; he will bear such suffering on behalf of humankind, enduring it with ecstasy and the knowledge that cata-clysm is a precursor of the redeemed future (Schweid, 61).

Consensual points in the disparate views on the messianic era itself include the arrival of the "Messiah king," the son of David, and his dominion over Israel, possibly even the entire world, and subsequent redemption. They also include an expectation of justice, vengeance against evil-doers, the eradication of idolatry, the return of the exiles to Zion, the re-establishment of the Jewish kingdom and the Temple service, bountiful crops that will require no toil, peace between Israel and all other nations, the resurrection of the dead, the elimination of pain and sickness, and an end to death (61).

These ideas, springing primarily from biblical texts, writings from the Second Temple period (538 BCE until 70 CE – notably the Book of Enoch in the Pseudepigrapha), rabbinic literature comprised of the Mishnah and Talmud, the works of Maimonides and Nahmanides, and mysticism (based for the most part on the Kuzari, a twelfth-century work by Spanish philosopher Judah HaLevi and the Zohar), as well as from modern religious movements ranging from Hasidism to religious Zionism (Bronner, 164–81), were fuelled by pervasive oppression and discrimination and the consequent need to safeguard hope (Werblowsky, 43). They are all parts of a theological position that views redemption "as an event which takes place publicly, on the stage of history and within the community" (Scholem, 1). Christian messianism, by contrast, operates "in the spiritual and unseen realm"; it "is reflected in the soul, in the private world of each individual and effects an inner transformation which does not need to correspond to anything outside" (1). Hence, Jewish messianism is "by definition doomed to failure in the historical sphere" (Werblowsky, 45), and its parameters repeatedly require reassessment in the face of recurring historical setbacks. Nevertheless, it has endured and recuperated from messianic outbreaks: impossible revivals and ill-fated movements throughout Jewish history, which are "tragic and moving witnesses of the powerful sway of messianic hope and belief over the Jewish people throughout their historic existence" (45).

By turning to the motif of messianic hope, Richler restates the dominance of hope in spite of historical evidence. In this sense, his novels, with their strong emphasis on moral codes, are very much a product of Jewish thought of the modern era, when many Jewish political groups – socialist, communist, nationalist, and Zionist – were committed to ideologies with a coherent worldview and often couched their views in the discourse of messianic aspirations: "the total rectification of all the perversities of the present and the realization of all the good" that is possible in the future (Schweid, 54).

Along with foundational conceptions of Jewish messianism, the narratives in Richler's fiction also refer, directly or obliquely, to false messianism, a phenomenon that pervades Jewish history and manifests in the novels as a tendency towards both comic folly and tragic despair. Examples of false or fraudulent messiahs and erroneous messianic longing have been well documented by scholars. In the second century CE, one of the most famed Jewish scholars, Rabbi Akiva, was eager to crown Bar Kochba, the leader of the Jewish revolt against the Romans (132–35 CE), as messiah. The rise of a saviour seemed the only escape from the Jews' torment under Roman rule in eschatological terms

(Werblowsky, 42). For similar reasons, in eighth-century Persia, Abu Issa al-Isfahani was regarded by many as the Jews' messiah, as was David Alroy, in twelfth-century Baghdad (46). Presumed messiahs also arose with increasing frequency throughout Western Europe in the century preceding the Spanish Inquisition. The most famous of all such impostors arose in the seventeenth century, Shabtai Tzvi, whose influence "had swept the whole Diaspora into orbit and had struck deep roots in the soul of the masses" (Scholem, 316).

Antinomianism, a recurring feature of false messianism, is explored in Richler's novels in regard to outright fakes, such as Ephraim Gursky, and more nuanced characters, such as Barney Panofsky's hero Boogie Moscovitch. Prominent in many movements of redemption and salvation, antinomianism seems to have evolved in Jewish messianic traditions from the rabbinic idea that the advent of the messiah would nullify the extensive and often restrictive ritualistic prohibitions of Jewish law. In a theoretical context, this expectation was generally tolerated by the rabbinical establishment. As long as nullification of halakhah, Jewish law as it pertains to the practice of Judaism, was a strictly abstract prospect, it was not considered a danger. But when messianic movements arose, they often advocated religious innovation and conflicted with rabbinic authority. Messianic leaders, usually charismatic and persuasive, attracted followers by calling for a new approach to Jewish law as a necessary harbinger of the messianic age (Scholem qtd in Saperstein, 297). It was an appeal rooted in Jewish tradition but may have been alluring because it offered Jews a way to be part of a teleological process without punctilious adherence to the rigid legal demands of the rabbis.

The Richler characters who flippantly disparage Jewish law tend to be delegitimized and ineffectual in the long run. The novels largely uphold traditional rabbinic rules as a framework for living an honourable and dignified, if untenable, life. The main actors – the protagonists and hero figures – rarely abide by these laws, but they respect them as well as those who attempt to comply with them in earnest. Thus, the novels' hero figures have strong messianic characteristics but are by no means antinomian mavericks. Richler's hero figures have the power to inspire the protagonists with hope in a world that makes moral sense. Antinomianism, in history and Richler's writing, is often seen as dark, self-interested, and nihilistic. Therefore the question is not whether the novels' hero figures are meant to be messianic, or even pseudo-messianic, but whether they are endowed with the moral gravitas to inspire faith in some positive vision of existential meaning.

Joey Hersh is a hero figure whose insistence on straightforward justice and moral intelligence – especially in relation to the aftermath of the Holocaust – is encouraging to Jake; there is a suggestion that all is not lost in the battle to uphold some form of ethical standards. Critics such as Carol Iannone, Rachel Feldhay Brenner, and Wilfred Cude view Joey Hersh as a monster-saviour, created to avenge the Holocaust by hunting down Josef Mengele, the *Doktor*, in South America, "taking him by surprise, gaining the advantage" (Richler 1991b, 11). However, Jake Hersh views his cousin's objectives in more complicated terms. On the one hand, he is obsessed with revenge for the Nazis' war against the Jews and convinces himself that Joey is, in fact, on the trail to capture Mengele. On the other, he has a murky vision of what kind of blame he assigns to Germans twenty years after the fall of the Third Reich. He wants Joey to deal with history, but the immediate reality of German men and women in the present day is another matter.

Jake's convoluted ideas about Germans reflect Richler's own thinking. In an essay first published in 1966, Richler wrote:

> The Germans are still an abomination to me. I do not mourn
> for Cologne, albeit decimated for no useful military purpose.
> I rejoice in the crash of each German Starfighter. No public
> event in recent years has thrilled me more than the hunting
> down of Adolf Eichmann. I am not touched by the Berlin Wall.
> (1973b, 81)

A little more than a decade later – taking his cue from Elie Wiesel, who found it hard to sustain his unadulterated hatred of the Germans two decades after the Holocaust (Richler 1993, xxvii) – Richler's perspective softened. While travelling through Germany in 1978, witnessing the residual bomb damage from the Second World War, he found himself, "moved to sympathy" until "freight trains intruded" and his rage was renewed (1998b, 126). Thus, the fury had not totally abated, but it was more nuanced.

Jake's conflicted attitude is encapsulated in his entanglement with the German au pair Ingrid Loebner in *St Urbain's Horseman*. In dealing with Ingrid, Jake is first rude and disrespectful but does not evict her from his house. He responds to her with controlled disdain, as a Jew who has tempered his hatred for Germans. However, when Ingrid is surprised that he is a Jew because his looks suggest otherwise and he is "so nice,"

Jake's self-control dissolves (Richler 1991b, 432). He roughly forces her out of the house in a state of disarray in the early morning hours with the anger of the unforgiving Jew, who harbours no pity for the Nazis' descendants. In taking this decisive step, Jake seems to be emulating the Horseman as golem. He does not tolerate Ingrid's comments; he responds with decisive action. Ironically, however, the decision is not recompense for Ingrid's insensitivity but the springboard for Jake's humiliating arrest on charges of rape and salacious criminal offences.

This experience suggests that the Horseman, as a golem, is psychologically necessary for Jake. He needs to believe in some kind of saviour, one who will ensure that evil is punished and the oppressed are redeemed. Yet when Jake assumes the role of moral avenger, the results are pathetic. In Rosenberg's rendering of the golem legend, the mythical creature can be not only a devoted servant, "but a threat to its creator and all who dwell in his house" (Kieval, 98). Jake, indeed, wreaks havoc upon himself and his family with his vengeful antics. Inspired by moral grandeur, he tries to act out his fantasy and perform deeds of moral restitution. Instead, he brings misfortune to himself and those he loves. When he assumes the persona of the Horseman, the transformation of faith into action illustrates how Joey's ethics, as imagined by Jake, constitute a useful belief system but not a maxim for action in ordinary life.

M.G. Osachoff argues that Richler views the past as the only source of genuine Jewish values. However, the strain of messianism in his novels suggests that there is a form of Jewish justice that could be available in the future as well (34). At times, Jake Hersh believes that his faith in Joey and a better future is futile, just like his family's hapless efforts to conjure the harbinger of the messiah, Elijah the Prophet, each year at the Passover Seder meal. Nevertheless, his search continues and he expects Joey to do more than provide a corrective for the evils of the Holocaust. He is "a sheet anchor, an assurance that evil will be punished, that the compromise of principles is not an inevitability" (Richler 1991b, 465). "Richler's characters are always looking for spiritual mentors" (Ramraj, 11), and Jake's search for the Horseman is not only related to his need to make sense of the Holocaust, it is a quest to find an uncompromised spirit who is a worthy "moral editor" (Richler 1991b, 309). Brenner insists that Richler sees only "meaninglessness and impotence of humanist values in a post Holocaust world" (1998, 76), but Jake never abandons his search for Joey or the belief that his cousin represents a life of meaning in a post-Holocaust context.

Even when he learns that Joey has died in a plane crash, he cannot bring himself to recognize that his cousin is finally gone. Though committed to a modern liberal outlook, he, like his pious forebears from previous generations, clings to shreds of evidence that allow him to sustain the dream of a different kind of future (Majer 2008, 157). Writing in Joey's journal at the end of the novel, he crosses out the notation he has added, "Died July 20, 1967," and inserts "presumed dead," allowing for his cousin's "resurrection" and the possibility of a future guided by this spiritual shepherd (Richler 1991b, 462). Reinhold Kramer points to the possibility that, as a result of Jake's decision to believe that the Horseman has not been overthrown completely, "the novel arrives at a kind of humanist faith" (2011, 177).

Just as Richler sets up his protagonists as a contrast to his hero figures, a divide that distinguishes between ordinary values and supererogatory propensities, he commonly pits messianic figures against messianic charlatans in order to differentiate between legitimate hope for a more humane world and inane faith in failed ideas and false prophets. While it is often left unclear whether the hero figures are genuinely devoted to a benevolent, redemptive mission, it is obvious that the messianic elements of the other characters are a charade, one that is sometimes pathetic, at other times decidedly pernicious.

The Ephraim Gursky subplot is a convoluted mix of holy and messianic satire. Clearly, Ephraim is not a genuine saviour. He seems more likely to be based on the historical figure of Jacob Frank, a disciple of Shabtai Tzvi, whom scholar Gershom Scholem described as a "depraved and unscrupulous" (86) messianist who scandalized eighteenth-century Eastern European Jewry with his ideas and leadership. Scholem politely refers to Frank's doctrine of "salvation through sin" as an ethics of libertinism that took on the status of binding religious obligation (136). With less delicacy many Jewish historians of this period depict Frank as a depraved, spurious leader who urged his coreligionists to spurn the laws of morality and conduct that had long governed the Jewish people. He was reputed to be a lapsed observant Jew who opportunistically assumed leadership following the vacuum of faith that developed among some of Shabtai Tzvi's followers after his death. Unable to relinquish their messianic hopes, they accepted Frank as their leader, clung to his doctrine that the "nullification of the Torah was its true fulfillment," and participated in his mandated orgiastic rites (Seltzer, 472).

Ephraim, thus, seems a derivative of Frank, replacing Frank's Jewish followers with pagan Aboriginals and downtrodden Canadian farmers. He is a creative con man whose success is as much an indictment of devout faith and pious gullibility as dictatorial exploitation. His ability to lead is not principally a result of his wily intelligence and captivating charisma but the outcome of what Nietzsche, in *Beyond Good and Evil*, calls the herd instinct, the long cultivated pattern wherein obedience has become "an innate need" (107). It arises, moreover, when the Western human mass "accepts whatever meets its ear, whatever any representative of authority … declaims into it" (107). The novel suggests that Ephraim is savvy, ruthlessly intelligent, and accrues proselytes because of human instinct; "a kind of *formal conscience* that bids 'thou shalt do something or other absolutely, and absolutely refrain from something or other,' in other words, 'thou shalt'" (107). His followers are not necessarily susceptible to a specifically Jewish demagogue with dictatorial and erotic proclivities but are amenable to any type of leadership, providing it is authoritative and explicit.[5]

The messianism associated with Henry Gursky is likewise satiric but less fantastical: it is more of a specific attack on modern messianic fervour and the willing naivety inherent in utopian belief. Convinced that an impending ice age will soon destroy the world, Henry plans to purchase "a three-masted ship modeled on turn-of-the-century schooners or possibly a windjammer" to endure the anticipated apocalypse (Richler 1991b, 258). The locals of his northern Canadian town are well aware of his plan but dismiss him as a harmless fool. In a particularly amusing episode, Henry tries to forewarn his cousin and head of the Gursky empire, Lionel Gursky, of the upcoming catastrophe:

> The men left and Henry, his eyes welling with tears, reached out and touched Lionel tentatively on the shoulder. In spite of everything, he was a cousin: he was entitled to know.
> "It's coming to an end," Henry said.
> "Family Control?"
> "The world."
> "Oh, that," Lionel said, relieved. "Good to see you again and thanks for the tip. Knowing you, it has to be insider information." (81–2)

Still, Henry cannot be dissuaded. Despite his trust in the biblical promise to Noah that God would refrain from flooding the world a second time, he is certain that man's wickedness has reached a new high and that global deluge is both warranted and imminent. This storyline portrays an alternate model of misguided messianism. If Ephraim is fashioned in the image of a corrupt messianic leader, such as Jacob Frank, Henry is both an emasculated saviour, empowered with little more than a rudimentary knowledge of astronomy, and a dupe of a devout messianic group, desperate to believe in a higher good despite the profuse evidence to the contrary.

Henry's innocence is eventually the cause of his demise. Blind to his son Isaac's delinquent, angry disposition, he takes him on a pre-Passover trip to supply an outlying Arctic community of the descendants of Ephraim's Faithful with matzah and sacramental wine. Then, in an inversion of typological roles, Isaac the son sacrifices his father. When the trip goes awry and the supplies are lost, Isaac cannibalizes Henry. Here the novel resorts to a biblical model but also "mixes Christian Messianism in the same phylum as Lubavitch messianism, culminating in Isaac's ghastly communion, in which he lunches on his father" (Kramer 2008, 317). Henry is referred to as "that good shepherd" for his outreach to Ephraim's zealously suicidal Inuit. Nevertheless, his martyrdom, rather than producing redemption, is a comic rendering of the Eucharist: his flesh is not ingested by devout followers but consumed by his faithless son. When Isaac is cleared of wrongdoing, his cannibalism attributed to self-preservation, he returns to his Lubavitch yeshiva in New York. There, he is promptly summoned for his use of marijuana and entanglements with the Puerto Rican maid. Isaac defensively quotes from the Book of Kings: "a king may take wives and concubines up to the number eighteen, and I am descended from the House of David" (Richler 1991b, 392). Like his father, grandfather, and great-grandfather, he has messianic attributes, yet he is not a moral arbiter, seeker of justice, or national defender. The portrayal of Ephraim, Henry, and Isaac is invested with messianic allusions, but none of them has the idealism, vision, or wisdom of an inspired messianic character because they are, respectively, a cruel narcissist, a good-hearted simpleton, and an immoral punk.

– ✳ –

Since the nineteenth century, one of the most debated aspects of messianic prophecy has been the "ingathering of the exiles," or the return of the Children of Israel to the Land of Israel. Foretold in the biblical Book of Daniel, the return of the Jews to the land God promised to

Abraham in Genesis has received special prominence in the modern era with the rise of Zionism and creation of the State of Israel. Even outside of the strictly religious context, most ideological Jewish movements in the late nineteenth and early twentieth centuries perceived messianic links in the rise of Zionism and the progress towards a Jewish state (Schweid, 54). Nonetheless, Richler's messianic hero figures are Diasporic Jews who have no interest in reaffirming the return of the Jews to Zion. Israel is not their home or their fantasy of a promised land. At no point do any of them attempt, or even consider, settling in the Jewish state for good. They are not staunch advocates of the Diaspora, like intellectuals such as George Steiner or Grace Paley, whose self-referential narrator in "The Used-Boy Raisers" says:

> I believe in the Diaspora ... Jews have one hope only –
> to remain a remnant in the basement of world affairs – no,
> I mean something else – a splinter in the toe of civilization,
> a victim to aggravate the conscience. (Paley 1987, 132)

Richler's messianic figures do not relish the vulnerability of the Diasporic condition. Still, they are never inclined to see Israel as their home or *the* Jewish home. For them, it is only a place to visit.

Joey Hersh is the hero figure who spends the greatest amount of time in Israel. He is rumoured to have been active in Israel during the 1948 War of Independence, taking part in the Jewish attack on the Arab village of Deir Yassin, suffering an Arab ambush at Bab el Wad and turning his gun on ultra-Orthodox Jews who attempted to surrender to the Jordanians. But Joey's residence in Israel seems to have ended a few years after the war and is obliquely linked to the assassination of Rudolph Kastner. Joey, when in Israel, operates as the golem of Jake Hersh's imagination. He takes part in a pre-emptive strike against local Arabs in much the same way that he organized vigilantism to counter anti-Semitic attacks in Montreal. He participates in a convoy to break the Arab blockade of Jerusalem during Israel's War of Independence, willing to enter the heart of combat in order to reassert his identity as a proactive, courageous fighter rather than a timorous, passive victim. And when he believes that Kastner must be punished for betraying masses of Hungarian Jews during the Holocaust, he barks his mantra at the residents of Kibbutz Gesher Haaziv: "what are you going to do about it?" (Richler 1991b, 257). In Israel, Joey acts more as a monstrous golem than a redeeming messiah. His *return to Zion* is not an idealistic endorsement of nation-hood or part of a utopian mission to foster a new Jewish reality. It is, rather, another opportunity for him to prove that Jews are not doomed to compliant victimization. He does not journey to Israel because the nascent state is the specific locus of Jewish honour and dignity, or the Jewish future, for that matter. For him Israel is just another locale where Jews have to resist physical assault, struggle for their survival, and revolt against degradation in any form. Joey includes Israel in his worldwide agenda of redressing Jewish vulnerability, but he is just as much his European alias, Jesse Hope, as he is Yosef ben Baruch, the name by which he is known in Israel. In other words, his messianic persona is as Western as it is Israeli. His insistence on Jewish strength and audacity is not specifically linked to reclaimed Jewish nationhood. For Joey, Jewish weakness demands a corrective whether it is embedded in the Jewish reality of Montreal, Jerusalem, or elsewhere.

Coming to the rescue of a burgeoning Jewish State is also part of Solomon Gursky's messianic bravado, but again, these actions are part of a broader determination to pluck Jews from the vise of their enemies and not a contribution to Jewish settlement in Canaan. After the Second World War, Solomon, posing as Sir Hyman Kaplansky, is implicated when a ship disembarking from Naples "tries to run the Palestine blockade" and is "diverted to Cyprus by a British destroyer." Then, the day after Sir Hyman claims to have lost money on a movie featuring a stunt air force that failed to go into production, "David Ben-Gurion proclaimed the State of Israel" – the insinuation that armed with newly acquired air power, the Jewish leader was ready to face the inevitable Arab wrath that would follow his announcement (Richler 1991b, 142).

Despite the emphasis on messianism in Richler's works, as well as the focus on Israel, redemption in these books is never bound to the end of exile. Henry Gursky is arguably the Richler character most invested with overt messianic concerns and imagery. Nonetheless, even when he envisions an impending apocalypse, it does not include the return of the Jewish people to the land of Israel or "an end to exile, an ingathering of the Jewish people, a messianic age, a restoration of harmony between God and man, a righteous judgment by the Judge, a postressurection existence" as predicted in rabbinic writings (Seltzer, 306). Henry imagines the apocalypse in universal terms: "God's punishment, Henry was convinced, would be another Ice Age. Then there would be floods" (Richler 1991b, 258). It is an image of the end of days that resembles the Noah story in Genesis, and God's decision to abolish evil and build the entire world anew. It does not, however, recall a specifically Jewish rendering of the "World to Come," typical of rabbinic messianism, nor does it include Israel as a geographic locus of redemption (Seltzer, 306).

− ✳ −

With their messianic allusions, Richler's novels are in conversation with a substantial corpus of works by twentieth-century Jewish writers, novelists who incorporated messianic figures into their novels, many based in historical reality, as a means "to interpret the events of their own time" (Wisse 2000, 154). One of the precursors of the trope of the messianic quest in Richler's novels is the pursuit of Melech Davidson in A.M. Klein's *The Second Scroll* (1951). The novel tells the story of a Montreal journalist who is assigned the job of investigating the effect of the rebirth of the Hebrew language upon the creation of the Jewish State. The protagonist uses this trip as an opportunity to track down his Uncle Melech, "the emblem of the Messiah" whose life journey "holds a promise of redemption no only for the Jewish People, but alsos for the entire world" (Brenner 1989b, 74). While the messianism in Richler's novels never suggests anything as promising or romantic as renewed national unity, the process of the open-ended search, as structured originally by Klein, offers "the idea of the metaphysical quest" (Kramer 2011, 176). Because the protagonists' yearning for the messiah is never satisfied, it allows for ongoing hopefulness. The lack of closure provides the protagonists with the unlimited imaginative space to conceive of an inspirational figure who insists on moral truths, real justice, and societies governed with more intelligence and integrity.

In a more general sense, Richler's use of messianism – including false messianism – is also preceded by a number of nineteenth- and twentieth-century European Jewish writers, such as Israel Zangwill, Jakob Wassermann, Sholem Asch, Leopold von Sacher-Masoch, and Josef Katstein, for whom "the Sabbatian movement functioned as a kind of cultural code" and was a linchpin in the struggle to "define borders between tradition and modernity" (Biale, 120). Writing several decades later, Richler tapped into the way in which these earlier writers conveyed ambivalence towards "issues such as rabbinical authority, conversion, intermarriage and erotic liberation" (120) through the fulcrum of messianic faith.

The messianic element in Richler's novels is likewise mirrored in the writing of Israel Joshua Singer and Isaac Bashevis Singer, even though the works of the two brothers contain diametrically opposed ideas regarding traditional messianic beliefs and their value. In the works of I.J. Singer, the urge to trust humanism as a palliative against human evil is repeatedly thwarted, and no alternate ideal, religious or otherwise, is proposed. At the end of his most ambitious work, *The Brothers Ashkenazi* (1936), the expectation that liberalism will finally bring amelioration for the Jews of Poland is unfulfilled. It is a disappointment that characterizes his fiction and resonates with the failure of salvation for the Jews or other oppressed groups of any kind (Wisse 1980, 162).

I.B. Singer's fiction is not as grim as his brother's. From the outset of his career he was interested in the redemptive potential of messianism. His first novel, *Satan in Goray* (1935), deals with the influence of Shabtai Tzvi in the mid-1600s. His second, which was serialized in the Yiddish *Forverts* but never published in book form or translated into English, *The Sinful Messiah*, was a fictional biography of Jacob Frank (Wiegand, 122). However, it is in the two versions – one Yiddish the other an English translation – of his third novel, *The Family Moskat* (1950), that a coherent vision of messianism begins to emerge. It is noteworthy that, in the abridged English text, there is no messianic redemption. Redemption is only in death, as the character Hertz Yanover tells the protagonist Asa Heshel: "Death is the Messiah. That's the truth" (608). Both the religious and secular ideas of redemption have failed. The pious ways of Meshulam Moskat and the other believers among Warsaw Jews have not heralded the arrival of the messiah, and Asa Heshel's faith in the rationalist path blazed by Spinoza has not shielded the world from the Nazi evil. "The ending expresses utter nihilism and despair in the face of the impending catastrophe awaiting Polish Jewry" (Wiegand, 123). In contrast, the original Yiddish version follows a different plot trajectory and suggests that, while all the new secular messiahs are failures, traditional Judaism, the Torah, and prophets retain their validity even as evil spreads across Europe.

None of Richler's novels romanticize Jewish piety or devout messianism. They do, however, share the sceptical approach to secular ideology and nihilism found in the Yiddish original of *The Family Moskat*. For example, in *St Urbain's Horseman*, Jake Hersh sardonically reviews the problematic condition of being a liberal in the twentieth century, theoretically committed to universal equality, sexual freedom, anti-authoritarian principles, anti-war policies, and counterculture attitudes:

He felt his generation was unjustly squeezed between two raging and carnivorous ones. The old-establishment and the young hipsters. The shits and the shitheads. Unwillingly, without justice, they had been cast in Kerensky's role. Neither as obscene as the Czar, nor as blood-thirsty as Lenin. Not having gone like sheep to the slaughterhouse, but also too fastidious to punish Arab villages with napalm.

He would have been willing to vote for the legalization of pot, but he couldn't feel that a sixteen-year-old was deprived if he lacked for a pack of Acapulco Gold. He was *against* puritan repression, *for* fucking, but not necessarily on stage. A born cop-hater, he still wouldn't offer one a sandwich with shit spread between the bread. Though he felt the university was too intricately involved with the military-industrial complex he didn't think it was a blow struck for universal love when students tore a professor's work of twenty years to shreds. Admittedly, Hollywood had lied, so had the *Satevepost*, but he didn't want Molly to feel like a wallflower if at fourteen she didn't submit to a gang bang. When Reb Allen Ginsberg preached to the unformed that all history was bunk, what first sprang to mind was Goering reaching for his gun when he heard the word culture ... For one day, Jake feared, they would be dismissed as trivial, a peripheral generation ... Their Gods and mine, he allowed, don't fail. At worst, they grow infirm. They suffer pinched nerves, like Paul Hornung. Or arthritic arms, like Sandy Koufax. (Richler 1991b, 307)

Expressing similar views, Barney Panofsky of *Barney's Version* lampoons his oldest child's liberal sensibilities:

He's a member of a trendy theater board, a promoter of in-your-face plays wherein top people's leggy daughters feel free to pretend to shit on stage and RADA guys simulate bum-fucking with abandon. *Ars longa, vita brevis.* He's one of the more than two hundred backers of the monthly *Red Pepper* magazine ("feminist, antiracist, environmentalist, and internationalist"); and, not without a redeeming sense of humor, he has added my name to the subscription list. (Richler 1982, 18)

In both of these examples, the protagonists denigrate indiscriminate and unhedged acceptance of progressive liberal thinking that is meant to foster a more generous, inclusive, and sensitive society. At the same time, neither traditionally conservative nor religious positions are ethical options according to Barney. However, Richler's works avoid this existential impasse. Already in *Son of a Smaller Hero* there is a polemic against nihilism: Noah Adler cannot suffer the burden and myth of closeness but realizes that he has to seek an alternative. "It's not enough to rebel," he muses. "It is necessary to say yes to something" (Richler 1989b, 25). In Richler's later works it is the belief in the hero figures and their ability to instigate some sort of redemption that triumphs over meaningless banality.

Moses Berger in *Solomon Gursky Was Here* compensates for his life's ample disappointments with faith in the Gursky middle brother. He had "come to be in thrall to Solomon" (Richler 1990b, 166). Moses explains his obsession as a reaction to the tirade Shloime Bishinsky had unleashed against his father, L.B. Berger, in the 1940s for becoming the in-house writer for Bernard Gursky, who had transformed the family's bootlegging venture into an empire. Distressed that L.B. was proffering his services to a notoriously crass, philistine, cold-hearted megalomaniac, Shloime berated him at a Friday night gathering of their social circle:

> What I'm trying to say, forgive me, is that such princes in America are entitled to their mansions, a Rolls-Royce, chinchilla coats, yachts, young cuties out of burlesque shows. But a poet they should never be able to afford. It has to do with what? Human dignity. The dead. The sanctity of the word. (18)

Moreover, Shloime believes the rumours that Bernard had arranged the death of Solomon in an effort to gain majority control of their family business. Moses assimilates this information and involuntarily becomes Solomon's acolyte. In his mind, his father and Bernard Gursky become symbols of hypocrisy, self-congratulatory arrogance, and moral degeneracy. Solomon is the only corrective to such contemptible moral decay because, in Moses's mind, he acts exclusively according to his own conscience, never suffers condescension, denies himself no pleasure, and possesses a flawless sense of moral outrage.

Barney Panofsky avoids nihilistic despair by remaining faithful to the "wonky system of values" that he absorbed from Boogie, his personal messiah (Richler 1998a, 8),

> whereby anybody who wrote an article for Reader's Digest, or committed a best-seller, or acquired a Ph.D., was beyond the pale. But churning out a pornographic novel for Girodias was ring-a-ding. Similarly, writing for the movies was contemptible, unless it was a Tarzan flick, which would be a real hoot. (76)

In other words, Barney finds meaning in an aesthetic standard, an assessment of taste that becomes a moral guide. For the rest of his life, he judges everyone in his life by these transgressive principles. As a result, he cannot abide anyone who shows too much faith in the establishment, popular culture, mainstream wisdom, or politically correct (PC) niceties. As a young man, Barney believes that Boogie is a "shining exception," superior to all the other aspiring intellectuals of their age, "a man destined for greatness" (8). Boogie's gospel sustains him even when Boogie himself proves a disappointment.

Thus the messianic motifs in Richler's novels are derived from a wide spectrum of references, Christian and Jewish, and go far beyond narrow medieval ideas of a Jewish avenger set loose to guard the Jews against evil, perfidy, and danger. Messianic expectation in these works combines a longing to redress persecution with a metaphysical need to be part of a more just world. However, that is only one function of the novels' messianism. It is also a vehicle for satirizing zealous subservience to would-be messengers of God and pious fanaticism, and, more seriously, an endorsement of the Jewish Diaspora and a strategy for rethinking Israel as a primary locus of Jewish pride. Moreover, it is part of a literary tradition, and puts Richler's novels in dialogue with a number of works by nineteenth-, twentieth-, and twenty-first-century Jewish writing, ranging from the stories of Rabbi Nahman of Bratslav (see Green) to Cynthia Ozick's *The Messiah of Stockholm* (1988) – texts that channel significant historical, social, religious, and cultural reflections through literary variants of messianism.

4

Hero Figures and Special Pleading

The concerns that preoccupy the hero figures in Mordecai Richler's novels – as they are imagined and perceived by the protagonists – overlap with many of the moral, ethical, and cultural issues that have been paramount in the second half of the twentieth century. Specifically, these larger-than-life characters are driven to resuscitate Jewish dignity in a post-Holocaust world fraught with moral instability, to unmask anti-Semitism and expose its cowardly underpinnings, and to defend the State of Israel when it is besieged by its enemies. Among them are anti-fascists who have typically played some role in battling Franco's forces in Spain, as well as aesthetes who cannot tolerate triteness in art and culture. In essence, the idealistic concerns of the hero figures reflect some of the defining events and phenomena of their times.

However, such concerns are offset in Richler's novels by the negative agenda of his far-ranging social and cultural satire. Indeed, the appeal of his novels is largely bound up with their witty and politically incorrect satire on late twentieth-century secular pieties.[1] With few exceptions, the hero figures dismiss the issues that are the targets of Richler's satire because they are irrelevant to their scheme of heroic values, too socially prim, or beneath their interest. His protagonists, too, are generally unsympathetic, though not indifferent, to political correctness. For instance, they often bemoan society's celebration of the minor achievements of disadvantaged groups as monumental progress and ridicule environmentalism as if it is some misguided form of religious doctrine.[2] The hero figures' disregard for political correctness, and the protagonists' grudging recognition of its contemporary relevance, imbue Richler's novels with a caustic discoure, one that champions unfashionable social attitudes and mocks feminism, homosexuality, racism, and other topics that headline the contemporary social agenda. This narrative perspective does not promise a better, more just social structure, but it is predicated on an ideal that insists upon personal integrity and a quest for justice. Moreover, it invites an assessment of liberalism that echoes twentieth-century philosopher Judith Shklar's perspective in *Ordinary Vices* (1984): "Far from being an amoral free-for-all, liberalism is, in fact, extremely difficult and constraining, far too much so for those who cannot endure contradictions, diversity and the risks of freedom" (5). Like Shklar, Richler demands that the hazards and folly of liberalism be acknowledged.

– ✳ –

Long before the term "politically correct" became a catchphrase used both to praise and disparage social awareness and affirmative action, Richler was vexed by preferential treatment based on anything beyond the disinterested recognition of merit. In the late 1960s, when the term "politically correct" was in vogue mainly in the American Black Power movement (Perry, 71) (and in wide use in communist countries where its meaning was different), Richler stated that "special pleading, whether by Canadian sports writers in Stockholm, kibbutzniks in Galilee, or proliferating Canada culture boosters, never fails to move me to mockery" (1968b, 10–11). When "politically correct" eventually became a mainstream epithet in the early 1990s after US president George Bush and his campaign staff began using it in reference to the ideology of extreme liberalism (Perry, 76–7), Richler had already been railing against what he called special pleading for more than two decades, and still "tend[ed] to make fun of it whether it [was] Jewish, homosexual, or feminist. "Special pleaders," he insisted, "parody themselves" (qtd in Hutcheon and Richmond, 45).

In the introduction to the 1995 collection of articles *Debating PC*, Paul Berman gives an overview of the socio-political spirit and impact of contemporary political correctness, despite his admission that it has no iron-clad philosophical foundations or coherent ideological structure. He suggests, however, that the PC ideology "might aptly be labeled 'race/class/gender-ism'" (14). In a landmark 1990 article in the *New York Times*, "The Rising Hegemony of the Politically Correct," Richard Bernstein explains "that a cluster of opinions about race, ecology, feminism, culture and foreign policy defines a kind of 'correct' attitude toward the problems of the world, a sort of unofficial ideology of the university. Pressure to conform." With his well-documented dislike of "special pleading" on behalf of any sector it is no surprise that Richler rejected the PC outlook that "Western civilization is inherently unfair to minorities, women and homosexuals" (Bernstein), and subverts its emphasis on conformity.

It is this abhorrence of special pleading, rather than a conservative political outlook, upon which Richler's satire is based. His novels can even be read as a fictional "laboratory" in which he formulates satiric narratological structures to present, challenge, or destabilize contemporary ethical postures.[3] Despite its wry humour, Richler's fiction insists upon a serious examination of socially prescribed chauvinism as well as the political and social conventions that are seemingly requisite in contemporary society. Yet Richler's fictive assault on special pleading does not evolve. It thus contrasts with models of "fiction as laboratory for ideas," such as, Sartre's "The Childhood of a Leader," considered "prophetic" by Menachem Brinker precisely because it "predicts the way [Sartre's] thought ... progress[es] from the study of individual self-deception to collective mystifications" (117). The static posture in respect to social attitudes in Richler's fiction accounts for a certain coherence but also suggests that the critique of special pleading may be reductive and even stagnant, a reflex rather than a substantive response. Except for a significant discursive shift in *Barney's Version*, the novels subscribe to a relatively fixed perspective on social attitudes – a perspective that remains an anchor to which Richler's imagination is moored.

Satire in Richler's writing often introduces an element of Swiftian quali-fied misanthropy, a tone likely to be associated with misery, spiritual despondency, and malice. Yet, when transformed into satire, misan-thropy can serve as "a fountain of intellectual creativity" and lead to an improvement in social self-knowledge (Shklar, 192–3). In his non-fiction writings, Richler emerges as Shklar's satiric misanthrope, one who is self-satisfied but "appears to enjoy the spectacle of human imbecility and of every kind of evil" (194). However, his protagonists are more of what Shklar calls self-righteous misanthropes, such as Molière's Alceste and Nietzsche – misanthropic optimists who find their contemporaries and immediate world abhorrent because they imagine a better, transformed humanity. Despite their highly critical view of society and individuals, they are still able to imagine a better state of affairs. They attach their hope for humanity to hero figures, resist the tendency towards nihilism, and pine for a loftier existence.

Whether a more honourable universal condition is possible is the central question in all of Richler's novels. The protagonists are never satisfied with the prospect of universal moral chaos and yearn for the kind of moral order that they think the hero figures demand. They are compelled to seek a decent code of living, and their fantasies of the hero figure allow them to believe that the search is not in vain. Ironically, the search is at odds with the novels' parallel satirization of a world in which there are no universal values of decency and goodness. By Richler's own admission, he repeatedly explores this contradiction: "How do you live with honour in a time when there is no agreement on values?" (qtd in Hutcheon and Richmond, 47).

In his novels, Richler sets a baseline moral standard by resorting to the strategies of the eighteenth-century satirists, namely, Alexander Pope, who tended to place one character in each of his satirical works as an approximate representation of his own moral, social, political, and ethical positions (Spacks, 362; Worcester, 160). It is an unusual approach for a modern writer, as the twentieth century is not generally characterized by even the minimally cohesive moral conditions that satire requires. Northrop Frye explains that "satire demands at least a token fantasy, a content which the reader recognizes as grotesque and at least an implicit moral standard" (1971b, 233–4). Richler, however, cannot assume that he shares an ideological platform with his obvious readership or, as described by Leona Toker, his "target audience":[4]

> The social, national, or cultural audience that the writer can reasonably expect will constitute his or her immediate contemporary readership. This readership, actual no less than postulated, usually shares the writer's cultural code (see Barthes 1974, 18–19) and is, in this respect though perhaps not in others, in a position to appreciate the shades of the text's meanings without extratextual aids, such as annotations, readers' guides, history books, etc. (2005, 282)

He consciously subverts too many mainstream positions on politics, culture, and society to assume an ideological kinship with his contemporaneous readers. Indeed, many of his assaults on political correctness may strike readers as morally obtuse. For instance, the depiction of Virgil in *The Apprenticeship of Duddy Kravitz* is an unapologetic indictment of special treatment for people with physical handicaps.

Virgil pleads with Duddy for a job as a driver, demonstrating his desire to be treated as an equal even though the work could be life threatening because he has epilepsy. At the same time, Virgil is the founding editor of an absurd newsletter, *The Crusader*, which calls for wide-ranging affirmative action for epileptics. Ultimately, Virgil has a fit while making a delivery in Duddy's truck. Though he is overworked by Duddy, who thus has to shoulder most of the blame, it is his seizure that precipitates his accident and leaves him a paraplegic. The subtext is that equal treatment is not in the interest of those with real physical challenges, and to pretend otherwise is to no one's advantage.

A similar attitude is evident in *St Urbain's Horseman*. Special pleading is transformed into black comedy when Jake is confronted by a woman who lobbies on behalf of mouth-and-foot painters and sells works created by disabled artists, such as a veteran of the Second World War battle at El Alamein and a street accident victim. The paintings remind Jake of the jigsaw puzzles of his childhood; still, he offers to buy one, feigning appreciation of its aesthetic merit. The woman insists that it is only for sale if Jake truly believes it is good because she abhors those who condescend to the handicapped. Her criterion, however, is ironic: her own efforts are a large-scale exercise in condescension cloaked in the trappings of good will and justice. She charges Jake twenty-five guineas, which is a small sum for a painting about which she had just raved, and proof that her praise is excessive, exaggerating the work's artistic virtue.

In *Joshua Then and Now*, the predilections of a Hollywood film beauty are presented as a microcosm of fashionable and banal politically correct censoriousness: She "wouldn't eat California grapes ... was for abortion-on-demand and ERA, but against Zionist duplicity and colored toilet paper" (Richler 2001, 319). The parallels drawn between popular socio-political issues and "coloured" toilet paper are a criticism of political correctness, an insinuation that many of its manifestations are ludicrous and its adherents unintelligent. Shklar observes that charitable patronage has long been suspect. "There were always people," she notes, "who detected a certain moral cruelty in the ministration of philanthropy" and felt "repelled by humanitarianism unshaken by scepticism and unmindful of its own limitations" (37). Richler's attitude towards philanthropic zeal includes this "scepticism" and takes into account the potential mix of benevolence and moral oppression, which "can readily ignite every sort of bossy and unfeeling private and public officiousness" (Shklar, 36).[5] Advocacy on behalf of populations who suffer various forms of discrimination and marginalization is a modern norm, but Richler's novels represent it as well-intentioned but wrong-headed.

For the satirist it is hard enough to create works that evoke clear, authoritative moral norms when there is little agreement regarding moral standards; it is all the harder for a writer like Richler, who mocks PC ethics, which are not universal but are widespread and socially fashionable. Despite such barriers, Richler's works invite a rethinking of moral values, while they satirically critique what they present as politically correct absurdities.

This approach can work, even in a time of moral uncertainty, if it causes a certain "uneasiness" that jolts the reader out of a state of complacency (Spacks, 363). Satire achieves the desired result when "we identify the victims as others and feel our superiority, only to find ourselves trapped a moment later, impaled by the scorn we have comfortably leveled against the rest of the world" (364). It is, in fact, Richler's method to provoke such a complex response. He integrates his own on-record views into his protagonists' moral attitudes and leaves the reader, and sometimes the protagonist, uncertain as to whether they are aligned with the novels' moral criticism or among its targets.

In 1957, by which time Richler had published only three novels, Canadian literary critic Nathan Cohen commented on his female characters: "Weak-minded creatures, they are stepping-stones leading his truth seekers toward their freedom bridge" (1971a, 54). "I fear a congenital weakness in the creation of women characters," Richler confessed in a 1959 letter to his close friend William Weintraub (Weintraub, 230). He reiterated these misgivings in a 1972 interview with Graeme Gibson: "the women in my novels tend to be rather idealized creatures, and not written about with the greatest confidence, I'm afraid" (288). Lawrence Kaplan comments that Nancy Hersh is "idealized and consequently lifeless and unconvincing" (186), while Canadian literary journalist Eleanor Wachtel considers *Joshua Then and Now* a work that generally vilifies women. She argues that Joshua loves his dad and hates his mom, which sets the groundwork for his life-long revulsion of Jewish women in particular, "fat harridans, all" (qtd in Craniford, 101). In his last two novels, Richler makes an effort to prove wrong those who consider him a misogynistic writer; there he adds complexity to his portrayal of women characters and his representation of gender relations. Still, these narratives are ultimately derisive of feminist beliefs, even ones that have become mainstream in the twenty-first century, and resonate with the sexist views that are pervasive in Richler's non-fiction writings.

In contemplating Richler's female characters it is also essential to evaluate how they are positioned in relation to the men in his novels. Throughout Richler's novels, female characters are mainly ancillary figures, portrayed as unlikable or even ridiculous. The others are idealized, slightly updated, but not altogether different from Coventry Patmore's Victorian "Angel in the House" (1862). They are the ever-constant women who keep the home fires alight while their husbands and lovers follow their creative pursuits. Though intelligent and talented, they are unmoved by feminism's call for a redistribution of power between men and women in their private lives, professional endeavours, and place in society.

In contrast to his fictional women, Richler's hero figures are endowed with outsized, stereotypical masculinity. They are domineering, intelligent, irrepressibly charming, and insatiably libidinous; women find them intensely alluring and passionate, though they are neither solicitous nor loyal. Fearlessly adventurous, they do not defer to anyone; they scorn weaker characters. At the same time, they readily accept the favours and good will of women, even those who they neglect or have abandoned, if it suits their purpose. Moreover, they operate with a suave machismo that not only defies any sense of gender equality but is so pervasive that it seems to obviate the issue of egalitarianism.

In the early pages of *St Urbain's Horseman*, Jake Hersh imagines his cousin Joey as an intrepid Nazi hunter, traversing the Upper Galilee, Mexico, Catalonia, or even Paraguay in search of Josef Mengele. Jake's Uncle Abe balks, insisting that Joey is such a delinquent that he would blackmail the notorious doctor rather than kill him (Richler 1991b, 41). The comment casts a pall over the fantasy of Joey as a moral avenger but buttresses the image of him as an ultra-masculine renegade "cantering on a magnificent Pleven stallion. Galloping, thundering. Planning fresh campaigns, more daring maneuvers" (41). He manipulates and uses women without compunction. He is not a dutiful son, concerned older brother, or his family's protector, though he does advise his sister, Jenny, to behave decently, teach his brother Artie that Jews do not have to cower when threatened, and bestow upon his mother occasional cash handouts. He is also known as a gigolo and blackmailer who "squeeze[s] women for money, sometimes even marrying them" (402). Women are drawn to him and even married socialites are willing to pay for his attention despite his modest pedigree.

The hero figure of *Barney's Version*, Boogie Moscovitch, is not as brawny or physically menacing as Joey, but he is a former soldier who fought the Nazis and survived the Battle of the Bulge. Like Joey, however, he is a sexual glutton and irresistible to women. With typical self-deprecation, he intones, "I will fuck just about any peasant girl who will have me" (Richler 1998a, 8), but then he appears in Paris after an unexplained absence accompanied by glamorous, exotic women (10). When he settles into midlife, women still stalk him. "Among them, to the amazement of onlookers one evening, Ava Gardner. He command[s] attention – no, something approaching reverence – of the young as well as beautiful women" (239).

Solomon Gursky of *Solomon Gursky Was Here* is the hero figure that embodies both daunting masculinity and hyper-sexuality. As a teenager, though "short for his age," he is a brazen horseman and a regular visitor to the boudoir of one of the local prostitutes (Richler 1990b, 261). Because he could occasionally be found at his father's convenience store, "the daughters were drawn to A. Gursky & Sons in swarms, blushing if he greeted them" (264). A local girl whom he seduces, Clara Teitelbaum, blames Solomon for disgracing her. "I'm a respectable girl," she taunts him. "I never even let another boy kiss me, but you, you animal, even a nun wouldn't be safe with you" (343). He eventually marries Clara because she is pregnant but only after unsuccessfully trying to cajole his younger brother, Morrie, into wedding her. Morrie, however, understands that no woman would accept him as Solomon's substitute.

Though Solomon returns from the Second World War with a leg wound, he has lost none of his physical or sexual prowess. When he falls in love with debutante Diana McClure, he is ready to abandon his family for true passion. Diana asks him how he can have such disregard for his wife and two children. "They mean nothing to me," he answers (301), admitting that he is callous but ardently passionate.

With his flying credentials, swagger, machismo, war experience, and war wound, Solomon seems to be a character based partially on Hemingway. This old-fashioned type of male bravado is often valourized in Richler's work. Joey Hersh, too, is "a romantic, adventurous Hemingway hero" (Ramraj, 106), while Joshua Shapiro's preoccupation with the Spanish Civil War also evokes the American writer (Bell, 70).

By assuming ultra-masculine personas, these hero figures implicitly reject feminist demands to redress the pre-existing socio-cultural assumptions that have historically defined gender relations. With their cavalier attitude towards women and aptitude for sexual conquest, they passively resist the call for a new gender-role paradigm. This construction of masculinity recalls the kind of virility advocated by the psychologist Abraham Maslow, an influential figure during the height of the counterculture era – a time when Richler was in the thick of his career.[6] Constantly invited to speak countrywide throughout the late 1960s, Maslow was so well received that some colleagues insinuated that his psychological approach had become a substitute religion (Nicholson, 86). Maverick social activist Abbie Hoffman and pioneering feminist Betty Friedan both cite Maslow as a major inspiration in their thinking and work (86, 88).

Maslow believed that men and women should both strive towards self-actualization, the highest achievement in his acclaimed order of physiological and emotional needs.[7] For him, it is a state wherein individuals exemplify "psychological integration and exhibit the fullest and most admirable potential of human identity" (Herman, 271). Such successful individuals are perceptive, self-accepting, spontaneous, autonomous, empathetic, and creative. They make their own decisions, display independence and free will, and are prone to orgasm-like mystical experiences – "peak experiences" (271). On the other hand, Maslow embraced a "vision of the world where male sexuality underwrote male control of society" and women's self-actualization was contingent upon their roles as mothers and nest builders (Nicholson, 88). He equated "intellectual ability with a highly energized and self-possessed male sexuality" and believed in the "'biological' reality of male dominance and female submissiveness" (89). Nascent feminists were appalled by Maslow's approach to women's self-actualization. "Friedan was alarmed at the almost complete absence of women on Maslow's list of peakers. (The only two exceptions were historical figures Eleanor Roosevelt and Jane Addams)" (Herman, 291). She believed that ideas such as Maslow's, heavily influenced by Freud, trapped women and ensnared them in "a psychological hell," or at the very least "a decidedly second-class emotional existence" (291). In response, she encouraged feminists in the 1950s and 1960s to appropriate the notion of self-actualization, reconceptualize it in non-chauvinist terms, and use it to help women strive towards "individuality and creativity" (291).

Richler's treatment of female characters is in tune with Maslow's idea of women's self-actualization. He struggles "to realize convincingly female characters" (Ramraj, 38), and his favoured women – almost always the wives of the protagonists, excessively beautiful with a quiet, reserved intellect – are alluring but not sexually aggressive; they are effortlessly graceful and domestic, never careworn or unkempt. They make few demands, and anticipate the needs of their men. In his opus, the archetype of ideal womanhood is arguably Miriam Greenberg of *Barney's Version*, the character thought to be modelled on Richler's wife, Florence Mann (Kramer 2008, 219). When Barney Panofsky catches a glimpse of her at his wedding to the Second Mrs Panofsky, he embarks upon a lifelong obsession: "the most enchanting woman I had ever seen ... Oh, that face of incomparable beauty. Those bare shoulders. My heart ached at the sight of her" (Richler 1998a, 176). Miriam is an intellectual, avid reader, and classical music aficionada, but, like Nancy Hersh, she is first and foremost a model wife, wholly devoted to her husband and children. These women's families – parents and siblings – are not troublesome (except in the case of *Joshua Then and Now*), and their careers are either nonexistent or irrelevant to their role as devoted caregivers.

Reinhold Kramer argues that Richler was hostile to the growing influence of politically correct attitudes partially because he knew it was a trend that could silence him as a novelist (2008, 281). He did not, Kramer adds, harbour misogynistic feelings – contrary to the accusations of literary critics such as Eleanor Wachtel, Carole Corbeil, and Patricia Craig. He approved of women's rights and accepted women in positions of economic and political power (281). Yet there is a strong anti-feminist tone in his novels. In *Joshua Then and Now* over-empowerment of women and emasculation of men are satirized as absurdities. For example, Colin Fraser, who is living with Pauline when Joshua first meets her, is portrayed as a weak-minded man, duped by the rhetoric of political correctness to the point of compulsive white-male self-flagellation:

Colin read *Peace News*, he subscribed to *Tribune*. He would,
Joshua was to discover, journey to any church hall or school
basement, no matter how difficult to get to, if only there was
a minister appearing on the platform there, who would rebuke
him for having been born white, an exploiter of Africa's soul,
or failing that, if there was some frizzy-haired matron in sensible

shoes who had just returned from liberated China to show
a jumpy, out-of-focus documentary about the joys of life
in a Cantonese bicycle factory. (Richler 2001, 270)

Such satirical attitudes are more pronounced in *Barney's Version*.
At the outset of the novel Barney pines for

the days when you could smooch with college girls with
impunity ... Moonlit nights on deck nice girls wore crinolines,
cinch belts, ankle bracelets, and two-tone saddle shoes, and you
could count on them not to sue you for sexual harassment forty
years later, their suppressed memories of date-rape retrieved
by lady psychoanalysts who shaved. (Richler 1998a, 5)

The passage foreshadows much of the novel's attack on normative
feminism, including campaigns against sexual harassment, professional
discrimination, and the objectification of the feminine body. It also
conjures nostalgia for a time when young women were obsequiously
feminine and non-threatening.

Richler's on-record views and comments invite readers to conflate
Barney's views with his creator's. Already in 1970 George Woodcock
observed that "the worlds he [Richler] creates ... belong to a fictional
continuum which perpetually overlaps the world in which Richler himself lives and feels, thinks and writes" (54–5). Years later, while interviewed by Joel Yanofsky, Richler explained, "it's all in the books," when
asked a personal question. It was as if one could piece together a biographical portrait of him through a survey of his oeuvre (27). Eventually
Richler tried to dispel this general impression. Specifically with regard
to *Barney's Version* he denied that the novel is fictionalized autobiography. "It's the only novel I've written in the first person," he notes, "so
obviously a number of people are going to take it to be autobiographical,
which is not the case. I was Barney Panofsky when I was writing it, but
not before and not after" (qtd in Posner, 303). He does, however, confess
that he shares Barney's outlook "that life is fundamentally absurd and
nobody understands anybody, but you make the best of it" (303).

Though Richler claimed that his characters were not autobiographical alter-egos, their ideological and cultural obsessions are topics that
he frequently revisits in his non-fiction. In a 1994 essay, "Sexual
Harassment," in the men's magazine GQ, Richler mocks a column
"about the unwanted touching by slavering males" in the *Montreal*

Gazette by Eve McBride. He accuses McBride of being one of the paper's "gaggle of knee-jerk liberal columnists" (Richler 1998b, 97) and then suggests that most women, unlike "oversensitive" feminists, enjoy random fondling. Dramatizing his point, he imagines a dinner party scenario wherein a man gropes his wife's friend's breast much to the latter's delight:

> "Whatever are you doing?" his friend's wife might ask.
> "Wiping the gravy off your blouse."
> "Don't you go away until you've removed every spec." (98)

Moreover, bemoaning the introduction of "leering" into the lexicon of sexual harassment, he insists that it is nothing more than the "girl-watching" that is celebrated in Irwin Shaw's short story, "The Girls in Their Summer Dresses": "an appreciation of passing grace and beauty" (99). Men who "whistle, leer, or assert office rank" are a blight, Richler concedes but then partly retracts this claim by lampooning the idea that women are blameless victims of rape in need of self-defence strategies to ward off unwanted sexual encounters:

> I am pleased to report that sweetly scented women who frequent singles bars, in search of a discourse on the politics of meaning, or well-brought-up college girls who repair to a young man's room at 2 a.m., hoping to exchange ideas on Kierkegaard only to find themselves jumped on the sofa, need no longer be victimized. They can ... apply for a license to pack musketry, preferably a pistol filled with live ammo. (99)

It is such passages that make the anti-feminism of Richler's novels seem sinister and more than a satiric appeal for greater balance within feminist rhetoric and activism.

Still, the novel's real assault on feminist zeal and white-male oppression focuses on the legacy of Barney's first wife, Clara Charnofsky, a modernist painter of violent pictures who, after her suicide, becomes a feminist icon. Seemingly based on real-life writers and suicide victims, Virginia Woolf and Sylvia Plath,[8] Clara's feminist "disciples" consider Barney the villain who is responsible for her demise, a parallel to the way Ted Hughes has been portrayed by a number of Plath scholars. Preparing to be interviewed about Clara by a woman from McGill University's student radio program, "Dykes with Mikes," Barney notes:

This will not mark the first time I have been interrogated about [Clara] ... the martyred Saint Clara's admirers are legion, and have two things in common: they take me for an abomination and fail to understand that Clara intensely disliked other women, whom she considered rivals for the male attention she thrived on. (Richler 1998a, 93)

Barney is rightly indignant to be libelled as Clara's tormentor. It is Clara who had tricked Barney into marriage when pregnant with another man's child. Moreover, during her life she was uninterested in any manifestation of feminism, even though her life-story itself could be read as a feminist statement. Thus, Barney's reaction forms a satiric assault on unexamined feminist catechisms and is an indirect defence of wrongly maligned heteronormative white males.[9]

Meanwhile, Clara's followers are depicted as indoctrinated foot soldiers in a feminist power struggle, and the novel portrays the evolution of the Clara Charnofsky Foundation as a model of left-wing extremism. When Norman Charnofsky, Clara's uncle, establishes the memorial foundation to honour his late niece, he appears to be sincere, a good-hearted man, an Orthodox Jew – but a moderate liberal. He "taught a remedial course one night a week in Harlem ... belonged to a group that collected clothes to be mailed to Jews in Russia ... was a blood donor, and had once stood as a Socialist Party candidate for the state legislature" (133). The evidence suggests that he has no motive other than the wish to pay tribute to Clara. And, in keeping with her supposed "legacy," he appoints board members to the foundation, "two African-American feminists ... Jessica Peters, whose poetry was published in both *The New Yorker* and *The Nation*, and Shirley Wade, who lectures on 'cultural studies' at Princeton" (211). While the choice of these women hints at Norman's interest in being true to Clara's fabled feminist agenda, it is, more piquantly, a satiric assault on the complexities, ironies, and even zealous impulse that are endemic to affirmative action on behalf not only of blacks in general but also of black women in particular.

Similarly, elected to the foundation's board is another woman, not black but Jewish, "an abrasive historian, Doris Mandelbaum, author of *Herstory from Boadicea to Madonna*."[10] The three women prepare a coup against Norman, the very individual who welcomed them to the board in an effort to make it more balanced. They claim that "it was a typical male power move, some might even say 'an oxymoron, gender-wise,' that the chairperson of the board of a feminist foundation should be a man, of the nuclear-family persuasion, his only claim to that office that he was a relative of Clara's, herself a martyr to male chauvinist insentience" (212). And later liberal fanaticism is framed as an outrage when Norman confronts the women about excessive expenditures that are charged to the foundation: a trip to Paris and lunches at some of New York's most expensive restaurants.

> "I suppose if we had gone to Tel Aviv, you wouldn't have
> questioned the trip."
> "... But I imagine it would have been kosher, so to speak, if we
> had met to discuss foundation business over chitlins in some
> greasy spoon in Harlem."
> "Please," said Norman, flushing.
> "We've had enough of your tripping on penis-power here, Norm."
> "The truth is we're all weary of your patronizing manner – "
> " – and your sexual hang-ups – "
> " – and your racism."
> "How can you accuse me of – didn't I appoint you and Shirley
> to the board?"
> "*Oy vey bubele*, but it made you feel good inside, didn't it?
> It warmed your kishkas."
> "You could go home and tell your wifey, we've got *shvartzes*
> on the board now." (212)

Sounding archetypally anti-Semitic, the women respond with accusations of Jewish particularism, racism, and patriarchal dominance, and appeal to liberal guilt to cover up their misuse of the funds. Ultimately, Norman's good intentions leave him denigrated as a man and a Jew, and spell his expulsion from the foundation. This narrative thread, consequently, is a lampoon of feminism and affirmative action run amok.

Eventually, Norman embezzles from the foundation and absconds with the money. When Barney encounters him years after Clara's death, he has destroyed his marriage and become convinced that he is guilty of the women's accusations. Barney, conversely, views Norman as a victim and, to avenge his demise, mocks the self-appointed triad of foundation directors by sending them a letter that is meant as an unmasking of their pernicious extremism. Impersonating a member of CRAP (Chaps Resolutely Against Prejudice), he lobbies the foundation for funds, proposing an event. He writes, "wouldn't it be simply magnifico if Mike Tyson … *could be challenged and beaten for the heavyweight title by a womyn contender*: Surely, this would be a LANDMARK in HERSTORY" (217). The prospect of the match is not only preposterous but a narrative detail that is designed to reduce unqualified gender parity to absurd hijinks.

Richler himself almost certainly found the idea of such a showdown entertaining, as he wrote about a similar matter in "Kiss the Ump," which he published in GQ magazine in 1992. In this article, Richler first asserts his pro-feminist credentials, confessing that he finds it "astonishing" that "women weren't enfranchised at the same time as their dim husbands" and had to endure myriad indignities "in order to win the right to vote" (2002b, 196). He then proceeds to erroneously mock a leading feminist because "this champion of women's lib" carried a designer handbag and "backcomb[ed] her hair and touch[ed] up her eyeshadow" before appearing on television (197). He also scoffs at the idea that women have traditionally compromised professional achievement for the sake of their families:

> I am often cornered by mature women who tell me how they have had to sacrifice a brilliant career in order to make a home for an unfaithful husband and ungrateful children. Nonsense. More often than not, it is clear that the only alternative career available to them is to serve behind the counter at McDonald's or possibly do something even less useful, such as become a sociologist or a professor of English Lit. 101. (197)

Further illustrating the limits of his own feminism, he adds, "I am not prepared to fight for the right of women to drive steamrollers, serve with impunity on submarines, interview inarticulate naked athletes in stinky locker rooms, box, play hockey with the guys, or umpire baseball games" (198).

However, it is the article's castigation of Pam Postema and her memoir recounting her experience as a minor league baseball umpire from 1977 to 1989 that resonates with the chauvinism found in Barney's epistolary gag regarding boxing. Richler finds humour in Postema's accounts of being kissed spontaneously by a player at home plate and having her bra pulled out of her shirt by team mascots. He suggests that a player's dugout joke is the unavoidable outcome when women assume inappropriate professions: "What's another name for a female umpire? The answer: A call girl" (200). Women's participation in traditionally male sports is ludicrous according to both Richler and Barney – an undesirable blurring of gender roles.

Even when Richler's positive female characters are resilient, they are still counter-feminist. Nancy Hersh maintains her dignity while Jake is on trial for rape, but her fortitude is almost pitiable. She is long-suffering to a fault and largely refrains from recrimination against her husband's foolish misadventures. Pauline Shapiro, too, remains loyal throughout Joshua's sexual misconduct scandal, though it is bizarre front-page news that shames her and disgraces their family. These characters stretch the bounds of plausibility with their steadfast fealty and, unarguably, pit Richler as a novelist with extremely outworn conceptions of gender relations.

Moreover, Richler's ideal female characters are expected to be brave for their family's sake but not for their own. Consistent with Maslow's idea of self-actualization for women, Richler's main female characters may have careers, interests, and hobbies, but self-actualization is only possible for them if they sublimate such interests and first embrace their roles as wives and mothers. Instead of running off with Solomon Gursky on the eve of his trial for illicit alcohol sales, Diana McClure confesses: "Realist (and possibly coward) that I am, I settled for my library and my music and my garden and Harry McClure and the children we would have together" (Richler 1998a, 303). These women are resilient but could never qualify as hero figures. They lack the bravery and incendiary passion of larger-than-life men. "I would have flown closer to the sun with Solomon," Diana muses. "However, the likelihood is that I also would have been burnt to a crisp long ago" (303).

With the creation of Beatrice Wade, Moses Berger's spirited girlfriend in *Solomon Gursky* – and even Miriam Greenberg, who eventually has the gumption to leave Barney – Richler tries to update his treatment of female characters. Charles Dickens attempted to atone for the anti-Semitic presentation of Fagin in *Oliver Twist* by creating the sympathetic Jew Riah in *Our Mutual Friend*. Richler seems to apply the same strategy regarding the chauvinism in his novels, fashioning these later women characters as a corrective to the sexist timbre found in earlier works. But, where Dickens over-reached, straining to make Riah "a strange amalgam of good-natured fairy and Biblical sage" (Stone, 248), Richler does not go far enough. Even these "empowered" women are the fodder of male fantasy. For example, after their first night together, Moses awakens to discover Beatrice reading a paperback edition of *One Hundred Years of Solitude.*

"Surprise, surprise," she quips. "I'm not just a sensational lay" (Richler 1990b, 45). She does not tolerate Moses Berger unconditionally and leaves him when his alcoholism becomes insufferable. She rebuffs his attempts to make her feel uneducated and obtuse. Nonetheless, she is ever the sex object: "A raven-haired beauty, with breasts too rudely full for such a trim figure and coal-black eyes that shone with too much appetite" (42); long after the end of their relationship, she acquiesces to his request to see a glimpse of her garter-clad thighs (240). In Richler's novels, favourably portrayed women must be reasonably clever but pervasively feminine, innately sensual and emotionally loyal. Ultimately, his novels "deal with a man-dominated society" (Cohen 1971b, 54), and his portrayals of women who are not profoundly domestic are fraught with "a deep distrust and contempt" (ibid.).

While misogyny in Richler's work has been much discussed as a rebuff of political correctness, less has been written about the novels' treatment of gay characters. In *Joshua Then and Now*, Joshua and his friend Sidney Murdoch fabricate a series of love letters in which they pose as gay lovers. The correspondence is both a lark and a money-making scheme that eventually sparks a scandal with Joshua at the centre. The two writers sell the material to a university, presenting it as the juvenilia of personalities whose past dalliance will one day become a source of scholarly research. Also addressing the issue of homosexuality is an episode in *Solomon Gursky*, in which Solomon seduces the wives of high-society personages by masquerading as a homosexual in need of a woman's erotic overtures to help him discern whether he has, indeed, heterosexual propensities. The bluff is an act of vengeance against a pretentious anti-Semitic elite, but it is also a sort of burlesque carried out for the sake of personal entertainment and social restitution.

Richler's novels are rich with such gay jokes, characters, and allusions, but, with few exceptions, they are woven into the texts primarily as comic relief at the expense of politically correct sympathies. The novels' moral and social perspectives are always filtered through the hero figures and protagonists, none of whom ever treat homosexuality with any gravity. In Richler's debut work, *The Acrobats* (1954), Derek, the only gay character, is portrayed as tragic but also dysfunctional and unlikable. The treatment of gay characters and issues in Richler's later novels is more lighthearted and satiric, but it parodies homosexuals more than the society that marginalizes them.

Gay advocacy, too, is presented as a farcical issue. For instance, it is an issue championed in *Joshua Then and Now* by Joshua's "loopy" mother, Esther, "not only active in women's lib … but on the executive board of Parents of Gays in Canada" (Richler 2001, 10). As Esther, in Joshua's estimation, lacks all authority, her views are not only invalid but ridiculous. A similar conclusion can be drawn when Barney comments on a lesbian student's "charming bosom." The young woman gives an ideologically saturated response:

> "Now look here Mr. Panofsky … cut out the funny stuff right now. The reason why gay women frighten you is because you are terrified of what this would mean to the quote, normal, unquote patriarchal, authoritarian system based on women's submission to men."
> "I don't mean to pry," I said. "but what do your parents think about your being a lesbian?"
> "I prefer to think of myself as a humansexual."
> (Richler 1998a, 123)

In this case, the "indirect characterization," is constructed through speech (Rimmon Kennan, 66). So, while the rebuttal might have merit, it is undercut by its strident tone, the sophomoric use of "quote" and "unquote," cliché feminist language, and the neologism "human-sexual."[11] Consequently, the student's views comes across as the rhetoric of some radical feminist fringe rather than as a reasoned condemnation of sexual harassment.

In his non-fiction, Richler seldom wrote about homosexuality. In his 1978 essay "The Great Comic Book Heroes," he critiqued the mid-twentieth-century crusade of Dr Frederic Wertham to ban comic books, who believed they were tainted with homosexual overtones. However, Richler's point was not to defend traces of homosexuality in mainstream culture. He only opposed Wertham's reading of the relationship of popular comic book characters, such as Batman and Robin, as figures of a gay romance, arguing that such interpretations strike him as "witch-hunting. Sexual McCarthyism" (Richler 1978, 121). Later, he wrote some newspaper articles in favour of a more positive approach to the gay community, but he still failed to address gay advocacy without recourse to humour. "Writing about the National Lesbian and Gay Journalists Association, he sa[ys], it [is] 'clearly an organization whose time has come, but one which I am not eligible to join'" (Posner, 305). His first cousin on his mother's side, Lionel Albert, recalled that Richler had a job in his youth at CBC (Canadian Broadcasting Corporation) and joked incessantly about the number of homosexuals working there. "He thought there should be a third room alongside the Gents and Ladies for them" (qtd in Posner, 74–5). His son Daniel recollects that Richler was prejudiced against gays and stubbornly opposed to gay marriage (306).

Solomon Gursky is Richler's first book to treat a narrative episode that addresses homosexuality with measured sincerity. Sam Birenbaum, Moses Berger's childhood friend, suffers because his son, Philip, is gay. "I could be appropriately liberal if it were another man's son," Sam thinks, "but it's an abomination in one of my own" (Richler 1990b, 229). More than any other passage in Richler's novels, this comment alludes to the cultural tensions associated with homosexuality in mainstream society, even in the age of greater liberal sympathies and widespread political correctness.

Expressing a more modern, sympathetic, and politically correct attitude towards her son's sexuality, Molly Birenbaum admonishes her husband: "Sam, he's our son. We've got to play with the cards that we were dealt" (232). Still, the novel ultimately frames Philip's sexuality in the context of comedy. The solemnity of Sam's heartfelt confession about having a gay son is deflated by Philip's flamboyant language – "You really are *quelque chose*, Dad," he says, while sipping champagne by the pool with his boyfriend (234) – and by Sam's rant describing Philip's boyfriend as a stage gay. "I wasn't going to make a crack about his boyfriend's earring or his black silk shirt open to his *pupik*" (230). The novel broaches the complexity of the issues around homosexuality but then retreats into trite, comedic portraits of gay stereotypes, complete with their fashion, speech affectations, and decadence.

When not exploiting gay allusions and references for comedy, Richler's main characters are non-committal regarding homosexuality. After Sam announces that his son is gay, Moses responds impassively, "Well, he isn't the only one" (229). Richler's fiction abounds with moments of gay drama, few of which are essential to the plot or the development of the protagonists, heroes, or even other central characters. On occasion they force an examination of the social stigma of homosexuality. This is the case in *St Urbain's Horseman*, when Jake conspicuously feigns gay behaviour, deliberately provoking the antipathy of his traditionally conservative brother-in-law, Herky. In a 1990 interview, Richler admits that he "dislikes" special pleading on behalf of gays and lesbians but belongs to an organization that raises money for AIDS (qtd in Hutcheon and Richmond, 45). The admission reveals his sympathy for the gay community, despite the fact that it has been a centrepiece of the PC agenda. Yet his fiction rarely includes such sentiments. More typical is the attitude of Barney, who refers to AIDS victims as "queers and druggies" (Richler 1998a, 304) and his cynical reaction to an advertisement for AIDS research:

> The most recent issue of *Red Pepper* includes a full-page ad,
> an appeal for donations by London Lighthouse, which features
> a photograph of a sickly young woman, her staring eyes rimmed
> with dark circles, looking into a hand-held mirror.
> SHE TOLD HER HUSBAND THAT SHE WAS HIV+.
> HE TOOK IT BADLY.
> What was the poor bastard to do? Take her to dinner at The Ivy
> to celebrate? (Richler 1998a, 18)

For the most part, in passages that deal with homosexuality Richler seems to enjoy taking advantage of opportunities to rehearse and satirize stock gay stereotypes, and enhance the novels' politically incorrect tone.

– ✳ –

Race issues are another component of political correctness critiqued in Richler's novels. Early in his career, Richler was accused of being a self-hating Jew because of his portrayal of Jewish characters as caricatures – mercenary, uncouth, morally dubious, and exclusionary. However, it is often Jews in Richler's novels who espouse racist attitudes. This might be seen as the reflexive defensiveness of a historically persecuted people finding succour by masquerading in one-upmanship that conceals an underlying sense of inferiority. But in Richler's writing it seems hard to make that case. In a short memoir, "Going Home Again," from his collection of autobiographical vignettes, *The Street*, Richler hints at this inferiority complex when describing a Gentile student in his high-school class.

> Our class at FFHS, Room 41, was one of the few to boast a true
> Gentile, an authentic white Protestant ... Our very own WASP's
> name was Whelan, and he was no less than perfect. Actually
> blond, with real blue eyes, and a tendency to sit with his mouth

hanging open. A natural hockey player, a born first-baseman. Envious students came from other classrooms to look him over and put questions to him. Whelan, as to be expected, was not excessively bright, but he gave Room 41 a certain tone, some badly needed glamour, and in order to keep him with us as we progressed from grade to grade, we wrote essays for him and slipped him answer at examination time. We were enormously proud of Whelan. (1969, 5)

The admiration seems more ironic than genuine, the faux praise hardly masking the condescension. The humour appears to be a jibe at Jewish self-doubt. However, the tone, especially embedded in the phrase, "as to be expected," regarding Whelan's lack of intelligence, suggests that it is not the Jewish students who are the butt of the jest.

This kind of racism towards non-Jews is prominent in Richler's fiction. In *Son of a Smaller Hero* Jews repeatedly use racist slurs. Wolf Adler, for example, has no compunction about calling blacks "niggers" (Richler 1989b, 27). In *Duddy Kravitz*, the protagonist, like many of the characters from Montreal's Jewish ghetto, disparages non-Jews. When he dreams of operating a movie rental business, he insists that it is imperative he find "a *goy*" to run the projector (Richler 1995, 78). Visiting his brother at a boarding house, he observes, the "whole lousy house was permeated with *goy*-smell. Bacon grease. The way they can live ... Jeez" (211). Duddy's mentor Mr Cohen boasts: "A plague on all the *goyim*, that's my motto" (313). These characters are drawn as small-minded bigots whose racism is not excusable, though it emanates from many first-hand encounters with anti-Semitism.

In later works, ironically, Richler, creates his hero figures and protagonists as Jewish advocates. While feminists, homosexuals, and the disabled are positioned as unworthy of special consideration, their claims fatuous, the hero figures are uncensored for their Jewish concerns and their moral and cultural arrogance.[12] When patronized by a quintessentially WASP guest at a restricted club in Quebec, Solomon Gursky's reaction is as much an expression of racist elitism as of Jewish triumphalism:

"Don't you dare condescend to me," Solomon said ... *More than a hundred years after Maimonides wrote his* Guide for the Perplexed *your ancestors, pledging each other's health in cups of their own blood, were living in mean sod huts, sleeping on bare*

boards wrapped in their filthy plaids ... Spinoza had already
written his Ethics *when your forebears still had their children*
wearing amulets to ward off the evil eye and carried fire in a
circle around their cattle to keep them safe from injury.
(Richler 1990b, 287)

In *St Urbain's Horseman*, Jake Hersh contemplates his Gentile wife's past, and his stereotypical imaginings are seemingly satiric, designed to mock Jewish superiority. However, they have an undertone of Jewish snobbery that cannot be completely discounted. An example is when Jake buys a house in an upscale London suburb and is repulsed by Nancy's enthusiasm to revive the garden.

Nancy's goysy Ontario childhood came to the fore, aglow
with the memory of ... old grandad pricking out beds in the
greenhouse. "Lookit, Nancy, it's such a big sky." *Ontari-ari-ario.*
Toronto-liberated mother enthralled to be shoveling pig shit
again, singing, Hi, Neighbor, as some Mennonite freak moseys
past. And, lookee yonder, it's the Ford v-8, Dad come out for
the weekend, escaping the incomprehensible city, where Jewboys
own the shoe factories and try, try, try, he couldn't sell enough
to please Mr. Goldstein, Goldarn it. (Richler 1991b, 281)

When plagued by insecurity, Jake involuntarily retreats to the Jewish sense of superiority carried over from his childhood community. Still, his tirade also satirizes his own Jewish paranoia.

Following this same pattern is Joshua Shapiro's lament when his future wife Pauline refuses to go out with him and prefers the attention of a talented black West Indian writer. Mired in self-pity, he rants: "I'm a wreck. I'm in love with a nigger-loving whore" (Richler 2001, 277). Joshua's racist outburst may be read as a tongue-in-cheek comment that emphasizes his exaggerated self-pity, but it may also reveal, under stress, an ugly side of his character. Uttered by a Jew who is preoccupied with the Spanish Civil War and the Holocaust, and who is ever alert to anti-Semitism, a racist slur, even if ironic, suggests a lapse into double standards.

Barney Panofsky, too, speaks condescendingly of non-Jews, for example, of "men, Waspy types" who start to buy him drinks and congratulate him for striking a blow "for the good guys" (Richler 1998a, 142), impressed by his reputation as Boogie Moscovitch's killer.

Their wives are equally enthralled. "They flirted shamelessly, my mean origins forgiven," Barney explains. "Imagine. A kike with a passion for something else besides money" (142). Barney has cause to view this upper-crust society as emotionally numb, saturated with anti-Jewish feeling. However, he goes beyond judgmental condemnation and voices a type of Jewish ethical superiority. He represents Montreal's WASP elite as a gang of amoral and depraved racists who are invigorated by the proximity of a suspected Jewish murderer.

Though these Jewish characters' true attitudes towards non-Jews are unclear, what is certain is that on record Richler insisted that the reader should distinguish between him and his fictional characters. Paradoxically, however, he considered authorial distance suspect regarding anti-Semitic content in the works of non-Jewish writers. Most famously, in 1968 he wrote a lengthy article in *Commentary*, "Bond," claiming that Ian Fleming's fictional series is deeply marred by strains of anti-Semitism and served as a model for other writers predisposed to anti-Jewish feelings. In the essay, he singles out Canada's former governor general John Buchan as a novelist who took his cues from Fleming (Richler 1973b, 56). A passage in Buchan's novel *The Thirty-Nine Steps* has been scrutinized by many critics for traces of its author's antipathy towards Jews: "[If you] get to the real boss, then the one you are brought up against is a little white-faced Jew in a bathchair with an eye like a rattlesnake" (qtd in Richler 1973b, 56). Some (see Waddel, 6) have argued that the quote only represents the point of view of the speaker and not that of Buchan himself. But Richler disagrees and claims that Buchan's personal diary is replete with anti-Semitic prattle, evidence that he and his characters loathed Jews equally. The issue was addressed as recently as 2004 in the *Atlantic* by Christopher Hitchens, who agreed with Richler but admitted that many still insist that Buchan was no more than a faithful chronicler of his times, who socialized with Jews regularly and, like all writers, was at liberty to create fictional characters with anti-Semitic views. Ironically, the excuse that the attitudes of fictional characters should not be mistaken for the author's viewpoint, or that fiction often reflects the ugly side of a society in the name of contextual authenticity, was often repeated by Richler when he was accused of Jewish self-loathing. Nevertheless, he would not accept these defences from his non-Jewish colleagues.

In *Solomon Gursky Was Here*, the population in northern Canada is comprised of dim-witted imbeciles, hardly a match for shrewd, clever, and even erudite Ephraim Gursky, who arrives in the icy mill town, Magog, with a collection of books, including a work by Shakespeare. The townspeople, in contrast, are barely literate. About to ply them with his missionary pamphlets, Ephraim asks those among them who can read to raise their hands. "Six of them raised their hands, but Dunlap was only bragging" (Richler 1990b, 7). Compared to Ephraim, the Gentile locals are ignorant. Equally uncivilized are the Inuit townspeople who become Ephraim's followers. Led to accept him as their deity – a cross between a pagan god and a foul-mouthed Yahweh – they willingly offer their wives and daughters to him: they "stepped forward one by one, thrusting their women before [him], extolling their merits in an animated manner. Oblivious of the cold, a young woman raised her sealskin parka and jiggled her bare breasts" (6). Here, too, Canadian Aboriginals are represented as primitive.

In his novels, Richler satirizes Jews on the lookout for anti-Jewish slander, such as Irv Nussbaum in *Barney's Version*. Richler's non-fiction essays, notably the ironically titled "Innocents Abroad," likewise mock different racial, ethnic, and political "sensitive types," including "Portuguese, Italians, Moslems, Catholics, Turks, Greeks, feminists, Arabs, American Indians" (Richler 1998b, 106). Yet his hero figures and protagonists are not meant to be viewed as ridiculous with their plaints of anti-Semitism and tendency towards Jewish superciliousness. Ironically, their self-reflexive special pleading appears in the novels as part of their function as observers and sentinels of ethical standards.

The issue of special pleading, as it is construed in Richler's novels, not only questions politically correct norms but also dovetails with the phenomenon of liberal guilt, auxiliary to the kind of "unhelpful" pity that liberalism often produces (Shklar, 36–7). Richler's characters must reckon with special pleading because much of society has become attuned to it. Special pleading has become a catalyst that provokes liberal guilt, a disquieting sense that the fortunate have come by their advantages unfairly. A number of Victorian and Edwardian authors explored the issue of liberal guilt before it was part of the vocabulary of political correctness and incorporated it into their novels. For these writers (Forster, Conrad, Dickens, Gaskell), "social collective guilt coalesces around two prime issues: imperial power abroad and growing urban poverty at home" (Born, 141; Breton, 51).

While Richler's novels pay some attention to the colonial enterprise – manifested as Canada's sovereignty over the Inuit – they dwell more extensively on the problem of inequity within society. In particular, liberal guilt in Richler's works recalls the "unresolved tension" in E.M. Forster's *Howards End* (1910): "How can liberal intellectuals reconcile the private activities of aesthetic contemplation, friendships, spiritual formation, with a broader concern for the public and social interest" (Born, 142).

In *St Urbain's Horseman*, there is, in fact, a reference to Forster. Jake admires his liberal stance as expressed in his essays collected in the volume *Two Cheers for Democracy* – "With Forster, he [Jake] wearily offered two cheers for democracy" (Richler 1991b, 307); the adverb "wearily," however, modifies the endorsement, suggesting that Jake's faith in democracy might be somewhat precarious. *Barney's Version* also pays tribute to Forster's liberal views, deliberately misapplying Forster's language: in a spoof of the hyper-sexuality of the twentieth century, Boogie Moscovitch imagines that sex will become as insignificant as a handshake and people will be able to have intercourse or "to 'only connect,' as Forster advised, while waiting for a traffic light to change" (Richler 1998a, 159). In this instance, liberal concerns are not at the heart of Boogie's joke. The reference to "only connect" – the point central to *Howards End* – mainly heightens the humour. However, it is also a tribute to Forster's appeal for meaningful interaction between the privileged and lower classes (or rather the lower middle class) as well as an allusion to double standards. Again in *Barney's Version*, the same idiom is used: when Boogie finally manages to inject heroin into his damaged vein, Barney jokes, this is what Forster must have meant by "only connect" (241).

That liberal guilt leads to "special pleading" – or a politically correct type of apologetics – is a theme Richler had already begun to explore in *Duddy Kravitz*. Benjy, Duddy's uncle, is the owner of a successful textiles factory and "wishes to become the replica of an English gentleman at the same time as he is a socialist radical well known enough to be denied entry to the United States" (Woodcock 1990, 46). As a result, he treats his workers with a mixture of noblesse oblige and democratic equality. When Duddy reports having seen an employee steal bolts of cloth, Benjy reprimands him – "I don't like squealers" (Richler 1995, 64): his socialist leanings lead him to assuage his liberal guilt by ignoring his employee's offence. Making Duddy's accusation even more problematic is Benjy's reluctance to side with another Jew, especially a family member, against a Gentile worker. The desire to believe in universal good faith makes such scenarios anathema to him but also portrays immoderate liberal guilt as loss of moral fibre.

By the end of his career, Richler represents liberal guilt through stinging parody. Barney Panofsky, for example, rants about the concessions his entertainment company makes to placate the entertainment establishment and ostensibly society's collective social conscience. These concessions may be inspired by class consciousness and sincere good will, but Barney references them as obligatory nods to mandatory political correctness:

> Our latest, godawful expensive pilot was rich in meaningful, life-enhancing action: gay smooching, visible-minority nice guys, car chases ending in mayhem, rape, murder, a soupçon of s & m, and a dab of New Age idiocies. (Richler 1998a, 106)

Barney mocks his rivals and enemies, too, as liberal guilt crusaders. When he thinks of Miriam's new husband, Blair, he alludes to his politically correct energies, his "habit" of "hugging trees or pasting Animal Rights stickers on fur-shop windows" (138). Terry McIver, an award-winning author and Barney's life-long nemesis, begins a book reading with a "statement opposing the use of clear-cutting and supporting the protection of British Columbia's Clayoquot Sound." He warns that the unbridled exploitation of the earth's resources will lead to global warming and the extinction of hundreds of species and then asks his audience to sign a petition on environmentalism. Solange, as one of Barney's cherished friends and one of the few voices of reason in the novel, insists that McIver is right, that animal life is endangered. However, her rebuttal is stonewalled. "Yours and mine, too," Barney replies. "But you know something? You're right. I worry in particular about the possible loss of hyenas, jackals, cockroaches, deadly snakes, and sewer rats" (144). Barney rejects the appeal on behalf of animalism, the environment, and the health of the ecosystem and insists that the human species – also in peril – not only matters more but need not be overly troubled by conservation alarmists.

However, liberal guilt is granted more serious attention in *Joshua Then and Now* and *St Urbain's Horseman*. In these two works, Richler's anti-PC tone is destabilized by the earnest liberal guilt experienced by Joshua Shapiro and Jake Hersh, respectively. In the throes of midlife,

Joshua Shapiro chastises himself for his own liberal inconsistencies. He asks himself how "he had ever become a television personality, a husband and a father of three, charged with contradictions. He sent his children to private schools and complained in other people's houses about being the father of children who attended private schools" (Richler 2001, 125). He loathes the assumed entitlement of the upper middle class but finds himself comfortably a part of it.

An even more complex portrayal of liberal guilt, which closely examines the dichotomy of liberal values that engaged Forster and others, is found in *St Urbain's Horseman*. Jake Hersh is prone to it; he chides himself with the knowledge that he enjoys a fortunate life available to few:

> In 1967 while 450 million people were starving and, in
> England, at least 18 per cent of this happy breed lived below
> subsistence level, and society's golden rule was alcoholism, drug
> addiction, and inchoate brutality, I, Jacob Hersh ... [was] paid
> £15,000 not to direct a fun film, made love to my wife on crisp
> clean sheets, sent my progeny to private schools, worried about
> corpulence gained through overindulgence and play hours
> lost through overimbibing ... I complained about our maid's
> indolence. I lamented the falling off in the British craftsman's
> traditional pride and a rise in the price of claret. While the
> rich got richer and poor got poorer, I survived very nicely.
> (Richler 1991b, 94–5)

Jake is troubled by the cosmic forces that have made him deserving of a successful (if not inspired) career, the love of an exceptional woman, and a comfortable home with an adoring family.

The aspects of liberal guilt that haunt Jake Hersh are similarly reminiscent of the liberal hypocrisies that preoccupy Orwell in *Down and Out in Paris and London* (1933) and *The Road to Wigan Pier* (1937): "the failure of middle-class liberals to connect with the working class" (Breton, 47). At the same time, *St Urbain's Horseman* lampoons the class-based liberal inclination, identified by Orwell, "to embrace the underdog, the marginal working class, because that is where the public's sympathy lies, and because liberals revel in the reputation of being 'decent'" (48). The novel dramatizes this tension through the unlikely relationship between Jake and Harry Stein, a character possessed of an exceedingly high IQ and vivid imagination, who has nevertheless suffered prodigious misfortune and a life typified by abject misery. He is a slapstick version of early twentieth-century lower-middle-class characters, such as Leonard Bast in Forster's *Howards End* (1910) or Jude in Thomas Hardy's *Jude the Obscure* (1895). Similar to them, he is physically frail, well-read despite the demands of long work hours, and tragically conscious of his unprivileged condition (Born, 149). In his case, however, he is also vulgar and shameless. Consequently, not all of Harry's unhappiness is a result of uncongenial circumstances. He is unapologetically lecherous and assumes no responsibility for the considerable misconduct that has contributed to his wretchedness. Still, Jake is troubled when considering the divergent paths that have led Harry to a life as a disgruntled, underpaid accounting clerk and him to a creative life with ample emotional and material comforts.

For example, "with his bleeding colonial heart," Jake feels guilty about his Hollywood image of the Second World War when he learns of Harry's actual war experience (Richler 1991b, 28). Together with a horde of bedraggled mothers and children straight from London's slums, Harry was sent to the English countryside and "finally disgorged on a station platform ... where the ill-tempered gentry, aghast to discover such urban pestilence in their midst, had nevertheless fore-gathered to take their pick" (29). While Jake was secure in Canada, imagining the war with cinematic grandeur, Harry was returned to the city and exposed to England's wartime anti-Semitism as well as to the anxiety of the Blitz, which caused his family to take nightly shelter in the Liverpool Street tube station. Though Jake realizes the absurdity of his war fantasy, Richler suggests that it was typical for Canadians, far from the battlefront, to feel that they were making great sacrifices for the sake of the war effort. In his introduction to *Writers on World War II*, he accentuates this point by recalling the wartime ad of Canada's most exclusive department store:

HOLT RENFREW has taken ANOTHER STEP in aid of the government's all-out effort to defeat aggression.

Beginning July 15 no deliveries will be made on Wednesdays. This will enable HOLT RENFREW to save many gallons of gasoline ... and many a tire ... for use by the government.

However, will it not THRILL you to think that non-delivery of your dress on Wednesday will aid in the delivery of a "block-buster" over the Ruhr ... Naples ... Berlin ... (Richler 1991c, xxv)

In the spirit of Richler's satire, the passage suggests that Canadian wartime "sacrifices" were expressions of liberal guilt; insipid gestures of good will that placated the conscience of those remote from the frontlines but hardly beneficial to the people who were genuinely in dire circumstances.

Harry, like Jake, is a Jew from a working-class background with a morose and cynical outlook on the world (though Harry's is decidedly darker). Accordingly, he can be seen as Jake's Doppelgänger (see McSweeney). As such, he evokes Jake's sympathy and functions in the narratives as an outlet for his guilt for having achieved worldly success. Jake attempts to befriend him and, in politically correct fashion, treats him as a peer and companion. Even when Harry's shenanigans embroil Jake in a rape trial, Jake finds himself "exhilarated" by the disgrace because it relieves his liberal conscience. He is oddly at peace because "he had expected the outer, brutalized world to intrude on their little one, inflated with love but ultimately self-serving and cocooned by money" (Richler 1991b, 93). Even so, the relationship, as Harry notes, is still an opportunity for Jake to alleviate his liberal guilt and realize the fantasy that he is, after all, "decent."

It may be tempting to also see Harry as an outlet for Richler's penchant for sophomoric mischief. Richler seems to take Harry's and Jake's antics too far, stretching their liaison beyond satire to childish farce. Nevertheless, Harry does not serve merely as a comedic digression. Jake genuinely admires his socially defiant attitude. When Harry visits the Hershes' well-appointed home, he discreetly burns a cigarette hole in the back of a chair. "Why the bastard, Jake thought, with sneaking admiration" (338). In the same way that he valorizes Joey for having the courage to do things that are "heroic," he values Harry's audacious, even malicious, subversiveness. But when Harry starts to harass Jake at home, unsettling his wife, Jake loses patience – and Richler cues the reader that the joke has expired. "Harry, I've been thinking," he begins. "Maybe I live in a house like this, possibly I make so much more money than you do, because I'm intelligent and talented and you're just a mindless little fart" (341). Ultimately, Jake refuses to be the recipient of Harry's endless rage. His liberal guilt does not override his desire to protect his family.

Still, Jake's relationship with Harry illustrates the predicament of the liberal suffering from contradictory social impulses. It is, as noted above, a dilemma that Orwell explores but fails to solve. Richler is attached to his working-class origins, the unsophisticated unpretentiousness of blue-collar society, as is Orwell, who "appreciates traditional rough-housing values: crass, silly, sexist humor; bawdiness and the carnivalesque for what it is (not for what it represents); empiricism or the real and tangible; the ordering of survival instincts over principles; and what might be said to be political incorrectness" (Breton, 55). However, in trying to persuade the reader to abandon his own class prejudice in *Down and Out in Paris and London*, Orwell "does not or cannot abandon his. He admits that the attitudes he attempts to absorb through his working-class enculturation conflict with his own class perspective" (Breton, 50). To his chagrin, he finds himself similar to others for whom the attempt to eliminate barriers and connect to the working class is founded upon disingenuous motives, the urge to expiate guilt, and a real repugnance towards the poor. Accordingly, Orwell contends that middle-class liberals "would connect to the working-class only if they could first scrub them down, de-class them – and even then, the sanitized, Disney version would be subject to patronizing and sentimental domination" (56).

The class impasse identified by Orwell is realized in the final scene of Jake Hersh's trial in *St Urbain's Horseman*, when the judge discharges him with a warning and punitive fines:

> "You have been a confounded fool ... You are a man with
> every advantage, obviously intelligent and talented, yet today
> you stand here disgraced ... Through folly, and sheer egoism,
> perhaps, you have formed an association with a man of obvious
> disreputable character, placing your family and your property
> in jeopardy. How in God's name could you form an association
> with Stein in the first place?" (Richler 1991b, 446)

The judge, no proponent of PC pieties, articulates the obvious paradox that makes an association between Harry and Jake inconceivable. In the novel, liberal guilt may accommodate the sympathies of privileged women towards disabled painters, but society cannot fathom how Jake could sustain a friendship with a poor man who is clearly malevolent. Ultimately, there is a cultural assumption that the divide between Jake and Harry is unbridgeable.

Despite their liberal proclivities, Richler's protagonists cannot tolerate the politicization of the underpinnings of liberal guilt. They nurse views, not unlike Richlers' – or Shklar's – that "the left tends to be smug and self-satisfied and shallow" (qtd in Cameron, 117). Furthermore, their moral mentors, the hero figures, subscribe to values that are outside the rubric of political correctness; they are, as a result, unresponsive to liberal guilt. Because the protagonists are ironic about liberal guilt and the hero figures ignore it, the novels ultimately satirize it as an affliction suffered mainly by those who are either too vapid or too self-righteous to grasp the real struggle of their generation: the struggle to correct historical and political wrongs through honour, decency, and justice.

Moreover, "special pleading" is discredited in Richler's novels because the hero figures, all self-made men, make no allowances for those who blame their failures on racism, chauvinism, or social distress. Despite being born into impecunious Jewish families in rural Canada, Joey Hersh and Solomon Gursky are fully empowered. Whatever hardships they face personally, these challenges are never attributed to economic disadvantages, anti-Semitism, or social marginalization. The narratives of Richler's novels endorse a given order or unlegislated caste system, where there are those – the hero figures, mainly – who are destined for greatness. By the time Solomon Gursky was seventeen, he "strode through the streets of the town as if he were a prince in waiting, destined for great things" (Richler 1990b, 264). Barney notes that "Alfred Kazin once wrote of Saul Bellow that even when he was still young and unknown, he already had the aura about him of a man destined for greatness. I felt the same about Boogie" (Richler 1998a, 8). Joey Hersh is not as clearly fated to be extraordinary, but Jake, even as a seven-year-old, recognizes that his cousin is exceptional. Though Joey is continually humiliated and aggrieved by his extended family, he refuses to be cowed. When he first meets the Hershes, he is a young boy from the disreputable branch of the family, but he still stands alone and smiles "scornfully" at his relations.

Meanwhile, those who are only good, mediocre, or worse are expected to know their place and accept their lot. Just as the novels do not endorse the liberal bent towards moral, cultural, aesthetic, or social pluralism, so they do not allow a pluralistic standard of individual worth. Some individuals are simply better than others – braver, smarter, more charismatic, morally astute, and aesthetically savvy – and to blame this inequality on political oppression or social disparity is an evasion. Richler explains this view in plain language in an oft-cited interview with Donald Cameron: "If you can't get a decent girl, if you're physically ugly, no political system is going to make life delightful for you. A man with cancer at twenty has had a bad deal no matter what" (290).

Thus, Jake Hersh is appalled by the attempt to promote a sub-standard artist as a burgeoning master because he has been injured at war. He demands objective standards of excellence and tolerates no excuses. He wants everyone to be as irrepressible as Solomon Gursky, whose war injury has no bearing on his sexual magnetism, business conquests, and indefatigable exploits. For him, it is pathetic to attribute failed ambitions to physical, financial, or social afflictions.

It is this attitude that underlies the satire of Virgil's campaign on behalf of epileptics in *Duddy Kravitz*. Composed of childish platitudes, his newsletter encourages epileptics to strive for greatness. Using Julius Caesar as an example, it intimates that epileptics need not be limited in their dreams and achievements: "Life was no breeze for young Julius, but ... he never once let his health handicap stand in his way" (Richler 1995, 318). However, the narrative of the novel suggests that having a congenital disease *is* a limitation, one that makes life trying. Accordingly, the novel poses the possibility that it would have been wise for Virgil to refuse the driver's job on account of his epilepsy. Liberal guilt is founded on the idea that an individual's achievements are enhanced or hindered by financial advantages and social support, but Virgil's accident makes such beliefs appear naïve and dangerous. In some sense, he becomes a victim of liberal guilt.

Richler's novels are more an indictment of liberal guilt than an appeal to examine society's countless inequities. They depict a world where material and emotional success is generally available through merit and toil as long as one is blessed with reasonable physical and intellectual assets. Those without such assets are expected to accept their predicament with grace. To expect special consideration, or grant such consideration, is to invite or practise condescension. At the same time, the niggling liberal guilt of Jake Hersh and Joshua Shapiro is not inconsequential. It suggests that compassion – even if tinged by concessions to political correctness – is not necessarily a fault and that the hero figures' ruthless code of values may be too harsh. Jake and Joshua are among Richler's most contented protagonists, as if the novels reward them for their more nuanced sense of liberal principles.

– * –

The expectation that political correctness could provide a sound basis for stimulating positive social change is satirized in Richler's novels. PC policies may spring from judicious attempts "to redistribute power, knowledge and resources" (Perry, 78), but that is not how they are depicted in Richler's fiction. They are, more often, a type of philanthropy tainted by the kind of "moral cruelty" that is described by Shklar as overly self-righteous "humanitarianism unshaken by skepticism and unmindful of its own limitations" (37). However, the anti-PC heroism in his novels is not a plausible alternative, and its value as a scheme of moral and social principles is significantly tempered by the fates of the hero figures. Joey Hersh may represent a type of hard-line, no-nonsense moral rectitude and personal dignity, but he is ultimately ineffectual – no saviour of the Montreal Jewish community, no war hero in Israel, no captor of Mengele. Solomon Gursky's ruthlessness, conversely, influences politics, war, and economics but leaves him romantically stymied and disconnected from the few people in whom he has a sincere interest. Boogie Moscovitch, Barney's intellectual mentor, is a tragic character, ruined by over-inflated literary expectations and addictions that both precipitate and exacerbate his ultimate failure. All of these men revile political correctness, or "special pleading," but their merciless personal ethics and codes of honour do not necessarily ameliorate social and political ills, contribute to cultural achievements, or set the groundwork for trusting, authentic personal relationships.

Moreover, it is unclear in Richler's novels with whom the reader is expected to identify. The hero figures are admirable but troublingly restless and too far beyond the limits of "ordinary" life to elicit empathy. The protagonists, generally the most sympathetic characters, are appealingly human but usually engage in behaviour that is slightly too passive and have attitudes that are a bit too impolitic to be the novels' real heroes. Thus, Richler's novels are manipulative, always prodding readers to re-evaluate their own ideological postures as well as the targets of the narratives' satire and social critique.

In allowing neither PC thinking nor the value systems of the hero figures to triumph, Richler's novels can be read as an apt illustration of Richard Rorty's argument that no single system provides the right "theoretical glue" for an improved society because conditions always vary in relation to "historical contingencies" (86). Secular societies, Rorty explains, have a need for stories about how conditions might improve. However, if stories that offer social hope have become less tenable lately, "this is ... because, since the end of WW II, the course of events has made it harder to tell a convincing story of this sort" (86). Richler seems committed to this view, especially as expressed by Rorty in relation to an ideal vision of society in the wake of the Holocaust.

Rorty also elucidates the reasons storytelling cannot provide a synthesis of the pursuit of individual perfection – heroism, in the context of Richler's works – and advocacy for better social conditions. To demonstrate this, he offers readings of Nabokov and Orwell. The former, he claims, wrote novels that provided "illustrations of what private perfection – a self-created autonomous human life, can be like." In contrast, Orwell, in his writing, "engaged in a shared social effort – the effort to make our institutions and practices more just and less cruel" (xiv). While these two approaches are seemingly opposite, Rorty believes that this is only true "if we think that a more comprehensive philosophical outlook would let us hold self-creation and justice, private perfection and human solidarity, in a single vision" – apparently, no single philosophical or theoretical discipline will let us do that: demands for self-creation and human solidarity must be seen as equally valid, even if incommensurable (xiv).

The values and personal codes of honour of the hero figures are not satirized in Richler's works nor, however, are they represented as ideal systems that necessarily result in social, political, or cultural improvement. Furthermore, they do not generally contribute to the personal happiness of the hero figures themselves or the people around them. At the same time, political correctness is not a feasible alternative to heroism in Richler's fiction, though it provides a contrasting social perspective that dramatizes the inability of a single value scheme to address the gamut of a community's social ills. Somewhat self-reflexively, Richler's novels explore the impossible intersection of literature and social activism and provide evidence for Rorty's claim that fiction cannot encompass and fully reconcile the pursuit of individual perfection and social progress.

5

Anti-heroic Canada

In *Solomon Gursky Was Here,* Solomon claims that Canada has no essence, "no tap root" (Richler 1990b, 286). Richler's entire corpus reiterates Solomon's accusation to varying degrees with regard to Canadian culture, society, and politics. It is, therefore, seemingly paradoxical that Richler repeatedly chose to weave Canadian issues into his fiction, presenting them as some of his protagonists' chief preoccupations. Richler's non-fiction provides some possible explanations for the apparent contradiction. As a journalist, he wrote rather passionately about Quebec, proclaiming, "this is my home and I care deeply about what is happening here" (Richler 1992, 257). Despite all of its problems, it is the place where he felt an intense personal investment, one that was integral to his fictional universe. He also recognized that, while Canada as a whole may have been an easy target for a satiric onslaught, it "is still a good neighborhood, worth preserving. So long as it remains intact" (260). Even if it was a minor player in the international arena politically and artistically, it was a fortunate nation – free and unsullied by the immeasurable bloodshed and oppression in which European history is steeped (Richler 1984, 291). Still, special pleading on behalf of Canadian society, which Richler viewed as patronizing officiousness, is always misguided and comical in his novels. For this reason, the hero figures (who are, nonetheless, Canadian except for Boogie Moscovitch) do not bother with it. They are men of action who value ends rather than means, and neither moral conventions nor socially conscious conduct advance their personal crusades. The protagonists, in contrast, whose lives are governed by ordinary values, cannot avoid grappling with the politically correct nationalism of their country. Thus, it is an important or, rather, ineluctable part of the foundation of their values. They mock and deride Canada and its society but feel compelled to confront them as formative influences that they cannot easily disregard.

– ✳ –

Richler had moved to England in the 1950s, convinced that Canada did not provide a nurturing cultural environment for a writer. In his 1957 interview with Richler, Nathan Cohen makes much of Richler's belief that Canada was too culturally impoverished to nourish his novelistic ambitions. The statement that Canada was not artistically inspiring probably did not endear Richler to some writers, critics, and other intellectuals. And yet, having had his first two books initially published by the British firm Andre Deutsch may, ironically, have added clout to Richler's status. Begrudgingly, some Canadianists might have felt some pride that a native-born writer still in his twenties had been recognized in a country with a particularly rich literary heritage.[1]

Among those who were irked by the depiction of Canada in Richler's work was Farley Mowatt, who accused him of having "no Canadian identity at all." Possibly, he bristled at the irreverent depictions of Canada in Richler's novels. More certain is that he questioned Richler's sense of self and the lack of a national constituent in his writing: "It's his Jewish identity and it's his little neighborhood identity" (qtd in Posner, 283). Mowat's observation may express the reticence of critics over the years to firmly recognize Richler as one of Canada's most important writers. Some even speculate that Canadian scholars and academics tended to downplay Richler's station among major Canadian writers because he was perceived as having been unfairly critical of Canada (Brenner 1998, 66). Backhanded compliments, such as Richler's 1970 confession, "Today, I believe, it is no longer necessary to apologize for being a Canadian writer" (Richler 1970, 20), were not perceived as sufficiently conciliatory to override earlier insults.

This view of Richler harks back to the early years of his career when he belligerently confessed that, as a Jew and a writer, he felt a greater affinity to the United States than to Canada. From the early 1950s onwards, such comments had become extremely unfashionable. After a 1951 report conducted by the Royal Commission on National Development in the Arts, Letters and Sciences (also known as the Massey Commission) "bemoaned the struggle that Canada's culture had to survive in the face of American books, magazine, radio, movies and … television" (Granatstein and Hillmer, 190), the government set out to cultivate the local arts. In 1957 it established the Canada Council for the Arts, which became the cornerstone of the Canadian cultural industry (191). Amidst a climate of Canadian cultural protectionism, Richler's outlook appeared "faintly treasonous" (Foran, 274).

Richler was candid about his tendency during his early career, in particular, to lambast Canada. As a young man, he felt that Montreal was "suffocating and excruciatingly boring and provincial." Canada, for him, was "a big lonely place" (qtd in Gibson, 281). It was "a country where there were only isolated voices of civilization, here a poet, there a professor and, between, thousands of miles of wheat and indifference" (Richler 1970, 22). But, like Davies, who later admitted that Canada had changed culturally and developed a "serious reading public" (qtd in Davis, 270), Richler, too, eventually modified his critique and became one of Canada's most concerned citizens, an engaging writer on Canadian politics, and an advocate of Canadian literary talent (21). He still idealized New York and felt a kinship with writers such as Norman Mailer, William Styron, and Herbert Gold. Nevertheless, he acknowledged that he was very much a product of his native environment. "All my attitudes are Canadian"; he insisted. "I'm a Canadian; there's nothing to be done about it" (qtd in Cohen 1971b, 25).

The tension between critics' discomfort with Richler's expatriate status and pride in his achievements seemingly dovetails with the oft-stated observation that Canada suffers from an inferiority complex. Canadians may have wanted their writers to be faithful patriots, but, arguably, they also sought validation in foreign approval of their nation's cultural endeavours. Richler referenced this insecurity during the Cohen interview: "I don't know any publisher who dares to publish a book in Canada without first sending it out to an American or British firm" (qtd in Cohen 1971b, 31). More than thirty years later Robert Lantos, who founded Canada's largest film and television company, Alliance Communications Corporation, and produced the film versions of both *Joshua Then and Now* (1985) and *Barney's Version* (2010), was frank about the Canadian drive for foreign plaudits. The American Academy of Film and Science (Academy Awards), for example, is especially important to the Canadian film industry, he argued, "because of the very nature of the Canadian inferiority complex. Canadians never truly believe they're good at something unless recognition comes from America" (qtd in Amsden, 9).

Canadians may have cause for believing theirs is an undervalued country. Canada was indeed slandered even before it was over-shadowed by American pizzazz. Richler, in contextualizing his satire, demonstrated how the country had been maligned over the course of its history by writers as diverse as Voltaire, Samuel Johnson, Samuel Butler, Oscar Wilde, and Wyndham Lewis, all of whom belittled the North American frontier as a snow-ridden outback rich in little other than furs and fish (1970, 16). To prove that contemporary Americans had an equally disparaging view of Canada, he went on to recount a story about a New York editor that he later incorporated into *St Urbain's Horseman*:

> One afternoon he and his associates compiled a list of twelve deserving but ineffably dull books with which to start a publishing firm that was bound to fail. Leading the list of unreadables was *Canada: Our Good Neighbour to the North.* (17)

While Richler was often accused of perpetuating the menace of American cultural domination, in fact, other Canadian writers have expressed similar feelings. In his 1960 essay collection, *Voices from the Attic*,[2] Robertson Davies describes Canada as an incomparably dull country incapable of producing its own literary canon in the European tradition (see Davies 1960). Anticipating Richler and Davies, the Yiddish writer J.I. Segal relocated from Montreal to New York for several years during the 1920s because he "loved the size and great scope a city like New York provided for a writer" (Robinson et al., 18). More recently, Neil ten Kortenaar shows how "migrant writers who chose Canada did so primarily because it was North America" (563). He points to the novel *Comment faire l'amour avec un nègre sans se fatiguer* (1985) by Dany Laferrière, in which the Haitian protagonist cruises for white girls on the streets of Montreal because he wants a piece "of America" (563). He also quotes novelist Dionne Brand, who confessed her feelings upon arriving in Toronto as an immigrant: the "plane landed in Canada, but I was in America" (563). Still, when Richler showed a greater appreciation for Canada in his non-fiction, praising Canada's cultural progress and new cadre of talented writers, he remained suspect. Regardless of his evolving on-record views, the cultural establishment resented his continued fictional portrayal of Canada as either dreary of risible.

The Canadian culture quagmire has prompted much dialogue on the issue of national identity and the effort to disabuse Canadians of their sense of being part of an underachieving nation of nominal importance – a nation mainly struggling to emerge from the political, economic, and cultural shadow cast by the United States. In his 1969 address to the National Press Club in Washington, Prime Minister Pierre Trudeau gave voice to this predicament: living next to the US, he said, "is in some ways like sleeping with an elephant. No matter how friendly or temperate the beast, one is affected by every twitch and grunt" (CBC Digital Archives). Likewise, in the introduction to his 1971 book *The Bush Garden: Essays on the Canadian Imagination*, Northrop Frye posits that many Canadians feel that, compared to the United States, their country is barely middling in every respect except its supply of natural resources (1971a, iv). It was a view he reiterated just over a decade later, insisting that Canadians, despite their growing cultural achievements, still suffered a sense of insecurity and inferiority (1982, 78).

Even by 2000, it seemed that such insecurities were still part of the Canadian national psyche. A Molson beer commercial, "I Am Canadian" (2000), which exploited the Canadian culture of self-deprecating humour, met with an overwhelming response (Seiler, 45). First broadcast during the National Hockey League play-off finals of that year, it soon went viral on the internet, receiving 600,000 hits a day. Almost immediately labelled "The Rant," the advertisement, a monologue delivered by "Joe Canadian," mocks the image, considered mainstream in the US, of Canadians as Americans' backward country cousins. Young Canadians identified with the commercial's message and began staging "ritualized performances" of it in public locations (52). Created by Canadian advertising executive Glen Hunt, who had heard scores of stereotypical comments about Canadians while working in advertising in New York, the commercial virtually morphed into Canada's unofficial national anthem (51). Like all advertising, "I Am Canadian" was intended to boost product sales, and indeed it fulfilled this function for the Molson company. At the same time, it reignited much discussion about the frustration that Canadians felt as part of an underrated country that was often belittled or ignored, especially by its next-door neighbour.[3]

Against this complicated cultural backdrop, Richler's novels typically include protagonists who believe they are subverting the Canadian predicament by becoming autodidacts and living a hardscrabble existence abroad among artists and intellectuals. Despite being reared in an atmosphere that they perceive as prosaic and pedestrian, they thirst for cultural sophistication and aspire to live according to lofty, universal ideals. The protagonists and some in their milieu achieve cultural sophistication but retain their interest in Canada, often as unforgiving critics. They refuse to sever their emotional ties to Canada but still feel compelled to ridicule what they consider Canada's philistinism.

In *The Acrobats* Canadian culture is scorned by the protagonist André Bennet: "Mediocrity draped in the maple leaf ... Sonnets by the ageing virgin grand-daughters of Tory tradesmen evoking the memories of rather un-Presbyterian passions" (Richler 2002a, 77). In *Son of a Smaller Hero*, Noah Adler, much like Richler at the age of nineteen, finds he can only realize his personal and artistic aspirations by trading his Montreal existence for life on the Continent. And, the fact that Noah's family – like Richler's, according to his account in "The Street" (Richler 1969, 16) – established itself in the northern port city of Montreal rather than New York is described as inadvertent, an accident rather than an intentional move to Canada instead of to the United States. The same is true of the coterie of L.B. Berger in *Solomon Gursky Was Here*, which regards Canada as "the next-door place," a consolation to immigrants who had not made it to New York, Boston, or Chicago (Richler 1991b, 11); like many characters in contemporaneous immigrant novels, they consider Canada a lacklustre refuge from bad conditions elsewhere rather than a promised land (see Atwood 1972, 151).

In *St Urbain's Horseman*, Jake Hersh believes that he must leave Canada and its provincialism for the sake of his ambitions as a film director. New York, he imagines, is his "spiritual home" (Richler 1991b, 112) and Canada's "true capital" (110). It is the entertainment mecca, home of *Partisan Review* and the *New Republic*, an oasis of opportunity and intellectual camaraderie. However, Jake's maiden journey to New York is unsuccessful. Because he is misidentified as Joey Hersh, who is banned from entry into the US, Jake is forced to seek intellectual refuge in England: he never considers remaining in Montreal. He cannot imagine a productive future in Canada, where the artistic community seems too small and the critical accolades for mediocre film productions too readily available.

The prevailing belief that Canada lacks literary excellence is further lampooned in *Solomon Gursky* when Bernard Gursky, ostensibly a paragon of Canadian patriotism, instructs his sycophant Harvey

Schwartz about finding a writer to pen his biography: "For this job I don't want a Canadian. I want the best" (Richler 1990b, 117).

A number of critics have laboured, specifically, to redress the notion that Canada, as a cultural environment, is not conducive to the production of rich, enduring art and literature. By 1970, even Richler offered a defence, though tepid, of Canadian literature in the introduction to *Canadian Writing Today*. "I believe it is no longer necessary to apologize for being a Canadian writer," he conceded. "There are more than a fistful who can be read with honest pleasure" (Richler 1991c, 20). But more recently, Coral Ann Howells and Eva-Marie Kröller, editors of the *Cambridge History of Canadian Literature*, tender a far more effusive endorsement of Canadian writing:

In 1917 Canadian Literature made its first appearance in *The Cambridge History of English Literature* as a modest twenty-page chapter ... Almost exactly ninety years later, this substantial *Cambridge History of Canadian Literature*, co-edited by two women scholars, with its thirty-one chapters written by a distinguished company of Canadian and international contributors, offers convincing evidence for the establishment of Canadian literature as an important scholarly field and for its current standing. (1)

Likewise, Reingard M. Nischik's *History of Literature in Canada* begins with an equally emphatic statement. The editor boasts that Canadian writing "has arrived at the center stage of world literature": it contains many international bestsellers and has "developed into a staple of academic interest" (1–2).

Nevertheless, Richler's satirization of Canadian artistic achievements is much more confluent with earlier criticism and invokes Douglas LePan's well-known 1948 poem, "A Country without a Mythology." It also coincides with Northrop Frye's claim that Canadian literature was inferior to other important national canons because Canada had not undergone "a period, of a certain magnitude ... in which a social imagination can take root and establish a tradition" (1971a, 219). It had never had this period, as did American literature, for example between the Revolution and the Civil War (219). Arguing that literature is conscious mythology, and evolves into the "structural principles of storytelling," Frye believed that Canadian writers lacked such a structure, with its inherent stories and images (233).[4] In later years, Frye softened his view of Canadian culture. It had developed, he claimed, "an inner composure and integration of outlook, even some buoyancy and confidence" (Polk, 82). Still, Canada's literature was not world class. "It is here," he said of Canadian literature, "perhaps still a minor but certainly no longer a gleam in a paternal critic's eye" (72). A statement that offered recognition but hardly exuberant validation.

Richler's stance on Canadian national identity, which aligned with Frye's insistence that a national narrative is a necessary, a priori backdrop to a great national literature, has generally fallen into critical disfavour and become "outmoded" (Carter, 6). Already by the late 1970s Canadian critics were shying away from the belief that literature was "an expression of a single national character" (New, xxxii). And, by the end of the twentieth century, it was a commonplace that "the idea of a national essence ha[d] long been recognized as a fiction" (Redekop, 263). In Canada, specifically, the idea of coherent national narratives, or "metaphors of unity," to use Frank Davey's term (19), was being contested by the time Richler was in the later stages of his career. Literary critics were becoming increasingly attentive to matters relating to colonialism, race, class, ethnicity, and gender, and were disinclined to consider "nation" as a unifying framework (Carter, 6). The thinking was that, in the formulation and promotion of national myths, "the conflictual and heterogeneous reality of any society is falsely neutralized" (6). Influential scholars, such as Robert Kroetsch and Linda Hutcheon, theorized that the constant of Canadian identity was not an overriding, shared quality but a national awareness that the country was rooted in "multiplicity and difference" (6). It was an "ironic identity," not bridged by any cogency but "characterized by the doubleness of the plural, differential, discursive and hence unstable nature of identity" (6).

However, Richler's lampoon of Canada and its culture never engages with these more nuanced conversations about Canadian identity. His work more closely echoes the ideas expressed by Davies, Frye, and Atwood, who claimed that Canada's most dominant myth is "Survival or Survivance," not only the survival of Canada's grim physical conditions but cultural survival too – the survival of French language and culture within the embrace of English Canada, and the survival of Canadian specificity despite the shadow of American cultural hegemony (Atwood 1972, 32).[5] Specifically in terms of the development of a national literature, "Canadians," Atwood teased, "are forever taking the national pulse like doctors at a sickbed: the aim is not to see whether the patient will live well but simply whether he will live at all" (33).

Atwood's argument is supported by Frye's remarks in *The Bush Garden* that, in an effort to boost the national cultural milieu, Canadians are apt to exaggerate national literary achievements. It is a tendency, he adds, that hampers writers by making them prematurely self-conscious: "Scholarships, prizes, university posts, await the dedicated writer: there are so many medals offered for literary achievements that a modern Canadian Dryden might well be moved to write a satire on medals, except that if he did he would promptly be awarded the medal for satire and humour" (Frye 1971a, 216). Still, he has compassion for Canadians yearning for their own literary tradition: "The efforts made at intervals to boost or hard-sell Canadian literature, by asserting that it is much better than it actually is, may look silly enough in retrospect, but they were also, in part, efforts to create a cultural community, and the aim deserves more sympathy than the means" (216).

Richler was likewise wary of the Canadian literary establishment's propensity to encourage young Canadian writers to over-value themselves. He recognized that Canada had produced good writers but believed that writers in Canada were liable to lose a sense of proportion in terms of their relative importance and achievements (qtd in Cohen 1971b, 30). Addressing this point in his 1983 article in the *New York Times*, Richler made light of one of his peers, a fellow expat whom he had known from his days as an aspiring writer in 1950s Paris. Naming the failed author only as "Harry," Richler notes how this former hopeful secured a steadfast Canadian publisher though his writing remained mediocre and his novels never sold more than fifteen hundred copies. He continues that other Canadian cultural institution also embraced Harry despite his want of talent or commercial success. The Canada Council was faithful, organizing, for example, a reading tour in the Northwest Territories. He was granted "a term as a literary resource person at an obscure Nova Scotia college, putting together an anthology of Canadian writing for Radio Finland" (1990a, 3). In short, Richler makes his point: Canada is a place where native artists will be feted first for who they are rather than for what they produce.

Accordingly, Richler only slightly modulated his fictional portrayal of Canadian art, society, and politics, making his protagonists stand out all the more for their desire to be cosmopolitan. Canadian literary taste is savaged in *Joshua Then and Now* when Joshua is visited by Detective Sergeant Stuart Donald McMaster, ostensibly on police business but actually hoping that Joshua will read his manuscript. As a night student in creative writing at Concordia University, "he had been working on a novel for ten years" (Richler 2001, 20) and assures Joshua that it is not a lightweight work:

> "I want you to know it's not one of your little one-character jobs. Shit, no. It has ten major characters and I've written the biographies of each of them ... Now I suppose you want to know why ten? ... There's one major character from each province of Canada."
>
> Joshua whistled impressed. "No one from the Northwest Territories or the Yukon?"
>
> "Minor."
>
> "If Quebec separates, will you have to revise?" (20–1)

In this exchange McMaster's idea of great literature (he probably dreams of writing "the great Canadian novel") is a microcosm of mainstream Canada's lack of literary sophistication. It suggests that the Canadian idea of a magnum opus is a mechanical document in which setting, characters, and plot are unimaginatively moulded to represent the country's geography, history, and politics. The reference to Concordia and the very name "McMaster" – an allusion to one of Canada's largest universities – are insults directed at local academia. Joshua's ironic questions about the northern territories and Quebec highlight the dearth of cultural activity within huge expanses of Canadian territory, the farce of Anglo-French politics, and a self-referential joke that such topics are suitable as literary fodder.

In *St Urbain's Horseman*, Richler lampoons the depiction of Canada as a public relations cause. After arriving in Montreal hours following his failed attempt to enter the US, Jake repairs to the train station bar. A waiter approaches and greets him with an assurance that Montreal is "the Paris of North America." For Jake, however, it is no great distinction to be a pale imitation of an iconic city. The waiter continues, miffed when Jake is unimpressed. "Canada's no joke. We're the world's leading producer of uranium. Walter Pidgeon was born in this country" (Richler 1991b, 122), as if Canada were little more than a swath of incidental natural resources and a reservoir of actors of moderate achievements.

Even the legend of the failed Franklin discovery expedition of 1845, one of Canada's few foundational myths, is hijacked by Richler in *Solomon Gursky Was Here* and transmogrified into burlesque. His adaption "is amusing enough by itself, but when read in context – *against* the reverential Canadian literary treatment of Franklin – it's like a fart in church: hilarious but, well, sacrilegious. As Richler intends" (Atwood 2004, 38).

However, it is Richler's fourth novel, *The Incomparable Atuk* (1963), that is most consistently devoted to parodying Canadian national legends, cultural protectionism, and social issues: "a satire on Canadian poses and pretences so sharply localized that it is in fact a roman à clef" (Woodcock 1970, 45). Whereas his later works espouse a values scheme with Canadian elements, which is realized through the nexus between the protagonist and hero figure, *The Incomparable Atuk* has no hero figure, only the eponymous protagonist who, without a guiding mentor, is a cynical and doomed anti-hero. He shares the sardonic misanthropy of Richler's typical protagonists but not the redeeming hopefulness that comes from their belief in larger-than-life seekers of justice. Without a main figure who believes in any positive values, the satirization of Canada is one-sided. There is no ironic narrative element to balance the critique. Rather than being represented as a good country with some cultural deficits, Canada emerges as a pitiful nation peopled by mercenary opportunists, inept intellectuals, and lacklustre legends but no authentic heroes. *The Incomparable Atuk* does, however, set a precedent in Richler's corpus as most of the Canadian follies it mocks resurface in subsequent novels. Still, lacking the protagonist/hero figure structure, it fails to allude to qualities that make Canada an inescapable concern for the protagonists in these works.

The story follows the rise of Atuk, a member of the Inuit of Baffin Island who is discovered by a communications magnate and then exploits the market for local art by producing deliberately trite Aboriginal poetry.[6] George Woodcock argues persuasively that the novel is modelled on Voltaire's *L'Ingénu,* which represents a Huron Indian who is introduced to corrupt Parisian society in the eighteenth century. Richler, however, modifies the plot by making Atuk a shrewd opportunist rather than a noble savage graced with "mythical primitive innocence" (Woodcock 1970, 44). It is an effective "inversion of the Voltairean equation" and demonstrates that "even a rapacious savage … can throw into absurd relief the flaws and follies" found in Canada's socio-cultural landscape (44). *The Incomparable Atuk* has been widely dismissed as a convoluted, insignificant farce without moral substance or narrative coherence. Yet it remains among Richler's most piercing attacks on Canadian society.

As a coming-of-age story, the plot – Atuk's rise in Canadian society and subsequent televised death as the first contestant on the game show "Stick Out Your Neck" – can be viewed as a tongue-in-cheek cautionary tale warning Canadians to resist the allure of the American dream with its promise of celebrity and riches (Davidson, 106). When Atuk first arrives in Toronto he meets a shady magazine editor who boasts that his publication stands for national identity and that the "American mags" have been trying to shut him down (Richler 1989a, 5). The joke is that while American publishers may well have been interested in exploiting the Canadian market, they were not likely to give much thought to the publications produced in Toronto and Montreal, or, in general, to what Canadians wrote, thought, or reviewed. When the local *mafioso* Twentyman jockeys for a government-controlled television franchise, he has to comply with the royal commission's standards: "a schedule that was at least forty percent Canadian in origin" (156). But upon reviewing the program proposal, even the commission is unexcited by a line-up comprised of "Canada Hit Parade with the Three Gassers of Galt & a Girl (all Canadian-born), Trans-Canada Amateur Drama Night, a national ping-pong competition, Wednesday Wrestling, and Championship bowling" (157). Twentyman responds with a sly appeal to the board's hypocritical proclivities. Prime time television, unlike the early show with the Gassers and ping-pong, would include mainstream (American) shows that featured stars who were, at the very least, Canadian-born, and a game show (a prophetic version of reality television) in which contestants would be threatened with execution.

Aside from cultural jealousies, the novel also takes aim at Canada's founding legends. Lacking a national icon such as Jeanne d'Arc, Florence Nightingale, or Amelia Earhart, Canada is home to a native-born heroine, Bette Dolan. Based on the real-life figure Marilyn Bell, a sixteen-year-old who did become a Canadian darling in 1954 after swimming Lake Ontario, she is not a self-sacrificing leader, tireless healer, or brave innovator (Kramer 2008, 164). Nevertheless, Bette attains unprecedented celebrity in Canada as the first woman to swim Lake Ontario in under twenty hours. Politicians hail her as "an example here for youth all over the freeworld." The paradox between "here" and "all over the freeworld" suggests pathetic attempts to turn Bette into an icon against the background of a rather dim idea of the world beyond the borders of Ontario. Bette, too, is portrayed as a starry-eyed naïf. In the wake of her new-found fame, she is pursued by high-powered men from all walks of life. She denies them because she cannot, as she claims, give herself to a single individual. She insists that she "belongs to the nation. Like Jasper Park or Niagara Falls" (Richler 1989a, 21). Only Atuk, who is savvy and eager to selfishly exploit local nationalism, is able to woo Bette, with a plea to help him overcome his feigned sexual inadequacy. He seduces Bette the same way that he takes advantage of Canadian patriotism.

The novel's ridiculing of Bette is consistent with Richler's dislike of Canada's penchant for fresh-faced humdrum idols. In an article entitled "Gretzky in Eighty-Four," he describes the hockey legend as a "curiously bland twenty-four-year old" (1998b, 239) who is "incapable of genuine wit or irreverence" (243). Gretzky as depicted by Richler is ever-ready to oblige his fans, promoters, and advertisers, suggesting that this is a character flaw, one that is also evident in Bette Dolan. And, like Bette, Gretzky seems to be perceived as national property. Peter Pocklington, owner of Gretzky's team, the Edmonton Oilers, refused to trade Gretzky to "the nefarious Americans because keeping Gretzky in Edmonton was 'almost a sacred trust'" (249). He explained that the locals had few entertainment options and that therefore Gretzky was their Pavarotti or Nureyev (241). Richler believed that "the worship of innocent idols such as Bell and Gretzky stunted the nation's intellectual culture and left Canadians unable to worship more worldly and cynical artists" (Kramer 2008, 164). What irked him was not that Gretzky was a hockey player and national icon – he had only praise for the Canadian hockey legend Gordie Howe, a player known as Mr Elbows, whom he considered a "complete artist" (228) – but the willingness of Canadians to embrace humourless achievers who exhibit no engaging intelligence, no appreciation of irony, and little or no role-distance.

In relation to Bette, Atuk's Indigenous origins are used as a spring-board to mock Canada's cultural heritage and presumed myth of national greatness. However, throughout the novel Richler also creates problematic portrayals of Canada's Inuit, reinforcing demeaning stereotypes that have long been part of popular racist perceptions in Canada of local Aboriginals.

In one of the few episodes that is focalized through Atuk, the Baffin Island Natives are presented as ignorant, lazy alcoholics. They use the kitchen sink to urinate and are awed by the inexplicable wonder of television, "the great magic" (Richler 1989a, 57). Having discovered the commercial market for Aboriginal sculpture, Atuk sets up his family as slave labourers but finds their ignorance tiresome, the indoctrination period too wearying. "Atuk, I am frightened. It is winter. Yet every twelve hours there is the miracle of light. Are the Gods angry?" Neither would he put up once more with ignorant nieces breaking up cigars to spice the stew or with gluttonous, ever-thirsty uncles boiling his tooled leather belts in the soup and pouring anti-freeze into the punch bowl. (54)

Such depictions of these locals as unworldly at best, and primitive at worst, persist throughout the novel. At the same time, the obviously exaggerated stereotyping is meant to produce a certain "uneasiness" (Spacks, 363) in the reader and reveal the commonplace bigotry against Canadian Aboriginals. It is an example of the kind of satire that Patricia Spacks describes – initially inviting the reader to view the subject as other, even inferior, but, in fact, censuring that very sense of superiority (363).

The complexity of the Inuit predicament is evident in *Solomon Gursky Was Here* but is still more a comic digression than social commentary. Solomon, as the hero figure, validates the community by sustaining enduring friendships with various Aboriginals, including a faded beauty and renowned prostitute, Lena Greenstockings. Still, satire of the Inuit is heavy-handed in the novel, which primarily makes light of anti-Inuit discrimination. For example, at an event in the northern town of Yellowknife, attended by Queen Elizabeth, Prince Philip, Prince Charles, and Princess Anne,[7] local organizers regale the royal audience with some local culture. The event is a farce because the puerile presentations are not only inane but extolled by the evening's master of ceremonies as an expression of high art:

Before dinner, the royal couple was entertained by a group of outstanding Inuit artists, flown in from remote settlements for the occasion. Professor Hardy rose to introduce the first poet. He explained that unimaginable hardship was the coin of the Inuit's daily existence, but, reflecting on the woop and warf of their lives, they made ecstasy the recurring theme of their anacreontic salute to the world. This remarkable people plucked odes of joy, *pace* Beethoven, out of the simplest blessings, enshrining them in their own form of haiku. Then Oliver Girskee stood up and recited:
"Cold and mosquitoes
These two pests

Come never together
Ayi, yai, ya." (Richler 1990b, 46)

Following the poetry recitation, locals perform the mouth-pull, "a
contest wherein the two opponents hook their fingers into each other's
mouths and pull away until one of them faints or admits defeat" (46).
Last, "the justifiably celebrated Cape Dorset throat-singers" take
the stage:

> "The distinctive sounds of throat-singing," Professor Hardy
> explained to the royal family and their entourage, "part of a
> time-honored native tradition, are made by producing guttural
> nasal and breathing sounds, rather like dry gargling. The art
> cannot be described, but it can be likened to the sounds of great
> rivers ... the gentle glide of the gull ... the crumbling of the
> crisp white snow of the mighty gale of the Arctic." (46)

These passages, with their caricature of the local population's music
and poetry, actually allude to mainstream Canada's patronizing attitude towards Inuit culture. They call to mind Shklar's notion of moral
cruelty and the way in which charitable good will towards a minority
can be demeaning, even morally repugnant.

The episode also accentuates the prevailing condescension of the
governing powers towards Canada's Aboriginal peoples. Under the
auspices of "white" Canadian intellectuals and governmental authorities, the Inuit are paraded in front of the Queen of England like a
circus side-show. While their cultural achievements are not the usual
fare of the Commonwealth, the organizers of the event are unmoved
by the prospect that the locals will be perceived as Arctic freaks. This
insensitivity is emphasized when the narrative relays how the Eskimo
of the Keewatin, the Central and High Arctic and Baffin region are
treated at the hands of Canada's national authorities: they "were
known to Ottawa only by the numbers on the identification disks they
wore around their necks" (47). In the context of a Richler novel, this
official emblem is immediately evocative of the numbers tattooed on
the arms of Nazi concentration camp inmates: identifying individuals
by numbers is dehumanizing.

The comparison, however, is limited because the novel frames the
numbered citizens as objects of cynical mirth. When the Canadian
government grants the novel's Inuit the right to choose surnames, the

narrative explains how the "rambunctious" among them exercised their sense of humour and chose monikers such as "Hotdog, Coozycreamer, or Turf'n'Surf" (47). These preposterous, lewd surnames insinuate that a fair number of these people are simply vulgar and dim-witted.

By satirizing both the Inuit people themselves and the discrimination they have faced historically, Richler addressed a topic that has been a touchstone of political rage for nearly half a century. As an Indigenous minority, the Inuit are widely considered a victimized group, historically treated with indifference or subjected to assimilationist policies by the Canadian government (Gruber, 414). A grassroots movement arose in the 1960s that demanded Aboriginal rights and the reclamation of Aboriginal identity. Consequently, when Prime Minister Pierre Trudeau introduced the 1969 White Paper, which called for the end of Aboriginal Canadians' special status and for the mainstreaming of services for Canada's Native peoples, activists mobilized quickly and accused Canadian officials of attempting to exterminate them through assimilation (415). In more recent years, cultural critics, too, have accused Canada of having previously implemented policies meant to pressure Indigenous groups to assimilate, abandon their oral culture, and embrace modernity, or literate culture. But, according to Canadian Aboriginal orature scholar Penny Van Toorn, policies are being adjusted because "such ideas are discredited as relics of a colonialist ideology that justified European cultural domination by picturing Aboriginal peoples as Europe's primitive ancestors" (24).

There are indications, especially with regard to on-record comments, that Richler was not indiscriminately insensitive to the plight of the Inuit. In his article, "North of Sixty," he acknowledges the complexities of their predicament in the Northwest Territories, resistance to Canadian urbanization as well as acculturation, and lingering resentment towards their loss of culture and territorial independence (Richler 1984, 218). Similarly, he notes the seriousness of the region's worst social ill, alcoholism, and how it exemplified irresolvable cultural tension. To combat excessive drinking, Richler explains, the government published *Captain Al Cohol Comics*, a series that dramatized the problems associated with alcoholism. However, the series, which figures in *Solomon Gursky*, was discontinued after Inuit groups deemed the protagonist, Captain Al Cohol, a racist because he was a fair, blond hero preaching to the Inuit locals. Thus, even when the government embarked upon well-meaning attempts to improve the lives of the Northwest Territories' youth, these actions, Richler contended, were interpreted by the local population as policies rooted in cultural condescension.

Richler's sympathy for the Inuit and their treatment at the hands of mainstream Canadians is also intimated when, in the novel, they are cast as a comical version of latter-day Jews. In his non-fiction, he frequently recalls instances of Canadian anti-Semitism in various periods during the twentieth century. Thus, the framing of their plight as a replication of the Jewish experience is Richler's empathetic nod towards their history as a mistreated Canadian minority. Richler ascribes to the Inuit many of the best known canards against the Jews in an attempt to dramatize their absurdity. Even Atuk is cast as a more self-assured version of Duddy Kravitz – a money-wise, ambitious con artist who is nonetheless highly alert to discrimination. While perusing the newspaper, he is on the alert for causes for offence:

> His investments, considering the present state of affairs in Canada, were not doing too badly. He also found the coverage of his reading for *group sixty-one* entirely satisfactory. Jean-Paul McEwen ... was especially complimentary – or was she writing tongue-in-cheek? ... No, he thought, I'm just being touchy. A thin-skinned Eskimo. (Richler 1989a, 55)

Ironically, Atuk himself is a racist. He mocks an admirer's gift of knitted socks as "Negroid," (56). Atuk's family is, moreover, represented as clannish. They are opposed to Atuk's relationship with a non-Aboriginal girl. In imagining Atuk's future family, his father foresees a half-breed grandchild and in-laws who would expect him "to wash and eat with cutlery" and ingest "condemned foods" (85) – references to intermarriage, alien etiquette, and kosher dietary laws. He also cannot abide Atuk's intention to abandon his responsibility as one of the world's "chosen pagans" (85). Atuk, in response, calls his father a "bigot," a man who has an "igloo mentality" (83). Their satiric conflict is reminiscent of the clashes between twentieth-century Canadian Jewish immigrants and their children, and the younger generation's desire to break free of their parents' "ghetto mentality." This narrative thread is suggestive of sympathy with the Inuit as a culture in conflict with that of the dominant society. However, the depiction of Atuk's broader community as uncivilized is too grossly exaggerated to be tempered by the Jewish allusions, even if the allusions are a double-edged jibe also meant to caricature Jews.

Relatively brief, characterized by cynicism and dark humour, *The Incomparable Atuk* is mainly a farce, even though, as Linda Morra notes, it foreshadows much of the cultural identity dialogue that has dogged Canada, even into the twenty-first century. It also deals with significant Canadian issues, many of which continue to be relevant in Richler's subsequent novels. Concerns about under-achieving writers and artists, the paucity of credible national heroes and legends, the social complexities associated with the Inuit, and the corresponding racist attitudes towards this population are all matters that continued to interest Richler and his protagonists.

– ✳ –

In writing satire that mocks inflated claims of Canadian importance, self-deprecation, and corresponding defensiveness, Richler's novels rely upon narrative techniques such as free indirect discourse, first person narration, and dialogue, which create collusion between narrator and protagonist.[8] Yet rather than coalescing to make Canada seem ever more pathetic, the overlapping voices serve to complicate the representation of Canadian society: if it is so insipid, how could it produce likeable protagonists and, even more inexplicably, extraordinary hero figures (even if their heroism is partially exaggerated by the protagonists).

In *St Urbain's Horseman,* free indirect discourse, "direct discourse shorn of its conventional orthographic cues, or first-person interior monologue" (Rimmon Kennan, 113) intensifies the narrative's satire. For example, the narrator refers to the character Doug Fraser as "one of Canada's most uncompromising playwrights," but the sarcastic description is inflected with Jake Hersh's perspective on Doug, an author of banal melodramas about business tycoons who only discover the importance of family when suddenly confronted with the imminent prospect of a premature death. In *Joshua Then and Now* free indirect discourse also renders Joshua's cynical attitude towards a segment on American cultural domination presented by CBC-TV's weekly public affairs program:

> Probing cameras caught out of corner drugstores which displayed the latest Harold Robbins but *no Canadian poets* on their paperback racks; they zoomed in on schoolchildren, *our kids*, who knew who the Fonz was but had never heard of Mackenzie King ... And now [the journalist], fulminating

on camera, revealed that innocent Canadian children were being taught geography from a text that *included a photograph of an American rather than a home-bred dinosaur.* This was more than loose talk, it could be backed up by hard fact. [He] held up the picture for everybody to see. Sneaky imperialist eyes, shrewd Yankee mouth. (Richler 2001, 193)

Although the above passage is voiced by the narrator, it is focalized by Joshua (see Genette on narrative voice distinctions) and reveals his humorous but embittered reaction to such a blatant display of Canadian insecurity. In this case, free indirect speech accomplishes one of the goals delineated by Shlomith Rimmon-Kenan: "the tinting of the narrator's speech with the character's language or mode of experience ... promot[ing] an empathetic identification on the part of the reader" (117). As a result, the satiric element is strengthened and Joshua Shapiro's perspective is given added validation. Thus, a perspective that rehearses Richler's journalistic writings addressing Canadian paranoia vis-à-vis the United States, and that presages his 1988 endorsement of the Free Trade Agreement between Canada and the US, is voiced with polyphonic authority. A viewpoint that was seen by most artists and writers as socio-economic capitulation to American domination (Granatstein and Hillmer, 218) is granted substantial narrative space, expressed without apology or qualification.

In a later passage, Joshua, as a Canadian, feels a "yearning for an inheritance, any inheritance; weightier than the construction of a transcontinental railway, a reputation for honest trading, good skiing conditions" (Richler 2001, 211). His need to have Canada, a country he can neither praise nor relinquish, provide him with a meaningful heritage is validated by the collaborative tone of the multiple narrative voices.

Barney Panofsky's views on Canada and its self-image as a caring, socially concerned but overlooked nation, in contrast, emerge from an entirely different narrative strategy. First, *Barney's Version* is a far more direct narrative than any of Richler's other novels – not a blend of the narrative voice and third person centre of consciousness but mainly straightforward first-person storytelling. It is a narrative form that tends to create reader identification with the speaker and sympathy with his perspective. Moreover, Barney is self-deprecating in a way that is endearing, heightening readers' compassion for him as a flawed but engaging individual and underdog Canadian. Accordingly, Barney's views, even when petty and bitter, seem somewhat valid. A reference to a new book by his nemesis, Terry McIver, illustrates this point. In mentioning the new release, Barney ridicules the publisher, "The Group (sorry, the group)," because of its fashionable policies and Canadian prejudice: "a government-subsidized small press, rooted in Toronto, that also publishes a monthly journal, *the good earth*, printed on recycled paper, you bet your life" (Richler 1998a, 2). The insinuation is that Canadians' excessive social awareness and progressiveness, symbolized, in this case, by the conspicuous use of lower-case letters in titles and allusion to environmental measures, are just another form of pretension. And, because Barney controls the description and repeatedly prejudices the reader against McIver, the comment is amusing and persuasive.

The irony of such attitudes is exposed later in the novel. Though he is cynical about the Canadian propensity to cower in the shadow of its next-door superpower, Barney manages to earn a fortune exploiting the very insecurity he despises. He produces Canadian-content films and television programs, heavily supported by government subsidies. Confessing that he harbours little sympathy for Canadian chauvinism, he explains how he could still "rumba as a later-day patriot":

> Whenever a government minister, a free-marketeer responding to American pressure, threatened to dump the law that insisted on (and bankrolled to a yummy degree) so much Canadian-manufactured pollution on our airwaves, I did a quick change in the hypocrite's phone booth, slipping into my Captain Canada mode, and appeared before the committee. "We are defining Canada to Canadians," I told them. "We are this country's memory, its soul, its hypostasis, the last defense against our being overwhelmed by the egregious cultural imperialists to the south of us." (6)

In a later episode, Barney's tirade on the political turbulence in the province of Quebec is a more direct critique of Canada:

> The truth is Canada is a cloud-cuckooland, an insufferably rich country governed by idiots, its self-made problems offering comic relief to the ills of the real world out there, where famine and racial strife and vandals in office are the unhappy rule. (329–30)

Though Barney is an impassioned raconteur, and his first-person narrative commandeers the reader's sympathies, he is also an unreliable narrator, which problematizes his account of reality. "The main sources of unreliability are the narrator's limited knowledge, his personal involvement, and his problematic values scheme" (Rimmon Kennan, 103). From the publication of *St Urbain's Horseman* onward, Richler toyed with narrative unreliability. By offering a multitude of authoritative perspectives through both direct and indirect characterization (31) and shifting to free indirect discourse, Richler created narrative uncertainty in many of these works that compelled the reader to constantly evaluate the locus of narrative reliability. However, in Barney's case, all three factors of narrative unreliability are constantly at play. There is no question that he is personally over-invested in his narrative and that his values, while frequently inspired by no-nonsense realism and insight, are often anachronistic and cynical to the point of malicious excess. Moreover, Barney's knowledge is also a weak link in his reliability. As he relates his story, he admits that he is steadily succumbing to dementia. Mainly, this admission intimates that any number of Barney's observations and recollections could be faulty. At times, Barney is aware of his lapses in memory. In more poignant, sorrowful moments though, it is only the reader who is in a position to adjudge his coherence. Jason Blake argues that "Barney Panofsky is unreliable both as a narrator and as a person. With him narrative authority and credibility are thrown out the window" (72). However, this seems to be an overstatement. Texts, such as *Barney's Version*, often make "it difficult to decide whether the narrator is reliable or unreliable, and if unreliable – to what extent." Such cases might be categorized as "ambiguous narratives ... putting the reader in a position of constant oscillation between mutually exclusive alternatives" (Rimmon-Kenan, 106). Barney's story bears the hallmarks of narrative unreliability, but, at the core, the reader recognizes that there is a certain sanity and clarity to his testimony. Bearing in mind all of these factors regarding narrative reliability, it is unclear whether Barney's scorn expresses his true feelings or if Canada is indeed deserving of his wrath. The very fact that the novel begins with his assertion that he is writing "the true story" of his life, in contrast to the account that is recorded in the autobiography of his archenemy Terry McIver (1998a, 3), insinuates that the story is, from the start, part of the struggle between alternative narratives. Accordingly, his observations on Canada's foibles are suspect, making it hard to ascertain whether his ranting against both the people he loves and abhors, as well as the social and political issues that grieve him, communicates his genuine sentiments, reveals the terror and helplessness that accompany the progress of his condition, or is a more direct result of advanced dementia. Such uncertainties, which intensify gradually throughout the novel, counterbalance Barney's overall cynicism, creating the impression that the issues with which he is preoccupied, Canada among them, are complex, multifaceted, and close to his heart.

Further undermining Barney's reliability are the footnote corrections added, as it were, post factum to his memoir by his son Michael Panofsky. Even though most of them are tedious notations – corrections of insignificant dates by a few days, car models, airport references, movie details, and hockey game statistics that have no bearing on the story, they cast further doubt on Barney's account of past events. But, the way in which this metafictive element destabilizes Barney's account of events is more self-reflexive, connected to the process of writing and reading literature. Because Michael's emendations are so persnickety, they also seem to be a criticism of readers who expect novelists to function as historians, cartographers, and statisticians rather than as artists and storytellers.[9] In writing about John Cheever, Richler noted his distaste for critics who feel compelled to respond to literature with "picky footnotes," correcting specific dates and other details in order to make a work more historically faithful (1990b, 157–8).

Thus, Barney's memoir and its abundant ire have to be read with circumspection. Its complexity in terms of narrative authority seems to be a testimony to the fact that, despite his disdain for "special pleading," he understands that Canada has to a certain degree been overlooked. Margaret Atwood has called *Solomon Gursky Was Here* Richler's most Canadian novel (2004, 37). Yet its double-edged view of Canada is even more obvious in *Barney's Version*, Richler's last and most reflective novel, and the only one narrated in the first person. This novel is written with a pervasive focus on Canada and probes the distinctness of a nation that is often accused of being unimpressively generic. The complexity, irony, and contradictions inherent in Barney's views and recollections imbue the story with ambiguity, and also imply that Canada, despite its shortcomings, may be more historically, culturally, and socially substantial than Barney admits, its problems real if not centre-stage in the international arena. This perception of Canada reflects Richler's own evolving views. Indeed, towards the end of his career, and especially in the wake of his high-profile commentaries on Quebec and Canadian politics, he had begun to praise not only

Canadian writers but Canadians for their savvy "cynicism" (qtd in Posner, 251). Two years prior to his death in 2001 he delivered an address at the University of Waterloo, where he admitted that Canada was no longer barren of culture; it was now "a far more sophisticated country than the one [he] tried to put behind [him] in 1950." Canadians were "the inheritors of two of the western world's seminal cultures, the English and the French, and a good deal more besides … in spite of our increasingly tiresome family quarrel," he went on to say, "ours is a country where the civilities are still observed for the most part" (Richler 1999). So, while Richler's career-long focus on Canada may seem to be a paradoxically intense scrutiny of a would-be unworthy subject, *Barney's Version* tends to represent Canada as a society and culture with sufficient depth to serve as fecund material for the novelist's imagination and a worthy concern for his protagonists.

Though Richler's embattled position vis-à-vis Canada was already known by the mid-1950s, it was only in 1991, with the publication of "Inside/Outside" (*New Yorker*), that his reputation fully developed as that of Quebec's most notorious enfant terrible. The article seemed to catapult him into the political fracas surrounding the language crisis and the separatism conflict that has always threatened Canadian unity. With its publication, Richler was "joining the battle for Canada, more precisely, Quebec" (Vassanji, 208). In the essay, Richler traces the evolution of Quebec's language laws from the 1970s onward, and the way in which the province's French-speaking leadership had turned the preservation of Quebec language and culture into a clash of civilizations. Quebec's francophones were outraged by the article (Gilbert, 492; Posner, 284),[10] insisting that Richler had unfeelingly disparaged his home province in front of the world, meaning the United States (Kramer 2008, 322).

In fact, the article was not Richler's first commentary on Quebec, the French language, and the predicament of the local Anglos. In a mid-1980s essay entitled "Language (and Other) Problems," he critiqued French chauvinism and the mounting conflict, increasingly focused on language, between the local French and Anglo communities. It is a relatively humorous piece that details the political dealings that were alienating the local Anglos but also creating a surreal reality in Quebec. As an example of this, Richler recalled how the Quebec government House leader Claude Charron's shoplifting was excused by Quebec's

French pundits because he had stolen from Eaton's department store, "a notorious Anglophone institution, its head office in Toronto" (1984, 224): the fight for French was becoming an Orwellian plunge into moral absurdity. Underscoring the zealousness of Quebec's language officials, Richler describes the threats of a thousand-dollar fine against a seditious proprietor of a jewellery shop who had violated Quebec's French-only rules for outdoor signs with a poster that read "Merry Christmas" (229).

Prior to the publication of these articles, Richler had already referenced Quebec's language and culture conflict in his fiction. While earlier works, notably *Duddy Kravitz* and *St Urbain's Horseman*, contain representations, however limited, of French Canada – *Duddy Kravitz*, in particular, features Yvette, Duddy's love interest, and the reality of Québécois anti-Semitism – *Joshua Then and Now* is the first of Richler's novels that addresses Quebec's political crisis. In this book, the Montreal where Joshua was raised has become a place where French nationalist Parti Québécois politicians can kill homeless people in traffic accidents and escape with impunity. It is a city in the process of losing large numbers of its English-speaking population because of zealous language policies, one of which, for example, required a bar with the iconic name, the King's Arms, to reinvent itself as the foolish-sounding "Armes du Roi" (74–5). In *Solomon Gursky Was Here*, published two years before the appearance of the *New Yorker* article, an even gloomier view of Montreal is presented. At a Westmount party attended by Anglo Montreal's highest echelons, one guest laments the city's demise, the fact that unofficial separatism is in place and that Toronto has become Canada's reigning metropolis:

Montreal Piss Quick is not where it happens anymore. It's all Toronto now, perfectly awful Turrono. Outright separatism doesn't matter. What we're going to get is *de facto* separation. We're going to be Boston in the new order of things. Or maybe even Milwaukee.[11] (Richler 1990b, 224)

Still, it is through the first-person narration in *Barney's Version* that Quebec's culture and language tensions are most prominently evoked. In the first chapter, Barney ridicules Montreal's emergency-service hotline as an example of the province's anti-English discrimination: "press 17 for service in the language of *les maudits anglais*," he opines, "or number 12 for service *en francais*, the glorious language of our oppressed collectivity" (Richler 1998a, 11). Later bemoaning

Quebec's language laws, he mourns the change of all English topo-nyms. As an example, he recalls how "Lake Amherst was renamed Lac Marquette in the seventies by the Commission de toponymie, which is in charge of cleansing *la belle province* of the conqueror's place names" (92). More seriously, he depicts a provincial judge as a typical "*québécois de vieille souche*," meaning, in Barney's personal lexicon, that he had spent his youth as a fascist from a privileged background, was devoted to the racist daily *Le Devoir*, and revered the well-known anti-Semite Abbé Lionel-Adolphe Groulx's *L'Action*. He had been a member of the Ligue pour la défense du Canada, which vowed to defend Canada to the death, but would not support Canada's British-aligned adventure in the Second World War. Even worse, the judge, Barney further speculates, "had been among that merry throng that had marched down the Main in 1942, smashing plate-glass windows in Jewish shops and chanting, 'Kill them! Kill them!'" (314).

The protagonists' sarcastic observations of Quebec seem to express their nostalgia for the Montreal of their memories, a general resistance to change, and some more practical concerns about the French separatist movement and its language policies. The hero figures pay no attention to Quebec's language struggles and politics, suggesting that they are insignificant, or at least a very local problem that excessively troubles the protagonists. However, in a chapter that is atypical in Richler's fiction, Quebec's fate is lamented by Michael Panofsky in his afterword to his father Barney's memoir. The tone is earnestly despondent about the present state of affairs and expressive of a heartfelt longing for Montreal's former glory:

All my recent trips to Montreal have been depressing. This, not only because of our father's condition, but also in recognition of what has become of the city I grew up in. When I got out the phone book, hoping to get in touch with old friends who had been to McGill with me, I discovered that all but two or three had moved to Toronto, Vancouver, or New York, rather than endure the burgeoning tribalism. Of course, looked at from abroad, what was happening in Quebec seemed risible. There are actually grown men out here, officers of the Commission de protection de la langue française, who go out with tape measures every day to ensure that the English-language lettering on outdoor commercials signs is half the size of, and in no brighter color than, the French. (352)

Most of Michael's notations throughout the autobiography debunk Barney's impassioned views and opinions, and present the people and circumstances in his father's life with more realism, if less colour and verve. Michael notes that Barney had "two cherished beliefs: Life was absurd, and nobody ever truly understood anybody else. Not a comforting philosophy, and one I certainly don't subscribe to" (354). However, it is significant that, despite his tendency to correct his father's errors and question his recollections, he reaffirms Barney's pain regarding the fate of Montreal. Rather than the hero figures' values scheme reinforcing the protagonists' views, it is the sober intelligence of Michael, a character-type who is outside the usual circle of authoritative voices in Richler's novels, that lends credence to the protagonist's opinion. The break in pattern suggests that, in this novel, the protagonist/hero figure union is not as secure as it is in early works and that there are worthwhile values outside of the hero figure's (i.e., Boogie Moscovitch's) priorities. Narratively, this is a subtle but complex manoeuvre wherein the authoritative perspectives in the novel, cultivated through "indirect" layers of characterization, shift, and characters whose ideals and values seemed unacceptable are suddenly invested with unexpected narrative clout.

Hinting at another refiguring of moral values in the novel is the positive characterization of several French Canadians, who are seen from Barney's vantage point as fully realized, sympathetic individuals. Most notably, Solange Renault, a Québécoise actress employed for twenty years by Barney's company, Totally Unnecessary Productions Ltd is wise and level-headed. She is a foil to the one-dimensional and pitiful Yvette in *The Apprenticeship of Duddy Kravitz*. Barney boasts that she is "the most admirable of women" (103) even though she is a proud nationalist who voices intelligent arguments for Quebec's separation. She is also his most rational and devoted friend. Barney puts his successful television series in jeopardy by retaining Solange as a lead character even though she is too old for her part. In Richler's novels, sentimental patronage is usually scorned, but in this instance Barney's relationship with Solange is an important counterweight to Anglo Montrealers' fractious relationship to French Quebec. With Solange, generous allowances are permissible since she emerges as deserving of uncommon kindness.

The portrayal of another Québécois character, Serge Lacroix, Totally Unnecessary Productions' chief director, likewise undermines the perception of Barney as a sophomoric racist. After Serge is violently attacked one night while cruising for a tryst in a park in Montreal's French section, Barney bails him out of jail and arranges for his medical attention. Here, a gay scenario is not, as in previous Richler novels, a comical digression but proof that Barney is capable of genuine compassion. Despite his anti-French bluster, he is able to see the conflict as a political crisis rather than as a personal battle.

Again, as with other Canadian matters, the complexity of Quebec's inter-ethnic struggles is not diminished because the hero figure – in this case Boogie (an American) – is indifferent to them. Instead, the issue is central, evident in the protagonist's distress about how Quebec's culture and language battles affect his important relationships with French Canadians, especially a self-sufficient woman and gay man.

Considering Richler's on-record views in *Oh Canada! Oh Quebec!*, a follow-up book to the 1991 *New Yorker* article, it is not surprising to discover an account of the following turn:

> Today there are probably more French Canadians and Jews
> rooted in the mansions of Upper Westmount than there are Scots
> Presbyterian bankers, which suits me just fine, incidentally ...
> And if the banker is still being chauffeur-driven each morning,
> it is surely to his French lessons and only later to his office on
> the street that has long since been born again as rue Saint-
> Jacques ... Something else. That legendary bastion of WASP
> privilege, the Ritz-Carlton Hotel, is now managed by French
> Canadians, and any day of the week you will hear more French
> than English being spoken in the bar, which is as it should be.
> (1992, 71–2)

David Brauner argues that, from an early point in his career, Richler had "recognized, and even identified with, many of the grievances of Francophone Quebecers" (77). He was disturbed by the "institutionalized racism of the WASP establishment" (77) and felt that French Canadians and Jews had suffered from the same discriminatory attitudes of Quebec's Protestant anglophones. Thus, the position held in the last years of Richler's literary career may have been not so much a change of attitude as an elaboration of ideas that had long been part of his consciousness.

– * –

In part, Richler was sidelined in Canada because of his long-running polemic opposing Quebec's language laws and separatist politics. A sign of his contentious position within Quebec was the fact that it took the Montreal municipality almost ten years following his death to finalize a tribute to him, eventually settling on the dedication of a dilapidated gazebo – a project slated to take two years, which ran three years beyond schedule and was finally unveiled in 2016 (Magder). *National Post* writer Barbara Kay likened the move to potentially naming "the change house at an outdoor skating rink after Margaret Atwood, a pellet dispenser at the zoo after Yann Martel, or a maintenance shed after Margaret Laurence." She admitted that Richler may have been deserving of the antipathy he provoked among Quebec's francophones, most notably because of, "Oh Canada! Oh Quebec!" Still, she argued that the gazebo was more of an insult than a tribute: "Richler put Montreal on the map. It doesn't matter whether you liked him or hated him; he was one of us and he achieved great things."

However, in "Is Richler Canadian Content?," Melina Baum Singer argues that Richler fell into critical disfavour because of factors that go beyond his prickly attitudes towards Canada, in general, and Quebec, in particular. She offers an altogether different interpretation of the conditions that have seemingly shunted Richler to the margins of Canadian literature. To begin with, she outlines the ideological assumptions, once commonplace in the Canadian literary tradition, that pit Canadian and Jewish as two opposing identities. As examples, she notes that, at the Richler Challenge Conference at McGill University in 2004, and in Coral Ann Howell's introduction to *Where Are the Voices Coming From: Canadian Culture and the Legacies of History* (2004), the question of Richler's "Canadianness" was asked while its underlying logic, which tacitly assumes a divide between Canadian and Jewish, was ignored. Baum Singer then goes on to attribute this oversight to foundational notions of Canadian identity. Historically, the ethos was that "you are either white and a Canadian or non-white and an outsider" (20). Jews were in the latter category. Richler was a landmark Canadian writer in this regard because his novels "animate[d] a trajectory that move[d] the Canadian canon from depictions of British-inflected cultural landscapes to include other cultures" (18). Still, his works expressed "a sense of otherness" that magnified "the ways in which 'white' Canada has *overdetermined* [his] identity as non-Canadian in racialized ways" (19). So, to a certain extent, Canadian critics have been hesitant to recognize Richler foremost as a Canadian novelist because the Jewish fibre of his novels seemed to place him on the margins of the Canadian literary establishment.

More recently, there has been a "whitening" of Canadian Jews (as well as Jews in the US) as a result of the surge in non-white immigration to Canada since the second half of the twentieth century. "Jews can now drop their 'colour' and become white, but only because there are new minority groups who are compelled to take up the lower social positions, once held by the likes of Duddy's father [in the *Apprenticeship of Duddy Kravitz*], who works as a taxi-driver and small-time pimp" (20). This shift coincides, Baum Singer explains, with the divide between contemporary globalization studies, a "white" area of study and diaspora studies, a discipline that focuses on "non-whites." Today, it is generally thought that Jews have "transcended the type of racialized otherness" that is found in Richler's texts (22). Despite their historical status as outsiders, they are considered part of the "white" majority within globalization studies, a field that examines "assumptions relating to privilege, mobility, and most significantly 'whiteness'" (21). This categorization is also founded on the idea that Jews are now "white" because the social, economic, and cultural barriers that blocked their upward mobility have been eradicated. It is a perspective that threatens to delegitimize Richler's novels, making them "a relic from the past, one whose depictions of injustices towards Jews are now outdated, because the injustices are presumed no longer to occur" (22). Accordingly, Richler's works can be read as too Jewish to be part of the "white" Canadian mainstream, or as anachronistic for insisting upon "otherness" at a time when Jews have theoretically been absorbed into the dominant, "white" ethnic, sociocultural strata.

Ironically, the Jewish Canadian hybridity of Richler's fiction might fit squarely within the rubric of Canadian identity as it is conceived by Kroetsch and Hutcheon. After all, it is a Canadian identity that enacts diversity and resists the plausibility of a national metanarrative (Carter, 10). If, as Hutcheon claims, the multiracial and multiethnic nature of Canada is made real to Canadians – is written into their consciousness of what it means to be Canadian – by the country's writers (Hutcheon and Richmond, 5), then Richler's work is indeed quintessentially Canadian. Her definition of Canadian identity makes space for the Jewish and "little neighbourhood" constituents of Richler's writing. Furthermore, in Hutcheon's thinking, Canadian Jews, as both "other" and participants in white privilege, have the kind of "split/splintered identity" that is typically Canadian. She sees this quality not as a paradox or infirmity but as a virtue (qtd in Carter, 10).

Setting aside the question of Richler's Canadian identity, what is unarguable is that Richler never ignored Canada in his fiction. Certainly, he appropriated many of the sacred cows of Canadian culture and history, supplanting them with comical and often unflattering representations of the country, its people, art, and media. He also satirized progressive attitudes towards Canada's Aboriginal peoples in a broadly condescending manner and presented Quebec without much recourse to any politically correct sympathies. However, this jaded view was punctuated by glimpses of Canada's many compensating features, a great number reinforced by his non-fiction. Richler's cynicism, regardless of the protestations of Mowatt and others, is not uniform. Repeatedly, Richler signals to readers his awareness of the country's redemptive qualities. Overall, Canada may only figure in Richler's opus as part of the protagonists' values, rendering them decidedly unheroic, but it still has its considerable merits, especially in his mature works.

6

Culture and Moral Values

Mordecai Richler often claimed that his central concerns as a novelist were "with values, and with honour" (qtd in Cameron, 124). A parallel preoccupation, however, pervades his work: an axiological concern with the relationship between culture – specifically literature, art, and aesthetic sensibilities – and moral values, or the necessary tenets of a moral life. In general, culture and values are not explicitly intertwined in his fiction, yet there is a connection, albeit an uneasy one, between the novels' moral positions and aesthetic claims. With the exception of the character of Boogie Moscovitch in *Barney's Version*, the novels' hero figures embody this connection, suggesting that, in Richler's cosmology, culture and moral values are closely related. This conceptual linkage, however, is thrown into question by Boogie, who is an aberration and proves that aesthetic savoir faire and artistic talent do not preclude moral sloth.

Richler wrote about his effort to infuse his novels with a moral agenda – a search for ethical beliefs, or what he himself called "values" and the need for standards of honour and dignity in an age lacking consensual norms or moral authority. While most of Richler's contemporaries rarely claimed this as one of their literary objectives, the topic of ethical theorizing in literature was crucial to George Orwell, and Richler mapped his own novelistic principles in the 1973 essay "Why I Write," borrowing Orwell's 1946 article by the same title as the blueprint for his agenda. In his article, Richler borrows directly from Orwell's claim that among his motivations are

aesthetic enthusiasm ... Perception of beauty in the external world, or on the other hand, in words and their right arrangement ... Political purpose – using the word "political" in the widest possible sense. Desire to push the world in a certain direction, to alter other people's idea of the kind of society that they should strive after. (Orwell, qtd in Richler 1973b, 10)

In a 1973 interview with Donald Cameron, Richler seemed to thumb his nose at hardline "art-for-art's-sake" crusaders when he insisted that, as a novelist, he was very much a moralist, deeply engaged with values (Cameron, 124).

At the outset of his career, Richler wrestled less with axiology and primarily explored the uninitiated naif's encounter with "beauty." Though André Bennet, the protagonist of Richler's earliest novel, *The Acrobats*, is a painter, it is Noah Adler, the hero of his second novel, *Son of a Smaller Hero* (an inchoate *Künstlerroman*), who first grapples meaningfully with art and beauty. Critics have paid little heed to the concern with aesthetic values in Richler's work, but in the early 1970s David Sheps identified it as one of Richler's recurring themes. Sheps argued that Richler's protagonists are often motivated by "the idea of the expression of sensibility itself" (1971, xix) and that some characters even aspire to achieve a "pure, exquisite sensibility; a form of ecstasy" (xx).[1] Almost certainly Sheps would have had Noah Adler in mind with regard to the sensibilities of typical Richlerian characters in the throes of aesthetic quests. As a young man Noah is unaware of intellectual traditions that attempt to apprehend the sublime, but his encounters outside the Jewish ghetto of his childhood expose him to art that provokes a visceral reaction – if not "ecstasy," something akin to the renowned "shiver down the spine ... a constriction of the throat and a precipitation of water to the eyes" that A.E. Housman describes as one's involuntary response to great poetry (33). After attending his first concert, a performance of Vivaldi's *The Four Seasons*, Noah is so overcome by the music that he feels "something like pain" (Richler 1989b, 69): "He had not suspected that men were capable of such beauty" (59). In this case, Noah's observation reads like sophomoric cant, but the passage does demonstrate Richler's early attempt to acknowledge the Longinian impulse and the thrill of the sublime.

Richler's aesthetic sensibility, in addition to his Orwell-inspired poetics – "aesthetic enthusiasm ... the perception of beauty in the external world" and "words and their right arrangement" – also included a poetics of extremes, grounded in high and low culture indiscriminately. He also valued a writerly commitment to subvert what is commonplace in human experience and revel in what is exceptional, rare, or liminal. It is a kind of artistic mandate that he admired in Saul Bellow:

> Bellow, a big cultural fisherman, casts his line both high and low, covering all the water, reeling in not only Tolstoy and Mozart, but also Chicago's Yellow Kid Weil, Bathhouse John Coughlin, and Facts-and-Figures Taylor. Far from regarding the rest of us as a junkyard where he forages for parts, he has, to my mind, always approached his world with morally informed appetite, and a sense of irony, providing in abundance the excitement that counts, and celebrating what is enduringly beautiful in the human spirit. (Richler 1998b, 95)

In his own work, this reverence for the heights and depths of cultural referentiality is evident. Krysztof Majer (2008) recognizes "artistic integrity" as one of the central themes of *St Urbain's Horseman* and notes the protagonist Jake Hersh's repeated references to Auden ("Not all the candidates pass," for instance) as evidence of the novel's preoccupation with artistic discernment (66). Indeed, *St Urbain's Horseman* is Richler's first novel to address the problem of mediocrity, especially commercial mediocrity, in culture as a moral infraction. Jake is a film and television producer, but he dislikes most of his own projects and loathes the maudlin commercialism of the film and television industry:

> If, on rare occasions, he eked some satisfaction out of his work, he was, for the most part, laden with contempt for his peers, too many of whom, he felt, presented with a script, knew instinctively what would play well, and that's all. Almost everybody in television was a lightweight ... a cliché monger. (Richler 1991b, 229)

Affirming Jake's middling artistic talent are the observations of Duddy Kravitz and Nancy Hersh, Jake's wife (Majer 2019). Duddy, deflating any pretentions his friend may entertain regarding inspired creativity, labels Jake a "crap artist" (455). Nancy does not confront Jake, but observes that Jake's "overweening ambition," "self-hatred and debilitating doubts" as well as his fears of being an impostor "would only have been acceptable ... had Jake been blessed with a talent of the first order, but, she sadly allowed, this was not the case" (228–30). He is, nevertheless, charmed by the entertainment industry's culture of caricature and loves its downtrodden underdogs:

> The only companions he sought out on any production, those he fooled and played poker with, were the cameramen, the grips, the stagehands, and that company of failed actors, the bit players of whom no wrong could be uttered, who were jokingly referred to as Jacob Hersh's Continuing Rep. Largely drunks, has beens, never beens, itinerant wrestlers, wretched drag queens, superannuated variety artists, decrepit Yiddish actors, befuddled old prized fighters, and more than one junkie. (230)

In *Solomon Gursky Was Here*, it is Sam Burns, an old friend of Moses Berger, who is troubled by the "philistinism" of popular culture and his own career as a high-profile television news anchor. Sam, along with all of Moses's childhood friends, considers Moses a genuine intellectual. Though he is a failure, a wasted *wunderkind*, they have faith in his scholarly and aesthetic intelligence. When Moses comes for a visit, Sam carefully scans his library "to make sure there [are] no compromising best-sellers on the shelves" (Richler 1990b, 232). He is uneasy in acknowledging that he has succumbed to middlebrow tastes. After dining with Moses, he is overcome by self-pity. He

> couldn't sleep. He was thirsty. He was dizzy. His heart was hammering. His stomach was rumbling. "They can take everything. The works. I would have settled for writing 'The Dead.' Never mind *War and Peace* or *Karamazov*. Am I greedy? Certainly not. Just 'The Dead' by Samuel Burns né Birenbaum." (232)

Sam's distress is also caused by the feeling that he has "sold out," forsaken his ethical commitment to the pursuit of art in favour of the glamour and handsome remuneration of news-broadcasting celebrity. The tension between inspired art and commercial writing is a recurrent theme in *Solomon Gursky*. Moses Berger holds his father, L.B., in contempt for agreeing to pen a poem for *Jewish Outlook* to mark the anniversary of liquor magnate Bernard Gursky and his wife Libby. He is further appalled that his father has preferred the post of the Gurskys' well-compensated in-house scribe over the life of a soul-bearing, socially conscious poet. "A committed socialist himself now, he lashed out at his father for having betrayed his old adoring comrades to become an apologist for the Gurskys, one of Mr. Bernard's lapdogs" (23).

Mediocrity is again pilloried in *Solomon Gursky* when Moses randomly picks up a book, *The Unquiet Grave* by Palinurus (a pseudonym for the highly regarded English literary critic Cyril Connolly), and turns to the beginning: "The more books we read, the sooner we perceive that the true function of a writer is to produce a masterpiece" (140). Moses, aggrieved by Connolly's pronouncement, especially in light of his own stunted career as a writer, throws the book across the room. This episode, which has no special function in the plot, can be read as a signal of meta-literary reflection. Excellence is the only goal of art, and writing that is less than masterful is not only inadequate but necessarily mediocre, even unethical. Richler went on record paraphrasing this idea: "there's nothing as boring as a seriously-meant novel which is bad" (qtd in Gibson, 279). Still, left unsaid is what constitutes the requisite standards of good taste and aesthetic achievement. As is the case with much of Richler's satire and social criticism, the positive value is left vague. It is also unclear whether Richler's readers are being pigeon-holed as Philistines or ranked among Auden's passing "candidates."

In *Barney's Version*, authentic art, according to Barney Panofsky, is only born of indisputable genius or outrageous burlesque. Everything in between is banal. This idea, gleaned from the ramblings of Boogie Moscovitch when he and Barney are young bohemians in Paris, explains why Barney feels that his career as a producer is an ethical compromise. He is able to reluctantly justify his popular, kitschy entertainment programming but despairs of his more serious work. He can endure his company's (Totally Unnecessary Productions) puerile television series about Royal Canadian Mounted Police (RCMP) but recoils from its more middlebrow content, such as earnest but uninspired documentaries about Canada's men of letters. He owes these attitudes to Boogie's principles, especially as they provide him with an organizing code that, however disjointed, makes the world less incomprehensible:

Anybody who wrote an article for *Reader's Digest*, or committed a best-seller, or acquired a Ph.D. was beyond the pale. But churning out a pornographic novel for Girodias was ring-a-ding. Similarly, writing for the movies was contemptible, unless it was a Tarzan flick, which would be a real hoot. "McIver of the RCMP" was strictly kosher but financing a serious documentary about Leacock would be *infra dignitatem*. (Richler 1998a, 76)

According to Richler's novels' cultural platforms, in addition to mediocrity, abstract art, and experimental art, "the artist as media darling" and "the academy" are also dubious cultural phenomena. In *The Apprenticeship of Duddy Kravitz*, the eponymous hero hires Peter John Friar, an alcoholic director with questionable credentials, to produce a film commemorating Bernie Cohen's bar mitzvah. It is a narrative element that provides Richler with an opportunity to show-case his satiric flair. When Duddy views it for the first time, he "is sick to his stomach" (Richler 1995, 170). However, the Cohens, their friends, and the rabbi of their synagogue, afraid of seeming reactionary, hail the film – a spoof of experimental cinema – as a masterpiece, their money well spent. They applaud Friar's amateurish attempt at mod-ernism with its mix of clichéd bar mitzvah images, advertisements for Maidenform bras, blood-covered windows, pretentious narration, and soundtrack, which includes, "Pomp and Circumstance," "Auld Lang Syne" and the sporadic beat of tom-toms (177).

Richler seems to take equal delight in casting doubt on the merits of abstract art, specifically, Jackson Pollock's experimental work. In *Solomon Gursky* a painting by Pollock hangs in the office of Bernard Gursky, "one of his daughter's *farshtunkeneh* acquisitions" (Richler 1990b, 87). As Bernard is undeniably a vulgarian, his assessment of the painting, which he likens to "curdled vomit," is not especially reliable. However, the painting is also mocked by Moses Berger, who the reader is encouraged to trust. When Bernard tells him that the painting is hanging upside down, Moses asks, "How can you tell for sure?" (87–9). The question is ironic. It belittles Bernard's ignorance but also hints that experimental art may be a con.

In the same vein, Barney Panofsky is amazed that the canvasses of his old friend Leo Bishinsky – smudged with random paint stains and embedded pieces of garbage and bodily debris – are on display at the Tate, Guggenheim, and other museums. He labels these paintings "atrocities" in much the same way as he accuses pop fiction writers of engaging in criminal acts and "committing best sellers." These works are not merely a matter of bad taste: they are moral trans-gressions, violations of the sanctity of culture. Barney recalls how Leo would create his paintings by soaking a mop in buckets of paint, "stand back ten feet, and let fly" (Richler 1998a, 7), even urging Barney to hurl colour at one of his canvasses. Barney believes that Leo's canvasses are meaningless and random. His criticism echoes the plaints of art critics such as Bruno Alfieri (see Karmel, 68–9) and the *New Yorker*'s Robert Coates (58–9) who famously panned Jackson Pollock's poured paintings in a similar fashion, calling them chaotic, infantile, and void of meaning. Though Pollock became known as one of the foremost American artists, detractors continually insisted that his work was haphazard,[2] and the novel insinuates that this may be the case with Leo.[3]

The description of the gallery owned by Barney's son Michael Panofsky is also an outright send-up of the shock-value element in modern art. Barney notes that the gallery "has proven itself, as it were, having twice been charged with obscenity" (18), as if provocation is the mark of a gallery's mettle.

Richler's own on-record reaction to abstract and experimental artistic forms echoed the views found in his fiction. He disliked the modernist tendency to appropriate art for the purpose of challenging conventional morality or redefining creativity. He expresses this view in "London Then and Now," where he slanders London's cultural élite as "vulgarians" (Richler 1998b, 181). He is troubled by the adulation for installation exhibits, such as "Linda Moulton Howe's photography of 'cattle mutilations thought to be carried out by aliens,'" or Ron Haselden's work at the Museum of Installations – a dark room decorated by a white sheet while a soundtrack plays noises of the building itself, which are meant to represent the hum of daily life (182). Even more irksome to Richler were reconceptualized productions of Shakespeare's plays at Stratford-on-Avon where one was likely to come upon an innovative staging of *Julius Caesar* set in "Berlin, circa 1938," or a Kremlin-based version of *Hamlet* (182).

Another target of Richler's satire is the writer as a pop-culture celebrity. After becoming a Canadian cultural icon with his facetiously primitive poetry, Atuk, the eponymous protagonists of *The Incomparable Atuk*, translates his fame into a career. His photo becomes ubiquitous in the local media. Toy companies want to produce dolls in his image. Strangers nationwide begin sending him gifts (Richler 1989a, 56). This kind of popularity is precisely what irks Richler about writers such as Norman Mailer. Richler was dismayed that Mailer had become "another wowser on the scene, a personality, rather than a working writer" (Richler 1968b, 103), and that some of his works were accepted by publishers not because they were good but because they were his. Even when the writer deserved recognition, Richler was repulsed by his embrace of the role of media sensation. "I deplore the writer as a personality," he proclaimed, "however large and undoubted the talent" (1973b, 9).

In *St Urbain's Horseman*, a rift develops between Jake Hersh and his long-time friend Luke Scott when the latter becomes a celebrity playwright. The tension between them seems to be fuelled by Jake's envy, but Luke's boasting of his Hollywood adventures is truly off-putting for Jake. After regaling him with stories of his exotic travels and the sexual escapades of movie moguls, Luke flippantly says: "Look here, baby. We're on the *Titanic*. It's going down ... Me, I've decided to travel first class" (Richler 1991b, 302). Envy aside, Jake finds Luke's artistic treachery insufferable, and the incident precipitates an estrangement between the two.

Equally libelled in Richler's essays and novels is the "academic" study of culture and literary works. In "Why I Write," he muses on his "road not taken," that of a literary scholar: "instead of having to bring home the meat, I would only be obliged to stamp it, rejecting this shoulder of beef as Hank James derivative, or that side of pork as sub-Jimmy Joyce" (Richler 1973b, 7–8). Less than a decade later, he reportedly disparaged his daughter Martha's studies at Harvard, believing that no university degree could equal the education of the autodidact living in penury in the capitals of Europe (Kramer 2008, 292).

The derision of academia in Richler's work dates back to his second novel, *Son of a Smaller Hero*. Not long after Noah Adler begins studying at Wellington College, he is mentored by Professor Theo Hall, an Oxford graduate who has forsaken a career at a prestigious American university to idealistically revamp the English department of Montreal's second-rate institution. Despite his credentials, however, Theo is a disappointment. His own wife recognizes that he is "a baffled man" and a "plodder" with "no insights" (Richler 1989b, 43). Street-wise but uneducated, Noah clearly has a better mind and is capable of more profound aesthetic insight. The novel suggests that classroom studies are no match for inborn intellectual powers and may even dim aesthetic and intellectual instincts.

In the early 1970s, Richler directly criticized English professors for their lack of critical inspiration, using their concern with the details of writers' lives as an example of petty, insignificant data gathering.

Lecturing to students at Carleton University in Ottawa in 1972, he expressed his impatience with the way in which the academic world is "too much concerned, sometimes even obsessed, with the writer's detritus. What I like to think of as the school of James Joyce's laundry list" (Richler 1975, 21). In *Joshua Then and Now*, the subplot involving Joshua's friend, the writer Sydney Murdoch, in which the two men fabricate correspondence to be auctioned off as erotic juvenilia, is a spoof on this phenomenon.

Also satirized in *Joshua Then and Now* are disillusioned scholars devoted to arcane research for the sake of job security and/or distasteful opportunists who bilk their institutions and exploit their academic credentials for lucre. An example of the former is Mickey Stein, a Harvard faculty member who lectures on "the nuclear family, male bonding, and cultural patterns among the Assyro-Babylonians in Persia during the Sassanian Dynasty" (Richler 2001, 358). Lamenting his chosen calling, Stein suggests that he would have been a more useful member of society if he had followed his father's career path as a milkman. He tells Joshua,

> you don't understand what publication means. I don't write
> for the masses. I compose a three-thousand-word argument for
> publication in a journal with a circulation of, say, fifteen undred.
> The editorial committee broods for six months before they accept
> my piece, and then we write to and fro for another six months,
> quarreling over commas. A year later my reflections on the
> eschatology of the heretical dharmas is published, I Xerox
> two thousand copies for other professors, the Ford Foundation
> gives me a grant, and I am able to take Sylvia to conferences
> in Tokyo, Stockholm, and Grenoble. (359)

An alternative academic "type" in the novel is the opportunist, Joshua's friend Benny Zucker, a dean at UCLA who brags of his ability to parlay his title and prestige into large honorariums:

> My services as an industrial consultant are fought over. I have
> an agent. And once a year he sends me down from the mountain
> with my tablets. To conventions for overachievers in Hawaii.
> Or orientation courses for top-level executives on an Arizona
> ranch … And wherever I go … I tell the movers and shakers that
> our research at UCLA, computer-programmed, tested in the

field, indicate that there is more stress among executives than bartenders and, furthermore, that there is a definite correlation between energy loss and age. And they shake their heads, delighted with me. (359)

Moreover, Richler's representation of academia touches on the issue of society's cultural impoverishment – especially as Richler uses Auden's phrase "tiefste Provinz" ("deepest Province," a place that has produced no cultural contribution of permanent value) to describe Canada (Greenstein, xi) – and the triumph of economic motives over cultural idealism. So, it is unsurprising that the hero figures and the protagonists who revere them are rarely products of the Canadian establishment or its universities. They, like Richler himself, are self-taught aesthetes, who seem to have cultivated their tastes and knowledge through osmosis and experience, and, even more important, as a result of their innate intellectual agility and discerning temperament.

Similarly, in one of his many anti-academia tantrums, Barney rates rank-and-file university students as unthinking conformists, remarking "that Vladimir Nabokov was right when he told his students at Cornell that D.Phil stood for 'Department of Philistines'" (Richler 1998a, 300). Indeed, Nabokov was repulsed by what he perceived as the vulgarity of sentimentality framed as high-minded conscientiousness (Richler 1998a, 110–12, 137), and Barney shares that view.

It is not, however, that literary biography is always scorned by Richler. When Solomon Gursky fantasizes about Diana McClure, he imagines her with a copy of Samuel Johnson's *Lives of the Poets* by her side. Writers' lives may be scrutinized, but such scrutiny has to be selective and relate intelligently to the writers' work. Ostensibly it must be distinct, for example, from the prying that is parodied in *Solomon Gursky* when an earnest biographer writes to Moses Berger to clarify persnickety details regarding L.B. Berger's life. The letter includes a "street map, detailing the exact route of L.B.'s afternoon strolls from the house with the garden and ornamental shrubs on a tree-lined street in Outremont, down Park Avenue, past Curly's news-stand, the Regent cinema, Moe's barbershop, the YMHA and Fletcher's Field, cutting left at Pine Avenue to Horn's Cafeteria." The biographer asks Moses "to correct any errors or add variations to the route" (Richler 1990b, 405). Richler himself writes about the lives and works of Woody Allen, Ernest Hemingway, Saul Bellow, and Norman Mailer, but their biographies are intertwined with

observations on artistic achievements, the artists' modus oper-
andi, and other artistic concerns, not to be confused with writers'
detritus details.

In Richler's mature novels, aesthetics and morals become not only
important but critical. It is in these works that the connection between
cultural initiation and moral integrity is made urgent. Barney not only
references Nabokov but also invokes Matthew Arnold when he lam-
basts universities as failed storehouses of culture and moral standards.
He doubts that "Dr. Arnold would have been impressed with the winds
that blew in the latter-day groves of academe" (Richler 1998a, 296).
The allusion to Arnold reflects the novel's axiological imperative and
voices sympathy with not just Arnold but dominant Victorian thinking
on art and culture as "implicitly 'moral'" (Buckley, 143). While
Victorian critics and writers from the mid-1800s predominantly
subscribed to the notion that the arts provided "some" kind of enlight-
enment (Moran, 17), Arnold went one step further in *Culture and
Anarchy* (1869), arguing that high culture, especially literature, provided the best inspiration for enlightened moral values since religion
was no longer adequate as society's moral guide (Moran, 128). For
him, culture was ultimately the "the pursuit of perfection" (6), perfection meaning a cultural work that contributes to moral and human
perfection, respectively (44–5). It is a vehicle for accessing the highest
calling – "not merely a method, but an attitude of spirit contrived to
receive truth" (Trilling 1949, 241). Richler's mature works do not
entertain Arnold's obsolete perspective on class. Nor do they, in any
way, share his disdain for bathos as endemic to lowbrow culture
(116, 119). Nevertheless, they echo Arnold's belief in the ennobling
power of culture and its ability to elicit the finer, if not the best, human
capabilities. In fact, Richler's novels so powerfully resonate with
Arnold's turn-of-the-twentieth-century ethical concept of culture that
Leslie Fiedler considered them anachronistically conservative. With
contemporary liberal disdain, he labelled them fodder for the "guardians of official morality" (103), hinting that the moral bent in Richler's
fiction is archaic, superficial, and reductive.

With regard to the protagonists, who are all producers of culture in
some sense, even if it is second rate, as Majer contends (2019, 61), the
distinction between cultural grace and cultural pedestrianism is blurred.
These men are not part of the undiscerning masses, but whether or not
they have the innate abilities to contribute to high culture is unclear.

Part of their attachment to the hero figures, whom they consider indubitable "men of culture," comes from the urge to feel a kinship with their greatness and benefit from their cultural acumen, even if it is acumen that exists mainly in the protagonists' imaginations.

— ✳ —

According to the memories and imagination of the protagonists, the hero figures are never guilty of endorsing mediocrity or pandering to the undeserving. To return to *Culture and Anarchy*, they are those rare individuals, "aliens," who possess "an original and humane instinct" (Arnold, 108). They have the required "curiosity about their best self" that drives them to seek noble standards.[4] Because they see "things as they really are" and have a poetic mindset that makes them keen observers of the human condition. They are also "disentangled" from the "machinery," or the pragmatic materialism that drives the philistinism of the middle class (101). With the ability to apprehend "reason," they can analyze the world around them with clear logic. Though they do not abide by "the will of God," they do "pursue perfection" through the bond between cultural sagacity and moral values (108–9).

Jake Hersh and Moses Berger idealize Joey Hersh and Solomon Gursky, respectively, in part because they see them as possessed of a type of rare wisdom, an awe-inspiring mix of aesthetic instinct and moral impulse. As an adolescent Jake first thinks of Joey's sister, Jenny Hersh, as his intellectual tutor. She reads modern novels and decorates her bedroom with a map of the Paris metro and line drawings of Keats. She is not only attractive but exudes a knowing sensuality absent in the other girls of Montreal's Jewish ghetto. She infiltrates Montreal's theatre community and is the first to show Jake glimmers of a cultural world beyond the confines of their immediate environment. However, Jenny's judgment is flawed. She marries Doug Fraser, an untalented but successful Canadian playwright, and is subsequently suffocated and then embittered by the cultural stagnation in Doug's theatre circle. But, more significantly, she confesses to Jake that she was never destined for greatness: "I applied myself to learning and literature with a kind of hatred for it, so that if I ever fell in with what I think of as the blessed, talented people, I could fit in" (Richler 1991b, 156). For her, culture is not its own reward. It is an instrument for leveraging social status. This, as well as her avowed mediocrity, is the kind of shortcoming that the protagonists cannot tolerate in their mentors. For them, hero figures must be born to greatness. They still need to toil to realize their potential, but they cannot cultivate greatness if it is not innate.

Jenny falls short of her aspirations because she is insufficiently gifted, not even on par with those she perceives as the moderately talented local literati. Her limitations, however, might also be associated with her ulterior motives. According to Arnold, those in the middle class cannot fully appreciate culture because they are preoccupied with power and pleasure, which is at odds with the disinterestedness of real culture. For all their polite rituals and outward grace, they are prevented from gaining access to true culture because of their narcissistic or hedonistic motivations (162). Though Jenny is not from the privileged classes, her study of culture is tainted by the stain of self-interest. She is a social climber, not a seeker of "perfection."

Jenny's life is a cautionary tale for Jake. First, he realizes that he must pin his cultural ambition on loftier stakes than social mobility. Second, he decides that for the sake of his artistic development he must leave Canada for a society that is more culturally inspiring. Here, too, there is confluence with Arnold, who maintained – with Eurocentric paternalism – that culture can only emerge from societies that create fertile grounds for it – predominantly, order rather than the destructive inclination towards anarchy (203). Jake's idea of a great society has little to do with order or the absence of anarchical tendencies, but he believes – with that same Eurocentric paternalism – that there are select societies that are equipped with better mythologies as well as historical and cultural traditions for the flourishing of culture. For him, great societies are those that offer cultural, if not civil, order, and deeming England such a society, he moves there.

Having recognized Jenny's inadequacy at a young age, Jake makes himself an acolyte of her brother Joey, who, he believes, is a genuine judge of culture and committed to its intrinsic moral mandate. Joey, or the Horseman, becomes Jake's "moral editor" (Richler 1991b, 309) and generally his ethical and cultural standard bearer. "Considering a script," for example, "he knew that in the final analysis he said yes or no based on what he imagined to be the Horseman's exacting standard. Going into production, whether in television or film, he tried above all to please the Horseman" (309). These decisions have an ethical component because, for Jake, shoddy culture lacks moral integrity.

Moses Berger never wavers regarding his tutelary figure, Solomon Gursky. Solomon's critical acumen becomes evident to Moses already in his childhood, when his father angrily tells him about a reading he once delivered in Montreal where Solomon was in attendance: "A dreadful man … he was the first with his hand up in the question period. 'Can the poet tell me,' he asked, 'whether or not he uses a rhyming dictionary?'" (Richler 1990b, 23). Moses listens while stifling a giggle. He immediately understands that Solomon has a superior mind, one far better than that of his plodding father. Moreover, it is not only Moses who recognizes Solomon's superiority. When Solomon builds a cherry-wood table for Diana McClure, the one woman he considers worthy, his brother Morrie, a mediocre amateur carpenter, is devastated by its beauty. Though Morrie has laboriously tried to hone his skills as a craftsman, Solomon, it is clear, is a born artist.

In his youth, Barney Panofsky considers his own hero, Boogie Moscovitch, a doyen of cultural wisdom. He recalls the assorted artists who constituted his Paris social circle as mere "contenders," except for the "shining example" of Boogie (Richler 1998a, 7). Not only Barney, but his friends too, considered Boogie a prodigy, comparing him to Heine, from whom he inherited "*le droit de moribondage*" (10). His superiority is further endorsed when, later in life, he is said to be sought out as a friend and confidante by Ernest Hemingway, John Cheever, Norman Mailer, William Styron, Billie Holiday, Mary McCarthy, and John Huston (239). Eventually Boogie's image fades. He is unequal to his potential. Whereas Jake Hersh and Moses Berger are able to remain enamoured with their heroes, Barney's faith in Boogie is destabilized.

Boogie, unlike the other hero figures, succumbs to weaknesses that the novel treats as intolerable. He falls victim to his own myth-making. The other writers in the novels who are willing to prostitute their over-valued talents for fame and wealth are not hero figures, so their capitulation to commercial temptations are pathetic but not destabilizing. Boogie, however, seems capable of greatness, thus his surrender to celebrity is all the more grievous. It is as though he is initially one of Arnold's "aliens," in possession of the necessary powers to create culture, who squanders his potential and settles for undeserved notoriety. Aware he has become unproductive, he still willingly feigns the pose of "the author of the greatest modern American novel yet to be written" (239) and uses his reputation to finance a decadent lifestyle and a debilitating drug habit. Shortly before his disappearance, Barney confronts his friend about his much anticipated novel that has never materialized. When Boogie dodges the question, Barney accuses him of being "just another druggie with pretensions" (334).

Barney's disillusionment with Boogie is a significant commentary on the interplay between culture and moral values. Judging novelists, poets, playwrights, and artists collectively as a result of Boogie's personal and artistic sins, Barney rages against a slew of writers and painters – Hemingway, Lewis Carroll, Picasso, Simenon, Odets, Lillian Hellman, Robert Frost, Mencken, T.S. Eliot, Evelyn Waugh, Frank Harris, Jean-Paul Sartre, Edmund Wilson, T.E. Lawrence – every one of them "a self-promoter, a braggart, and a paid liar of a coward, driven by avarice and desperate for fame" (158).[5] It is an accusation that Joshua Shapiro makes in *Joshua Then and Now*, more specifically against late twentieth-century writers: "Once, writers had been committed to revolutionary change, not their own absurdity. Instead of *Catch-22*, there was *La Condition Humaine*; rather than Portnoy, Robert Jordan" (Richler 2001, 258).

It is widely thought that Boogie is closely based on Richler's friend Mason Hoffenberg, an American expatriate writer who Richler had met as a young man in Paris (Kramer 2008, 354; Foran 623). Like Boogie, Hoffenberg was a member of the American troops that liberated Paris; he was a well-read, hard-partying raconteur and an intimate of Sartre, Becket, Henry Miller, and other intellectuals of mid-twentieth century Paris (Kramer 2008, 86). Richler considered Hoffenberg the star of his expatriate circle of writers, and others in Richler's social group thought him a talent worthy of the Nobel Prize. Later Richler admitted that his Paris acquaintances, including Hoffenberg, lacked ideological originality: they were not non-conformists but "fumblers" or "misfits," committed to their own "particular conformities" and "anti-bourgeois inversions" (1973b, 19), hardly the intellectual heroes they believed themselves to be (23). *Barney's Version* reflects this disillusionment. Barney remembers his time spent in Paris with his Bohemian clique and how the group smugly, but mistakenly, considered themselves original free-thinkers. Richler eventually came to see the kind of cultural impulse Hoffenberg represented – "hipsterdom, later called Beat," – as barren, just as Barney perceives the feminism inspired by Clara Charnosfky, the Afro-American identity politics of Cedric Richardson, the art of Leo Bishinsky, and Boogie's intellectual pose as fraudulent.

As Boogie has always been Barney's cultural and aesthetic mentor, the realization that he is a fraud is painful. Boogie's slide into the life of a drug-addled "personality," as well as his unfulfilled promise and moral decline, dramatize the tenuous relationship between ethics and cultural commitments. Throughout *Barney's Version*, there are hints – some subtle, others not – that Boogie is lazy, unprincipled, and disloyal. His innate abilities as an art and culture critic are never in doubt, but as the novel progresses it becomes increasingly evident that those abilities have not made Boogie a more decent individual, committed artist, or great writer. Boogie demonstrates his imaginative powers, but, without moral backbone, he is insufficiently equipped to produce real artistic achievement.

Nevertheless, Barney is unable to wholly relinquish his affection for Boogie or his belief that Boogie, before disappearing, was still destined for greatness. When Boogie visits Barney in Montreal years after their sojourn in Paris, he proves to be petty and spiteful. Knowing that Barney and Terry McIver had been rivals, he praises Terry's writing, suggesting that Terry, unlike Barney, was among the chosen – those blessed with innate greatness (241). The reliability of Barney's repeated criticisms of Terry's literary abilities and general character are suspect, as Barney is vindictive, prone to pettiness, and hardly a reliable narrator. However, a letter from Terry to Barney confirms that the former is, in actuality, egotistical, pompous, and a poor prose stylist. In his correspondence, he accuses Barney of having always been "consumed with envy" for his talent; he also writes, somewhat maliciously, that the disappearance of Boogie is "a larger loss to drug dealers than the world of letters" (156). His sentences are studded with pretentious clichés and pompous expressions such as "unpaid factotum," "*la condition humaine,*" and "maledictory gesture" (157). Ultimately, the letter supports Barney's claim that Terry is an untalented fraud who has sated the Canadian thirst for a national author by assuming that role rather than by delivering good work. Hence, by trying to provoke Barney with praise of Terry, Boogie emerges as a vengeful failure, reduced to unkind antics in order to buttress his ego.

Still, Barney cannot sever his relationship with his long-time friend. The realization that he has misjudged Boogie or, even worse, that Boogie – his mentor – has proven unworthy, is too daunting. Faced with disillusionment, he admits: "I couldn't handle any more. I was too frightened. So, natural coward that I am, I retreated into humor" (334).

Indifferent to moral norms, uncaring about his closest friends, plagued by self-destructive energies, and haunted by the sense of unfulfilled greatness, Boogie may be seen in literary terms as a modern satiric version of a Byronic hero garbed as a cosmopolitan Jew.[6] By the time Richler was mid-career, David Sheps observed that protagonists in Richler's seminal novels cherish the notion of romantic heroism: "Byronism filtered through Hollywood films." Even though these characters sense that their belief in the hero figures is founded upon "a false sense of reality," one that "they know to be anachronistic," they cannot overcome their attraction to them (1971, xxi–xxii). Barney certainly cannot be cured of his devotion to Boogie even when it is evident that he is far from heroic. In light of this dynamic, Boogie's relationship with Barney, his protégé, resembles the bond between another model of the Byronic hero, Charles Dickens's James Steerforth and his acolyte David Copperfield.

David Copperfield (1850) is "a novel with a basic conflict between the comic myth of the successful hero on one hand and the powerful realization of tragic implications on the other" (Kincaid, 197). The rift between potential greatness and untrammelled egoism in Steerforth is associated with the novel's linkage of "good and bad in a single character," represented as a "Byronic hero, a character type whose fascination for the romantic period stemmed at least in part from this very combination" (Harvey, 306).[7] He is defined by contradiction. Steerforth "despises the world, he puts other values above work, he sometimes wishes he was not wasting his life, he has the vestiges of a power to love or at any rate to want to be loved" (Wilson 2006, 88). As such, he has no identity predicated upon the kind of moral code that is necessary in forming the basis of the self.

Boogie, too, is a paradoxical character – a grandiose personality and the source of his own ruin. Sometimes he is cavalier and flippant. At others, as Barney notes, he has "his dark side, disappearing for weeks on end" or isolating himself in his hotel "high on horse, or … compiling lists of the names of those young men who had fought alongside him and were already dead" (Richler 1998a, 10). His superiority and magnetism invite comparisons to Steerforth, who is "portrayed as a cut above his companions, a leader with ability and charm" (Harvey, 307). Both characters are intolerant of opposition or criticism, unmoved by the worries of their friends and the cares of the world. They are supercilious about their own talents and abilities, and both abandon their studies, as if they consider themselves above the rigours of the classroom of even the most famed schools. Regardless of such failings, David's admiration of Steerforth endures. He witnesses repeated instances of his cruelty and selfishness. Nevertheless, like Barney, he refuses to properly acknowledge his friend's immorality or to renounce him.

For David, Steerforth likewise remains a hero: his charm and beauty never ceasing to suggest a refined character. Steerforth, however, unhesitatingly destroys the lives of those who have been awed by his charisma. David eventually has to confront this reality, but he fails, or refuses, to fully disown Steerforth. He clings to his vision of his long-time friend as his personal hero, who is fated for a life of greatness. Even after Steerforth has seduced and defamed David's childhood friend Emily and left her family devastated, the mortified David still thinks of Steerforth with affection. Gazing at his face minutes after he has drowned at sea during a violent storm, David reminisces:

> No need, O Steerforth, to have said, when we last spoke
> together, in that hour which I so little deemed to be our
> parting-hour – no need to have said, "Think of me at my best!"
> I had done that ever; and could I change now, looking on this
> sight! (Dickens 1986, 650)

In David and Barney's minds, Steerforth and Boogie are forever heroes despite their unconscionable behaviour – Byronic heroes who are "beyond the rules and regulations of more ordinary men" (Harvey, 309). In adapting and modifying this type or relationship and enhancing its importance to the general narrative (making it almost a literary topos), Richler inscribes himself into a predominantly Victorian novelistic tradition.

Indeed, the flawed protégé/mentor relationship is portrayed to varying effects by Charlotte Brontë and George Eliot, and demonstrates ways in which the protagonists' position can be reaffirmed regardless of the fate of their tutelary heroes.[8] In *Jane Eyre* (1847), Rochester, the quintessential Byronic hero, becomes a suitable hero after being subjected to enough tragedy to render him adequately humble. His path to redemption is circuitous, but his underlying decency eventually sublimates his tendency towards demonic antics. He is thereby reformed, and Jane, who is unfaltering in her ethical views, can accept him.

In Brontë's *Villette* (1853), the mentor figure M. Paul, seemingly irascible and scheming, yields to his nobler inclinations and becomes worthy of the protagonist Lucy Snowe's love and admiration. Interestingly, M. Paul, like Boogie and Steerforth, dies, or seems to die, at sea after his three-year absence. He evolves to become Lucy's deserving hero and then perishes. It is a perplexing ending as Lucy describes the three years of waiting for his return as the happiest of her life, when she hovers between reality and fantasy, familiar enough with M. Paul to be his devoted student but also enchanted with the fantasy of him while he is abroad. This plot manoeuvre invites comparison to the protagonist/hero figure narrative pattern in Richler's novels. When M. Paul's death is apparently confirmed, Lucy's happiness erodes though she has been apart from him for a lengthy time. In Richler's novels, with the exception of *Barney's Version*, the protagonists' peace of mind does not ebb precisely because the death of their heroes is never proven. They are comforted by the ambiguity that enables them to believe that heroic values are possibly still being enacted.

In contrast, Dorothea Brooke in George Eliot's *Middlemarch* (1871 72) maintains her integrity by modifying her values and becoming critical of her mentor/husband, Edward Casaubon. Shortly after her marriage she discovers that a learned mind and a degree of cultural knowledge are not necessarily matters of moral merit. She sees that Casaubon, who she has imagined as a noble, religiously fervent scholar dedicated to lofty goals, possesses an uncharitable temperament and flawed intellect. When she tacitly disowns him as her moral and cultural mentor, she retains no nostalgia for the man she had envisioned in near-saintly form; she continues to care for him, but not as her superior, only as an infirm ward. The experience causes Dorothea to adjust her values, which are then part of the novel's composite of defensible moral positions. In contrast, neither Barney nor David revamp their views in response to Boogie or Steerforth's villainy: personal loyalty and attachment trump moral judgment.

Despite their faith in true artistic greatness, Richler's protagonists become disappointed in artists, generally, and writers, specifically, because they fail to provide an adequate scheme of ethical values that could help make the world more intelligible. Richler himself appears to have faith in writers. In a nod to Shelley's pronouncement that "poets are the unacknowledged legislators of the world," he once called them "unfrocked priests" (qtd in Gibson, 298). In an age when religious authorities have lost their clout, he suggested that the writer had become a voice of intellectual and moral authority. Though he was writing in the twentieth century, his axiological approach to culture to a large extent stemmed from Victorian attitudes: he reiterated Matthew Arnold's "faith" that the moral precepts once based on religion are best realized through culture (Wilson 1966, 41). Richler's protagonists, though, are sceptical of the writer's moral function. With a decidedly twentieth-century consciousness, they are not prepared to accept any hallowed beliefs about culture's moral integrity. Their contemporary view is encapsulated in a comment by the character Iris Griffin in Margaret Atwood's *The Blind Assassin* (2000). Describing her grandmother, Iris says,

> She went in for culture, which gave her a certain moral authority. It wouldn't now; but people believed, then, that Culture could make you better – a better person. They believed it could uplift you ... They hadn't yet seen Hitler at the opera house. (Atwood 2000, 59)

Jake Hersh decides that literature, "once his consolation, [is] no longer enough" (Richler 1991b, 301). His dismay does not, however, preclude his belief in truth. He continues to yearn for "answers, a revelation, something out there, a certitude, like the Bomb before it was discovered" and cherishes the hope that his cousin Joey Hersh will one day proffer this kind of wisdom (301). In Jake's case, the failings of literary texts do not obviate the possibility of *veritas*. He does not despair of moral principles or universal certainties because literature, even the great literature that inspired him as a young man, has been found wanting. He may find "men of culture" inadequate but not culture itself.

In *Solomon Gursky*, the child Moses Berger experiences a similar disillusionment with writers when Shloime Bishinsky, a family friend, accuses Moses's father – at that time the doyen of literature and intellectual wisdom of the Montreal Jewish ghetto – of prostituting his writing when he becomes the Gursky family ghostwriter. Even though it seems apparent that L.B. Berger lacks talent, at that moment, he becomes "the personification of Richler's low opinion of writers who betray what he perceived to be literature's higher calling" (Yanofsky, 47).

Richler, himself, never seemed to lose his trust in the Great Books of the Western literary tradition and in high culture. He "hated everything pretentious and academic and fake in the literary world yet [he] had an unshakable reverence for literature" (Gopnik). He writes cynically about critics and journalists who condemned Saul Bellow as a Eurocentric elitist for asking, "Who is the Tolstoy of the Zulus? The Proust of the Papuans" (qtd in Richler 1998b, 91). Unimpressed by Bellow's subsequent qualification of the statement (1994) – that he was only distinguishing between literate and pre-literate societies – Richler preferred to read Bellow's statement as a jab at cultural relativism. Overlaying his own prejudices, he insinuated that Bellow was implying that some societies, as Arnold argues, are better positioned than others to foment great culture (203). He unapologetically privileged traditional Western literary standards, insisting that "in the end the major novelists so many of us cherish did not fail us" (Richler 1998b, 92).

Like Richler, veteran journalist, art, literature, and music critic Max Wyman argued impassionedly for a re-engagement with the axiology of Arnold and his fellow Victorians: "[Arnold's] idealist Victorian social rectitude is out of fashion these days, but the humanist basis on which his thinking is built (the thought that art addresses our most profound concerns and improves us by exposing us to the highest levels of thought and morality) remains valid" (67). He adds that, while it is also in vogue to downplay the importance of "the classics," those very books (and he includes Richler's) contain the "great themes of art," which are not only timeless but "resonate throughout our lives" (92). Whereas Fiedler, very much an exponent of twentieth-century criticism, found the axiology of Richler's writing to be disconcertingly conservative, Wyman pleads for a revaluing of the critical approach of the mid-1900s, which considered aesthetics and morals inseparable. He insists that the arts do "have the power to change us and to comfort us with the recognition of human potential" and credits the Victorians for recognizing that this is "one of art's chief virtues" (67).

Richler, however, does not entirely embrace a neo-Victorian view of culture. He is devoted to the literature and the cultural exclusivity associated with the traditional Western canon and reaffirms the axiology of the Victorian "men of letters." Yet he still has a penchant for lowbrow burlesque as well as anti-establishment and anti-authoritarian irreverence. His protagonists, in contrast, are less convinced that culture – mainly literature – is necessarily morally illuminating; they find that it does not provide enough of a sense of what constitutes a moral life. Instead, the hero figures, as the protagonists imagine them, are their guides, and it is their cultural principles that help them make sense of the world. The hero figures are not just writers, artists, or thinkers – they are "men of culture" whose tastes are essential to their scheme of moral commitments. Moreover, the hero figures are suitable moral guides because they reject the popular fads – admiration for modernist art, academia, and the celebrity writer – that the protagonists, and the narrative voice, deem unethical cultural shams.

The one exception to the hero figure construct, Boogie Moscovitch of *Barney's Version*, succumbs to one of these follies, the lure of literary fame, and turns into a failed idol. Whether it is his faulty moral values, lack of character, or uneven cultural sensitivities that precipitate his decline is not clear. Yet his fall from the status of an intellectual of great literary promise to that of a treacherous junkie makes plain that the seeds of cultural refinement do not inevitably develop into moral strength. His downfall casts doubt over the connection between culture and moral value schemes. It also poses questions regarding the strength of that bond and what happens if/when "men of culture" stray from their roles as moral beacons. The problem with Boogie may be, however, that Barney has too much access to him and is unable to indefinitely nurse his hero figure fantasy when directly confronted with the unarguable fact of Boogie's failure. Seemingly, the idea of culture's moral force can only thrive in theory as an ideal in Richler's works. When it is imposed on characters who are relatively accessible and open to close observation, it is prone to collapse.

Conlusion

Contrary to the views of some early critics (McSweeney, Iannone), I believe there is ample evidence showing that moral values are affirmed in Richler's fiction, particularly in his last four novels. In his study of *St Urbain's Horseman* and *Solomon Gursky Was Here*, Krzysztof Majer defines these values – albeit under the rubric of the picaro messiah – as

> a means to substitute the stereotype of the Jewish compliance and benevolence with a myth of rugged dignity, courage and defiant transgression ... rescue Jewish literature from political correctness ... a tool with which to examine contemporary Jewish spirituality by gauging the current strength of its foundational myth, while simultaneously bearing in mind the long historical procession of false messiahs. (2008, 259)

However, the moral positions evident in the majority of Richler's novels are more extensive than Majer notes, relating to Jewish resistance, an imprecise contract of Jewish ethics, social norms ranging from Victorian liberal sympathies to au courant PC principles and cultural and aesthetic mandates. They are then woven into the novels through a merger between the consciousness of the protagonists and the topos of hero figures, larger-than-life men whose integrity helps remedy the moral deficiencies of modernity. That does not, however, suggest that the hero figures are classically "heroic." They are daring and principled but hardly saintly or even "good" according to common social expectations. With their own self-defined parameters of moral behaviour, they are not bound by the norms of any single community's values or assumptions. According to Judith Shklar's assessment of "ordinary vices," they are even guilty of cruelty, snobbery, betrayal, and misanthropy. Yet these characters are revered by the protagonists because they are true to their best values – Jewish dignity, moral backbone, personal accountability and cultural integrity. Thus, they are positioned as models of heroism because they are almost always faithful to their self-imposed moral ideals.

In analyzing the intersection between many of the predominant issues and attitudes in Richler's novels and the characterization of the hero figures, I show that the nexus between the novels' character construction and extra-textual elements demands inquiry into the novels' social, historical, and cultural contexts. In some cases, the concerns that bridge Richler's texts and their contexts began to garner critical attention already with the publication of *Son of a Smaller Hero*. Nevertheless, this kind of holistic reading of Richler's entire career has not received attention. Thus, in this work I respond to and expand upon the substantive but incomplete Richler scholarship, aiming to encapsulate a more comprehensive understanding of his worldview, including his novels' engagement with Canada, PC issues, and the way they link cultural authenticity to moral sophistication.

In addition, it is my intention to refute charges – held by some scholars and writers (Wisse, Laurence), and some in Montreal's Jewish community – that Richler's fiction suffers from anti-Semitic, or even self-hating, overtones and makes a mockery of most Jewish concerns. It is true that Jews who jockey for upward mobility but suffer from "philistinism" are disparaged in Richler's novels. Moreover, knee-jerk support of Israel is satirized, and the Jewish establishment is often portrayed as both timid and over-reaching. Nonetheless, family devotion, Old World religious sincerity, resistance to anti-Jewish provocations, and general temerity are represented as laudable Jewish virtues. Even some notorious stereotypes – the "good" Jewish husband, the sexually voracious Jewish man, the "smart" Jew – are reconceived as positive forms of traditional masculinity. Sander Gilman explains that "self hatred results from outsiders' acceptance of the mirage of themselves generated by their reference group – that group in society which they see as defining them – as a reality" (2). Richler may seem to traffic in these "mirages," but he usually enlists them in a ploy to upend stereotypes and uncover hypocrisy.

In examining the place of the Holocaust in Richler's novels, there has also been a departure from mainstream critical opinion. There is no argument in this regard with the widespread view of Richler's hero figures as pseudo-messiahs determined to avenge the persecution and indignities endured by Jews in the modern era. However, I claim that the impact of the hero figures on the novels extends further than has been acknowledged. Rachel Feldhay Brenner and Wilfrid Cude argue that these characters reflect a historical urge to enact vengeance, replicating the feats of the mythical Golem of Prague – another messianic type. However, in looking at Richler's work as a cohesive body, the hero figures become not only enforcers of justice, similar to the Golem, but a link in a Jewish literary tradition that has invoked the messiah model to varying effects. In the case of Richler's novels, the hero figures' messianic qualities inspire optimism in the protagonists. It enables them to sustain hope in human decency, despite the modern age's environment of moral chaos, and cling to faith in the future at a time when the Holocaust has forced a rethinking of the darkest human impulses.

I also consider the validity of complaints, such as those of Farley Mowat, that Richler's fiction contains unfair diatribes against Canadian society and culture. Mostly, these accusations have been vague, rarely targeting specific textual references in the novels. They have, as well, mainly been spurred by Richler's comments in interviews, magazines, or compendiums of Canadian writing. There is merit to some of these grievances. The early novels paint a dour picture of Canadian cultural achievement and the national psyche plagued by patriotic insecurity. The later ones are less bitter but still engage in what some might perceive as Canada-bashing. Eventually, Richler went on record, confessing his admiration of Canada and guardedly praising the country's most decorated literary lights. Still, his novels never celebrate Canada as a country capable of producing a cadre of serious intellectuals, world-class writers, or legendary cultural institutions. It is ultimately cast as a nation doomed to remain overshadowed by its southern neighbour. The attitude of Richler's hero figures towards Canada is also tepid, which is important because their views, or perceived views, hold much sway in the novels' narratives. As a result, their acolytes, the novels' protagonists, sustain a certain reticence with regard to Canada, even when they confess their enduring attachment to the country that is their home.

By contrast, there can be no argument with those who have asserted that, in Richler's novels, there is a running, somewhat malevolent critique of issues associated with political correctness and au courant social politics. Yet there is little explicit scholarship identifying and explicating the implications of these assaults on progressive thinking. While scant textual evidence has been produced to support claims that Richler's novels are anti-Canadian, specific references with regard to the novels' politically correct timbre are virtually non-existent. As early as the 1950s, Nathan Cohen found Richler's fiction socially outdated and his women characters drawn as products of conventional male fantasy. Long-time host of CBC's *Writers and Company*, Eleanor Wachtel, labelled Richler's novels sexist. Neither of them, though, substantiated these observations with specific examples from the texts. Nonetheless, both confessed to a general impression that conventional male chauvinism is woven into the novels. Here I address these matters in relation to the texts and, as a result, show that, as Richler evolved as a novelist, concessions to PC thinking began to appear in his fiction even though this shift was subtle and hardly a repudiation of the overall conservatism in his oeuvre.

Finally, I examine the relationship between culture and ethical systems in Richler's novels. Beginning with *The Acrobats* and continuing all the way to *Barney's Version*, the novels implicitly engage in a polemic on the importance and dangers of associating culture and aesthetic sensitivity with moral integrity. While there are instances in which culture appears ennobling and essential to the moral personality, it is also used as a mean instrument for self-interest and pretension. Art, especially experimental modern art, is often portrayed as amateurism masquerading as cultural sophistication. And one of the ugly aspects of culture appears to be the emergence of the celebrity artist, happy to sacrifice authentic achievement for mass popularity. The most probing explorations of these phenomena are found in *Barney's Version*. In previous novels, the hero figures understand culture well, but moral justice is their primary interest. In this final work, however, Boogie Moscovitch – an early hope in the quest for the next great American novel – disappoints as a hero figure because he is indifferent to ethics in personal relationships, even though he is an astute student of culture and aesthetics. While the protagonist-narrator Barney Panofsky remains awed by Boogie, he is sufficiently honest to represent him as a failure.

The modified characterization of the hero figure is one of the most complex discrepancies between *Barney's Version* and the rest of Richler's corpus. Yet there are other significant differences that underscore this novel's unprecedented moral possibilities. For one, *Barney's Version* is a departure in terms of narrative style and character construction. It is

Richler's only novel to be written in the first person, focalizing the narrative exclusively through the perspective of the protagonist, Barney Panofsky (with the exception of some quasi-paratextual additions by his son). The narrative voice communicates the protagonist's mindset directly and not through the third-person centre-of-consciousness technique characteristic of most of Richler's works. As a result, Barney seems more vulnerable than Richler's other protagonists, his personal follies more tragic. Because the reader has greater access to his interior heartache and remorse, he elicits more sympathy.

Also, this novel is distinct because of "its fascination with the unreliability of narrative and memory" (Shapiro). Barney himself admits that, at times, he has fiddled with the truth, "tinkering with memory, fine-tuning reality" (Richler 1998a, 199). It is an unsettling and unprecedented narrative move in Richler's work, one that compels the reader to constantly assess whether Barney is a sympathetic character or a voice to be challenged. Compounding suspicions that Barney's account of events is untrustworthy is the fact that he is writing while experiencing a slide into dementia. In addition, much of his autobiographical tale is a desperate attempt to disprove the widespread accusation that he murdered Boogie. Moreover, this defence, as first-person testimony, at times seems manipulative, and its inconsistent reconstruction of the past invites scepticism.

Experimenting with this narrative point of view, Richler tests a new plot construct, one that opens up a discursive space for a different type of character – a hero figure without integrity or high-minded principles. Majer argues that "Richler's writing always presupposes moral codes, even if they cannot be wholly reconstructed by the reader" (2008, 259). Usually, these codes are a fusion of the "ordinary" and "heroic" values that are upheld by the protagonist and hero figure, respectively. But in *Barney's Version* this is not the case. An ethical code emerges specifically in reaction to Barney and Boogie's problematic conduct.

In the novel, the most conspicuous repudiation of Barney's resistance to social change is the dissolution of his marriage. Barney dislikes the feminism that has infiltrated modern life and is confounded by the wish of women to be more than just guardians of hearth and home. Accordingly, he discourages his wife Miriam's budding interest in pursuits beyond her "calling" as wife and mother. His recalcitrance triggers a series of events that lead to his divorce and Miriam's subsequent marriage to Blair Hopper, a progressive academic with enlightened views on women and other PC matters. Presumably,

Miriam, who is perceptive and level-headed, is presented as one of the novels most authoritative characters. Accordingly, she would not accept Blair if she thought his views – which are radically at odds with Barney's – irrational or faddish. Conversely, in divorcing Barney she rejects the retrograde principles that underlie his moral outlook. At bottom, the novel acknowledges that conventional postures regarding gender roles are no longer, ipso facto, workable.

Earlier protagonists in Richler's novels, regardless of their most shameful behaviour (though they are never unfaithful, as Barney is), have wives who remain devoted to them and their children. But Barney is living in another era, and Miriam refuses to absolve him of his one-night stand. The affair seems to be Barney's rebellion against a world that no longer sanctions a patriarchal status quo, homage to an earlier time when a wife was supposed to find contentment solely in caring for her man. He knows that his behaviour is unpardonable, but he cannot quell his urge to defy progressive cultural norms. As a result, it is evident that his traditional, "ordinary" values, which Richler's other protagonists also hold sacred, are out of step with the world he inhabits.

Boogie, for his part, is an exception to the hero figure model as he has no personal code of cogent and strong ethical values. This type of code, explains Charles Taylor, is a "framework" – a background founded upon a conception of integrity that informs our moral positions – which is necessary because we cannot have an identity unless we know where we stand on matters of "crucial importance" (27). According to Taylor, for each of us

> identity is defined by the commitments and identifications which provide the frame or horizon within which [we] can try to determine from case to case what is good, or valuable, or what ought to be done, or what [we] endorse or oppose. In other words, it is the horizon within which [we are] capable of taking a stand. (27)

Boogie is glamorous, intellectually sophisticated, and worldly. Yet he never commits to the kind of moral foundation that makes the other hero figures honourable champions of their beliefs (despite their dishonourable exploits in other matters). He can be a generous teacher but is a disloyal friend. A glutton for pleasure, he is also self-destructive. He offers his acquaintances little besides the enjoyment of his company and celebrity aura but heedlessly allows them to accrue debt in order to supply him with resources for his self-destructive habits. On the one hand, he positions himself as the eiron – somewhat self-deprecating despite the widespread consensus that he is a part of the literary cognoscenti and a talent worthy of a future poet laureate; on the other hand, when he spirals downward into addiction and ignominy, he is more the alazon, unjustifiably supercilious, condescending, and abusive to Barney, his faithful friend and defender. While forgoing discipline and diligence, Boogie "gradually acquire[s] a reputation as author of the greatest modern American novel yet to be written" (Richler 1998a, 239). However, due to cowardice or sloth, he never really tests his writing ability. Instead, he gambles away his advances. As Barney puts it: he "drank, sniffed and mainlined the rest into his arm" (240).

Eventually, it becomes clear that Boogie is a spurious hero figure. Though his formative background appears to provide him with an identity – in Taylor's sense – it proves to be an insufficient springboard for Richlerian heroism. Boogie is ever the unapologetic Jew, confirms his worthiness by having served in the US army during the Second World War, and is perceived by friends and the literary establishment as a *wunderkind*, but these factors do not outweigh his lack of decency and idealistic ambition. He is not redeemed by his engagement with culture and belief in "the life of the mind," which seem almost frivolous in the absence of ethical beliefs and moral commitments. The Arnoldian model, linking cultural sensitivities with moral goodness, seems implausible in his case. Consequently, the novel calls into question the notion that authentic culture is bound to moral refinement.

The protagonist/hero figure configuration based on "ordinary" and "heroic" values in Richler's last novel, *Barney's Version*, becomes a criticism rather than a reaffirmation of the value system that can be teased from the earlier novels. Consequently, it calls into question, retroactively, many of the moral positions in all of Richler's mature works as well. Possibly, "ordinary" values, which are conservative – though not prissy or abstemious – no longer guarantee the protagonist a secure marriage, loving family, or contentment. Furthermore, an unconventional but unmistakable sort of Canadian Jewish identification, loyalty to family, intellectual autonomy (expressed as a rejection of political correctness), appreciation of culture, and, most important, faith in an ideal if complicated and impractical moral impulse may be found wanting as a personal code of decency. All of these ideals may simply be too reductionist for an era when the social and political thinking is no longer patriarchal simply by default. In response to the breakdown of this formula, the question looms whether the static value system adopted by Jake Hersh, Moses Berger, and Barney has been too myopic, too antagonistic towards what they see as Jewish establishment and bourgeois norms, and overly rigid regarding ideas about society, culture, and their relationship to a moral life.

At the same time, there is a sense that hero figures and, by extension, their "heroic" values would inevitably prove flawed if submitted to direct scrutiny. It follows that, in hindsight, Jake Hersh and Moses Berger are over-eager in imagining Joey Hersh's and Solomon Gursky's lives as models of courageous adherence to principle. The two protagonists do not "know" their "idols," can confirm only sketchy details of these men's' lives, and refuse to consider the families' and acquaintances' accounts of their criminal, unethical, and merciless inclinations. Boogie, then, is the counterproof to these mythical hero figures because Barney knows him from more direct, sustained experience and cannot deny his friend's disloyal, self-absorbed, and shiftless character. It is impossible to mistake his life for a paradigm of greatness. With this full disclosure of Boogie's shortcomings, Barney's commitment to him is the most extreme version of a protagonist's cognitive dissonance: faith in a hero figure who has repeatedly proved to be unworthy.

Ultimately, *Barney's Version* destabilizes the trajectory of existential and moral thinking found in earlier works and forces a reconsideration of the ordinary/heroic values framework. As a result, the hero figure framework collapses, forcing a rethinking of the values model that has been the focal point of Richler's development as a writer. This is a meaningful shift since, up until *Barney's Version,* this framework is the only value-paradigm that appears viable; almost all other value systems and social mores are satirized. If those values no longer circumscribe a moral vision for the modern world, then either the values have to be reconceptualized or contemporary culture is, indeed, condemned.

Still, in *Barney's Version* the world is not wholly beyond repair, and faith in the possibility of moral standards, which can be parsed in earlier novels, is not negated. The novel is, however, a cautionary tale about the perils of a fixed value system, impervious to social, political, and cultural change. It casts a shadow of doubt over the symbiosis between static "ordinary" values and unexamined heroic values, even if they inspire a belief in a legitimate moral standard, one that makes everyday living not just bearable but meaningful. However, it does not preclude such a symbiosis. Instead it hints at the need for a different or additional measure of moral commitments attuned to evolving social and cultural thinking – one conceptualized by those who are bound to "ordinary" values but inspired by real or imagined hero figures who enact "heroic values" through fantastical exploits.

Notes

1 This field dominated the first half of the twentieth century and is nearly synonymous with "the intentional fallacy" and "affective fallacy," terms coined by W.K. Wimsatt and Monroe C. Beardsley (1946, 1949).

2 This study focuses on the importance of the doubling feature in Richler's novels: a synergy that results from the protagonist/hero figure binary. If any aspect of Céline's novel is striking in this regard, it is the enigmatic coupling of Bardamu and Robinson. Though Céline's pairing suggests an entirely different meaning, it is worth noting that this was yet another example of the literature that Richler encountered in his youth, with doubling central to its development.

3 Also in 2010, journalist John Barber took Canadian universities to task, accusing them of near total disregard of Richler.

4 An internet search of Canadian literature courses showed that Richler's works appeared on syllabi at McGill, Queen's, the University of Toronto, the University of Montreal, the University of Ottawa, the University of British Columbia, Athabasca University, Université Laval, the University of Calgary, Carleton, Brandon University, York University, Huron University, St Mary's University, Ryerson, and Concordia.

5 In 2011, Professor Ira Nadel of the University of British Columbia told me that students were simply not interested in reading Richler because they did not relate to his novels' protagonists, social issues, or humour. With many coming from a wide range of immigrant backgrounds, he continued, they want to read Canadian literature that depicted their reality, "their" experience of having a hybrid identity, often blending a Canadian sense of self with Asian origins. However, Professor Norm Ravvin of Concordia

and Professor Ruth Panofsky of Ryerson University did not identify with Nadel's account, and both said that students found Richler compelling and that their engagement with his work, particularly *The Apprenticeship of Duddy Kravitz*, was always lively.

6 With uncommon urgency, Richler insisted that *Solomon Gursky* was fiction, not fact. He demanded that his years of toil not be reduced to a rehashing of Montreal gossip – a position that contradicted his claim to be the storyteller of the Montreal of his youth (Foran, 535).

7 It is widely acknowledged that Leonard Cohen, too, was deeply influenced by Klein. And Irving Layton not only entitled his memoir *Waiting for the Messiah*, a reference to Klein, but wrote movingly about his relationship with him. In addition, Henry Kreisel published *The Almost Meeting* in 1981, which is both a paean to *The Second Scroll* and to Klein.

8 Indeed, the novel so enraged the Bronfmans that their friends, associates, and employees were reluctant to mention the name of Richler at all and avoided having any of Richler's works on their bookshelves (Charendoff).

CHAPTER ONE

1 Just as Noah allows one value to supersede another – his need for independence triumphs over family commitment – Richler himself opted for pursuing literary goals at the expense of family considerations.

2 The episode involving Clara is yet another instance of a Richler protagonist's life conspicuously resembling Richler's own biography. At the age of twenty-three, Richler married Cathy Boudreau, reportedly an acid-tongued woman who alternately worshipped and ridiculed him (Posner 94). They were expatriates together in Paris, living among a group of other writers, artists, and intellectuals. It was believed (Weintraub, 216) that Richler married her out of a sense of obligation and that he also pitied her after she miscarried their child in 1955 (Kramer 2008, 119). Although Cathy, unlike Clara, never committed suicide, she had an erratic life after their marriage ended, and Richler sent her money from the time of their parting (Weintraub, 216) until the end of her life (Kramer 2008, 238).

3 Richler was well aware that the values championed as well as those satirized in his novels would arouse the anger of Canadian Jewry but was unmoved by a potential backlash (Gibson 282). In a 1970 article originally printed in the *Montreal Star*, Richler thoroughly ridiculed the publication of *The Jewish Community in Canada*, volume 1, *A History*, which he described as follows:

A catalogue, ostensibly boring, but inadvertently hilarious. Writing in the language of Shakespeare, as well as the Geritol commercial, the author owes something to Polonius, even more to the school of failed advertising copy writers. But his compendium, to be fair, radiates generosity. For if ... there are some 280,000 Jews in Canada, then it seems that at least half of them are enshrined in the history, and even to be mentioned by the rabbi is to be fulsomely praised. (Qtd in Richler 1973b, 143)

CHAPTER TWO

1 Glenn Deer rightly points out that, in his first three novels, Richler's fiction was bleak, focused on "weak male characters who are unable to compete with bullies, patriarchs, and opportunistic predators" (41). In these works the protagonists "are men who cannot physically protect themselves or their lovers from ... assertive antagonists ... or who are dominated by women." An example of this is

the ineffectual communist sympathizer, Norman Price, in *A Choice of Enemies*, who suffers a downward spiral in life. After serving as an RCAF pilot, he is forced to abandon his university teaching position due to his socialist ties in McCarthy-era America, then moves to London where he loses his girlfriend Sally to an East German refugee and disaffected Communist, Ernst Haupt, who has killed his brother, Nicky. (49)

From the publication of *St Urbain's* onward, however, Richler's invention of the hero figure/protagonist doubling proved a solution to the problem of male weakness. It enabled the protagonists to uphold a dialectic that encompasses both deeply felt compassion and ruthless self-preservation.

2 Richler maintained exacting standards, was easily disappointed, and readily found fault with his acquaintances, anonymous strangers, celebrated personalities, even dear friends. When asked why he presented so many of his characters in a critical light, he responded that "hardness has always been like a measure of my concern or regard, maybe a very perverse measure, but that's the way it is" (qtd in Gibson, 296).

3 Translated by Israel Efros, 1948.

4 Cynthia Ozick likewise sketched the contours of this contempt in her 1970 address at the Weizmann Institute when she noted that "Israeli rejection of Diaspora becomes not a revulsion against the millennial victimization of *galut* experience, but a revulsion against the victimized Jew himself" (1994, 21).

5 The idea that Israelis are somehow more authentic Jews than their
   Diaspora brethren did not necessarily fade as the Jewish State matured.
   A.B. Yehoshua, one of the giants of Israeli literature, provoked Diaspora
   Jews, especially Americans, with his host of twenty-first-century remarks
   on the transience of Jewish identity outside of Israel. Speaking to
   American Jews in Haifa in 2012, Yehoshua angered his audience with the
   following comments, which indicate that a supercilious attitude towards
   the Diaspora continues to resonate in Israel as the country surges into its
   eighth decade.

   > They are partial Jews while I am a complete Jew. In no way are we
   > the same thing – we are total and they are partial; we are Israeli and
   > also Jewish … Israel is the authentic, deep concept of the Jewish
   > people … in no siddur is there a mention of the word "Jew" but only
   > "Israeli." The name of our country and the territory is Land of Israel –
   > and it is about this deep matter that we must defend against a Jewish
   > offensive. (Qtd in Brosgol)

6 In Yehuda Bauer's opinion, such acts of heroism are indeed another form
   of resistance because they are "consciously taken in opposition to known
   or surmised laws, actions or intentions directed against the Jews by the
   Nazis or their supporters" (246).

CHAPTER THREE

1 In his 1974 article, "Waiting for Joey: The Theme of the Vicarious in
   St. Urbain's Horseman," David Sheps was among the early critics to
   offer a detailed account of the messianic characterization of Joey Hersh.
   However, Sheps does not understand it as hopeful and, instead, sees it
   as anti-establishment militancy (89–90).
2 The "Maharal" is an acronym for the Rabbi Judah Loew Betzalel, a
   sixteenth-century figure from Prague who published important works
   of Jewish mysticism and biblical commentary but is best known for being
   the legendary creator of the mythical Golem, a Frankenstein-like creature
   conjured to protect Jews from anti-Semitic attacks.
3 Depending on the speaker, in *Solomon Gursky Was Here* the Inuit are
   referred to variously as either the Inuit or Eskimos.
4 Lubavitch has been heavily criticized by leaders of other ultra-Orthodox
   communities, such as Rabbi Aharon Kotler, founder of the reputed
   Lakewood Yeshiva in New Jersey, Rabbi Elazar Menachem Shach, the
   former head of Israel's renowned Ponevezh Yeshiva and the one-time
   spokesman of the Satmar Hasidim, for its messianic obsession (Berger, 7).

5 It is tempting to view this mockery of religion generally in terms of Nietzsche's anti-religious doctrine. However, it is important to bear in mind, first, that Ephraim is addressing "pagans," not monotheists, and certainly not monotheistic Jews. Richler's satire of Jews may be stinging, but it does reach the levels of utter burlesque evident in this passage. Second, Ephraim may be twisting Judaism into some Machiavellian comedy, but he is hardly the mouthpiece of authentic Judaism – more a conniver than a satirist.

CHAPTER FOUR

1 Throughout his career, Richler frequently went on record bemoaning what he described as "special pleading" – exceptional treatment of any specific population because of compassion or guilt rather than genuine aptitude or achievement. For him, special pleading, which he saw as morphing into a pandemic of political correctness in the 1990s, was perennially in need of rectification – a position that is prevalent in his novels. Because of this attitude, in the early 1970s Leslie Fiedler deemed Richler's novels disturbingly conservative (103). This attitude, a sort of politically incorrect zeal, played a decided role in the critical backlash against Richler.

2 In retrospect, Richler might be seen as an early opponent of post-humanism.

3 An earlier model of such a laboratory is, for instance, Sartre's short story, "The Childhood of a Leader" (1939). In this work "human situations" resonate with the notions that dominate Sartre's philosophical text *Being and Nothingness*, which was published four years later and "anticipate[ed] later theoretical writings" such as *Reflections on the Jewish Question* (1946), *Saint Genet: Comedian and Martyr* (1952), and Critique of Dialectical Reason (1960) (Brinker 1994, 101). However, the story, which Menachem Brinker reads as a satire dealing with two of Sartre's distinct philosophical interests, self-deception and social conditioning, presents ideas in a more abstract fashion than do Richler's novels (102).

4 In contrast to the "target audience," Toker also describes the hurdle audience: "a segment of the work's contemporary readership but one that can impede access of the target audience to the work. The notion of the hurdle audience is needed because it is broader than the notion of censorship" (2005, 282). Her discussion mainly addresses Soviet writers, but it also addresses the kinds of constraints faced by Jane Austen and the three strategies enlisted by writers to surmount the hurdle, decoy, camouflage, or self-censorship (283).

5 Some readers have been charmed by the satire of philanthropic good
   will in Richler's novels, even those published well into the PC era. By
   2001, Richler had become somewhat of a celebrity in Italy, where *Barney's
   Version* had sold more than 200,000 copies and had evolved into a
   cultural phenomenon (Yanofsky, 267). It was heralded as a manifesto
   for those who delighted in Barney's politically incorrect zeal (Knelman).
   The editor of the conservative newspaper *Il Foglio* had championed the
   eponymous Barney Panofsky as a twenty-first-century rarity – a lovable
   sexist (Kramer 2008, 372), and *Richleriano* had become a code word for
   witty but socially unfashionable comments and observations (Yanofsky,
   267). Following Richler's book tour of Italy the same year, *Il Foglio* ran
   a column, "Andrea's Version," by Andrea Marcenaro, who "felt that
   Barney gave him a voice with which to attack the political left without
   being mistaken for a right-wing fascist" (Kramer 2008, 372).
6 See *The Journals of A.H. Maslow* (1979) for an overview of the differences between men and women and the process of self-actualization.
7 Maslow sets out his view of the motivations that underlie humanity's
   essential priorities – the hierarchy of physiological needs, safety, love,
   esteem, and self-actualization – in *Motivation and Personality* (1954).
8 Clara's anti-Jewish quips are suggestive of Woolf's eclectic anti-Semitism
   (see Trubowitz); and a following of acolytes develops after her death,
   evoking the posthumous career of Sylvia Plath, immortalized not only
   for her work but also for her importance to feminism.
9 The categorization of Jews as "white" has evolved and become more
   prominent as the discussion of identity politics has surged in the twenty-
   first century.
10 This is yet another example where Richler casts a cringeworthy shrew
   as a Jewish woman, a frequent pattern found repeatedly in his fiction.
11 When Richler released *Barney's Version* in 1998, "humansexual" seemed
   like an ultra-progressive neologism. Though the word still does not appear
   in the Oxford English Dictionary (web), it is included in more popular
   dictionary sites, such as Urbandictionary.com.
12 I am indebted to Ariela Freedman for her comments on Richler's tendency
   to respond to anti-Semitism with "special pleading," though he decries
   similar reactions when they are lodged by other social, political, and
   ethnic groups.

CHAPTER FIVE

1 In a similar vein, Robertson Davies claims that his novel, *Fifth Business*, only attracted Canadian readers after the book had "gained very warm recommendation in the United States and elsewhere" (1996, 59).

2 The very title of Davies's work is a barb about Canada's inferiority vis-à-vis the US as it invokes Patrick Anderson's "Poem on Canada" (1946), which refers to Canada as America's attic.

3 In concluding his article, Seiler notes that, ironically, the Nova Scotia actor who played Joe Canadian, Jeff Douglas, moved to Los Angeles a year after the commercial aired to try to parlay his fame into Hollywood success. In the wake of Douglas's move, the media decried Canada's inability to retain local talent, especially those in the arts (such as Jim Carrey, Martin Short, Mike Myers, Michael J. Fox, William Shatner, Shania Twain, and others). One journalist even quipped that "Joe" had really become a Canadian by migrating south (61).

4 It would be inaccurate to portray Frye's views in *The Bush Garden* as utterly dismissive of Canadian literature. He identifies individual works of excellence and credits Canadian authors with producing "an imaginative legacy of dignity and high courage" (1971a, 250). While unapologetic in proclaiming that "Canada has produced no author who is a classic in the sense of possessing a vision greater in kind than that of his best readers" (213), he grants that what is most important for present and future Canadian authors and readers is not isolated works of genius but "the inheritance of the entire enterprise" (251) – the whole composite of Canadian literary texts.

5 Carter, in tracing Kroetsch's and Hutcheon's views on Canadian culture and identity, shows how both scholars specifically illustrate the Canadian condition, one that celebrates plurality and diversity, in contrast to the American tendency to guard ideas of unifying national myths. The urge to frame Canada's situation through this juxtaposition may hint at an unintended self-reflexive quality. Canadians may proclaim that their country no longer hovers in the shadow of its southern neighbour; however, the tendency of scholars to repeatedly outline the Canadian socio-cultural landscape specifically in relation to the United States suggests otherwise.

6 In *The Incomparable Atuk* the Inuit are referred to by the term that was formerly popular for the native people of northern Canada, "Eskimos."

7 Queen Elizabeth and her entourage did, in fact, visit Yellowknife in 1970 to mark the centennial celebration and there was an awkward

presentation of Indigenous talent and culture. See Pat Carney's *Tiara and Atigi: Northwest Territories 1970 Centennial – The Royal Tour.*

8 See Frank Davey for a fuller discussion of the narratological structure in *Joshua Then and Now.*

9 In reviewing *Barney's Version*, both James Shapiro and Charles McGrath note that the editorial remarks recall the annotations of Charles Kinbote to the poem by John Shade in Nabokov's *Pale Fire* (1962). The two novels otherwise bear little resemblance, but the footnotes are suggestive of the self-referential aspect of *Barney's Version*, which registers the collapse of assumptions regarding the relationship between truth and reality in fiction.

10 Veteran Québécois government official and businessman Michel Bélanger responded to Richler's *New Yorker* article with an attack on his right to be a Quebec resident: "Foreigner is not the right expression [for Richler]. I think the right expression is he doesn't belong" (qtd in Posner, 284); and Gilles Duceppe, previously a member of the Canadian Parliament and former head of the Bloc Québécois, called Richler "a consummate racist with a totally decayed mind" (qtd in Posner, 284).

11 "Piss Quick," is a reference to the French name for Quebec, Province du Quebec, as well as the province's French separatist party, the Parti Québécois (PQ), which was founded upon the belief that Quebec should separate from Canada and become independent.

CHAPTER SIX

1 Leslie Fiedler also notes the prominence of attacks on mediocre aesthetics and low-grade intellectualism in Richler's work. However, in making this point he mainly claims that Richler's style was unimpressive and even characteristic of the exact type of mediocrity that his novels mock: "middlebrow satire ... however deliciously gross, an anti-genteel defence of the genteel tradition" (103).

2 "People thought it was arbitrary, that anyone can fling paint around" (Helen A. Harrison qtd in McElroy).

3 The belief that any novice can create a Jackson Pollock-like creation is still widespread. Helen Harrison's book, *The Jackson Pollock Box*, contains a kit with supplies and guidelines for creating a splatter-paint painting to prove that the technique is actually difficult; that it is only deceptively facile. The idea, according to Harrison, is to educate people about Pollock's work. "They should appreciate that there was more to it than the way it appeared" (Harrison qtd in McElroy).

4 In "On a Book Entitled Lolita," Nabokov cites curiosity as an essential component of aesthetic bliss. Richler quotes Bellow's appreciation of Nabokov's call for "aesthetic bliss" (Richler 1998b, 96).

5 This critique may hint at an autobiographical grievance. As a Canadian writer – rather than an American writer – Richler seems to resent his diminished chances of achieving major wealth and fame. In his non-fiction, he refers to such American writers as Norman Podhoretz, Mary McCarthy, Susan Sontag, Norman Mailer, and Lionel Trilling snidely as the "progeny" of New York intellectuals – "brilliant, influential, but astonishingly smug" (1973b, 95). He then notes that he is only "a country cousin" of this "family" (96), an outsider and therefore unwelcome in their inner circle.

6 Richler once wrote that as a young man he had fantasized about swimming across the Grand Canal as Byron did in 1818 (1990b, 2). *Barney's Version* centres on the suspicious circumstances of Boogie's death – whether he was shot by Barney or died while swimming in Lake Memphremagog – the answer to which appears in the above mentioned quasi-paratextual additions of his son.

7 Angus Wilson and Jerome Hamilton Buckley also view Steerforth very much in the mould of a Byronic hero, though Wilson mainly focuses on Steerforth's powers of seduction – powers that are inextricable from the Byronic hero archetype and present in Boogie's portrayal as well (Wilson 2006, 88–90; Buckley, 28).

8 Since the publication of *The Mad Women in the Attic* by Sandra Gilbert and Susan Gubar (1979), feminist critics have viewed the protégé/mentor relationship in works by Victorian women writers as both a subversion and accommodation of the normative literary tradition, casting women as either angels or monsters. Although I am considering these works in a different context, it would be remiss to overlook the importance of feminist theory regarding this issue.

Bibliography

WORKS BY MORDECAI RICHLER

As Writer

1968a. *Cocksure*. London: Panther, First published 1960.

1968b. *Hunting Tigers under Glass*. Toronto: McClelland and Stewart.

1969. *The Street*. Toronto: McClelland and Stewart.

1973a. *A Choice of Enemies*. Great Britain: Quartet Books Limited and Paperjacks. First published 1957.

1973b. *Shovelling Trouble*. Toronto: McClelland and Stewart. First published 1972.

1975. "Playing the Circuit." In *Creativity and the University*, edited by Andre Fortier and Rollo May, 7–28. Toronto: York University Press.

1978. *The Great Comic Book Heroes and Other Essays*. Toronto: McClelland and Stewart.

1984. *Home Sweet Home: My Canadian Album*. New York: Knopf.

1987. "Deuteronomy." In *Congregation: Contemporary Writers Read the Bible*, edited by David Rosenberg, 51–8. San Diego: Harcourt Brace Jovanovich Publishers.

1989a. *The Incomparable Atuk*. Toronto: McClelland and Stewart. First published 1963.

1989b. *Son of a Smaller Hero*. Toronto: McClelland and Stewart. First published 1955.

1990a. *Broadsides*. Toronto: Viking.

1990b. *Solomon Gursky Was Here*. New York: Knopf . First published 1989.

1991a. "Inside/Outside," *New Yorker*. 23 September, 40–92.

1991b. *St Urbain's Horseman*. Toronto: McClelland and Stewart. First published 1971.

1992. *Oh Canada! Oh Quebec!* Toronto: Penguin.

1994. *This Year in Jerusalem*. New York: Knopf.

1995. *The Apprenticeship of Duddy Kravitz*. Toronto: Penguin. First published 1959.

1998a. *Barney's Version*. New York: Knopf. First published 1997.

1998b. *Belling the Cat*. Toronto: Knopf.

1999. "Canadian Conundrums." The Stanley Knowles Lecture, University of Waterloo, 23 March.

2001. *Joshua Then and Now*. Toronto: McClelland and Stewart. First published 1980.

2002a. *The Acrobats*. Toronto: New Canadian Library. First published 1954.

2002b. *Dispatches from the Sporting Life*. Toronto: Knopf.

As Editor

1970. *Canadian Writing Today*. Middlesex: Penguin Books.

1993. *Writers on World War II*. New York: Vintage.

SECONDARY SOURCES

"104 Report of the Commission of Inquiry into the Events at the Refugee Camps in Beirut – 8 February 1983." 1983. Israel Ministry of Foreign Affairs, 8 February. https://www.mfa.gov.il/mfa/foreignpolicy/ mfadocuments/yearbook6/pages/104%20report%20of%20the% 20commission%20of%20inquiry%20into%20the%20e.aspx.

Allan, Ted. 1981. "Lies My Father Told Me." In *The Spice Box: An Anthology of Jewish Canadian Writing*, edited by Gerri Sinclair and Morris Wolfe, 82–7. Toronto: Lester and Orpen Dennys.

Allen, Woody, dir. 1983. *Zelig*. Perf. Woody Allen, Mia Farrow, Patrick Horgan. Orion Pictures Corporation.

Amsden, Cynthia. 1998. "Robert Lantos: The Singular Prince of Serendip." *Take One* (Fall): 7–11.

Arnold, Matthew. 1966. *Culture and Anarchy*. Cambridge: University Press.

Atwood, Margaret. 1972. *Survival: A Thematic Guide to Canadian Literature*. Toronto: Anansi.

– 2000. *The Blind Assassin*. New York: Anchor.

– 2004. *Strange Things: The Malevolent North in Canadian Literature*. London: Virago.

Barber, John. 2010. "Why Mordecai Richler Isn't Being Studied in Canadian Universities." *Globe and Mail*, 22 December.

Barthes, Roland. 1974. *s/z*. Translated by Richard Miller. New York: Hill and Wang.

Bauer, Yehuda. 1982. *A History of the Holocaust*. New York: Franklin Watts.

Baum Singer, Melina. 2010. "Is Richler Canadian Content? Jewishness, Race and Diaspora." *Canadian Literature/Littérature canadienne* 207 (Winter): 11–25.

Bell, Pearl. 1980. "Singing the Same Old Songs," *Commentary* 70, no. 4: 70–4.

Bellow, Saul. 1963. *The Adventures of Augie March*. Greenwich: Crest Book.

– 1994. "Papuans and Zulus." *New York Times*, 10 March.

Berger, David. 2001. *The Rebbe, the Messiah, and the Scandal of Orthodox Indifference*. London: Littman Library of Jewish Civilization.

Berman, Paul, ed. 1992. *Debating PC*. New York: Dell.

Bernstein, Richard. 1990. "The Rising Hegemony of the Politically Correct." *New York Times*, 28 October.

Biale, David. 2002. "Historical Heresies and Modern Jewish Identity." *Jewish Social Studies* (New Series) 8, nos. 2/3: 112–32.

Bialik, H.N. 1948. "The City of Slaughter." In *The Complete Poetic Works of Hayyim Nahman Bialik*, vol. 1, edited by Israel Efros. New York: Histadruth Ivrith of America.

Blake, Jason. 2004. "'The Truth Will Out' – Mordecai Richler's *Barney's Version*." *Central European Journal of Canadian Studies* 4, no. 1: 69–79.

Bloom, Harold. 1973. *The Anxiety of Influence*. Oxford: Oxford University Press.

Bonnycastle, Stephen. 1986. "Structure and Consciousness in *Joshua Then and Now*." In *Perspectives on Mordecai Richler*, edited by Michael Darling, 159–78. Toronto: ECW Press.

Born, Daniel. 1992. "Private Gardens, Public Swamps: *Howards End* and the Revaluation of Liberal Guilt." *NOVEL: A Forum on Fiction* 25, no. 2: 141–59.

Braine, John. 1957. *Room at the Top*. London: Eyre and Spottiswoode.

Brauner, David. 2010. "Writing the Triple Whammy: Canadian-Jewish-Québécois Identity, the Comedy of Self-Deprecation, and the Triumph of Duddy Kravitz." *Canadian Literature/Littérature canadienne* 207 (Winter): 76–88.

Breines, Paul. 1990. *Tough Jews: Political Fantasies and the Moral Dilemmas of American Jews*. New York: Basic Books.

Brenner, Rachel Feldhay. 1989a. "A.M. Klein and Mordecai Richler: Canadian Responses to the Holocaust." *Journal of Canadian Studies/ Revue d'études canadiennes* 24, no. 2: 65–77.

– 1989b. *Assimilation and Assertion: The Response to the Holocaust in Mordecai Richler's Writing*. New York: Peter Lang.

– 1998. "Canadian Jews and Their Story: The Making of Canadian Jewish Literature." *Prooftexts* 18, no. 3: 283–97.

Breton, Rob. 2002. "Crisis? Whose Crisis? George Orwell and Liberal Guilt." *College Literature* 29, no. 4: 47–66.

Brinker, Menachem. 1994. "A Double Clearing of the Fog: Sartre's 'The Childhood of a Leader' and Its Relation to His Philosophy." In *Comments in Reflection: Essays in Literature and Moral Philosophy*, edited by Leona Toker, 104–17. New York and London: Garland.

Bronner, Leila Leah. 2011. *Journey to Heaven*. Jerusalem: Urim Publications.

Brosgol, Dan. 2012. "A.B. Yehoshua and 'Partial' Jews: An Assault on Jewish identity." *Jewish Boston*, 20 March. https://www.jewishboston. com/read/a-b-yehoshua-and-partial-jews-an-assault-on-jewish-identity.

Brontë, Charlotte. 1985. *Jane Eyre*. London: Penguin.

– 1992. *Villette*. London: Macmillan.

Buchan, John. 1994. *The Thirty-Nine Steps*. New York: Dover.

Buckley, Jerome Hamilton. 1981. *The Victorian Temper: A Study in Literary Culture*. Cambridge: University of Cambridge Press.

Cameron, Donald. 1973. *Conversations with Canadian Novelists*. Toronto: Macmillan.

Carney, Pat. 1971. *Tiara and Atigi: Northwest Territories 1970 Centennial – The Royal Tour*. Vancouver: Mitchell Press.

Carter, Adam. 2003. "Namelessness, Irony, and National Character in Contemporary Canadian Criticism and the Critical Tradition." *Studies in Canadian Literature/Études en littérature canadienne* 28, no. 1: 5–25.

Céline, Louis-Ferdinand. 2006. *Journey to the End of the Night*. New York: New Directions.

Charendoff, Mark. 2009. Interview. Jerusalem, July.

Cohen, Nathan. 1971a. "A Conversation with Mordecai Richler." In *Mordecai Richler*, edited by David Sheps, 22–42. Toronto: Ryerson Press.

– 1971b. "Heroes of the Richler View." In *Mordecai Richler*, edited by David Sheps, 43–57. Toronto: Ryerson Press.

Cooke, Nathalie, and Norm Ravvin, eds. 2010. "Mordecai Richler." *Canadian Literature* 207 (Winter): 6–9.

Craniford, Ada. 1992. *Fact and Fiction in Mordecai Richler's Novels.* Lewiston, NY: Edwin Mellen.

Cude, Wilfred. 1986. "Jacob Hersh, Dr. Johnson, and Joseph K.: Literary Allusion and Comic Resolution." *Perspectives on Mordecai Richler,* edited by Michael Darling. Toronto: ECW Press.

Darling, Michael. 1986. "Introduction." In *Perspectives on Mordecai Richler,* edited by Michael Darling, 1–13. Toronto: ECW Press.

Davey, Frank. 1993. *Post-National Arguments.* Toronto: University of Toronto Press.

Davidson, Arnold E. 1983. *Mordecai Richler.* New York: Frederick Ungar.

Davies, Robertson. 1960. *A Voice from the Attic.* Toronto: Penguin.

– 1996. *The Merry Heart: Reflections on Reading, Writing and the World of Books.* New York: Penguin Books.

Davis, J. Madison, ed. 1989. *Conversations with Robertson Davies.* Jackson: University Press of Mississippi.

Dawidowicz, Lucy S. 1976. *A Holocaust Reader.* New York: Behrman House.

Deer, Glenn. 2010. "Early Richler, *Las Fallas,* and Sacrificing the National Self." *Canadian Literature* 207 (Winter): 90–102.

Dickens, Charles. 1986. *David Copperfield.* New York: Penguin Classics.

– 1994. *Oliver Twist.* London: Puffin.

– 1997. *Our Mutual Friend.* Hertfordshire: Wordsworth Editions.

Donovan, Kevin, dir. 2000. *I Am Canadian.* MacLaren Lintas. 1 min.

Eliot, George. 1994. *Middlemarch.* London: Penguin.

Ellison, Ralph. 1982. *Invisible Man.* Middlesex: Penguin Books.

Fiedler, Leslie. 1971. "Some Notes on the Jewish Novel in English." In *Mordecai Richler,* edited by David Sheps, 99–105. Toronto: Ryerson Press.

Foran, Charles. 2010. *Mordecai: The Life and Times.* Toronto: Alfred A. Knopf.

Forster, E.M. 1954. *Howards End.* New York: Vintage.

Freedman, Ariela. 2011. E-mail correspondence. 25 December.

Frye, Northrop. 1957. *An Anatomy of Criticism: Four Essays.* Princeton, NJ: Princeton University Press.

– 1971a. *The Bush Garden: Essays on the Canadian Imagination.* Toronto: Anansi.

– 1971b. "The Mythos of Winter: Irony and Satire." In *Satire: Modern Essays in Criticism,* ed. Ronald Paulson, 233–47. Hoboken, NJ: Prentice Hall.

Fuchs, Daniel. 1961. *Summer in Williamsburg*. New York: Carroll and Graf.

Furman, Andrew. 1997. *Israel through the Jewish-American Imagination*. Albany: State University of New York Press.

Genette, Gérard. 1980. *Narrative Discourse: An Essay in Method*. Translated by Jane E. Lewin. Ithaca, NY: Cornell University Press.

Gibson, Graeme. 1972. *Eleven Canadian Novelists Interviewed by Graeme Gibson*. Toronto: Anansi.

Gilbert, Sandra M., and Susan Gubar. 2000. *The Madwoman in the Attic*. New Haven: Yale University Press.

Gilbert, Teresa. 2009. "Ghost Stories: Fictions of History and Myth." In *The Cambridge History of Canadian Literature*, edited by Coral Ann Howells and Eva-Marie Kröller, 478–87. Cambridge: Cambridge University Press.

Gilman, Sander L. 1986. *Jewish Self-Hatred*. Baltimore: Johns Hopkins University Press.

Gopnik, Adam. 2006. "Mordecai Richler: A Local Boy at Home in the Word." *MacLean's*, 27 October.

Granatstein, J.L., and Norman Hillmer. 1991. *For Better or for Worse: Canada and the United States to the 1990s*. Toronto: Copp Clark Pitman.

Green, Arthur. 1992. "Nahman of Bratslav's Messianic Striving." In *Essential Papers on Messianic Movement and Personalities in Jewish History*, edited by Marc Saperstein, 389–432. New York: New York University Press.

Greenstein, Michael. 1989. *Third Solitudes: Tradition and Discontinuity in Jewish Canadian Literature*. Montreal and Kingston: McGill-Queens University Press.

Gruber, Eva. 2004. "Literature of the First Nations, Inuit, and Métis." In *History of Literature in Canada*, ed. Reingard M. Nischik, 413–28. Rochester: Camden House.

Hammel, Yan. 2005. "Yvette, Solange et Chantal: Les Québécoises de Mordecai Richler." *Voix et Image* 30, no. 3 (Spring): 57–71.

Harrison, Bernard. 1994. "Sterne and Sentimentalism." In *Commitments in Reflection: Essays in Literature and Moral Philosophy*, edited by Leona Toker, 63–100. New York: Garland.

Harshav, Benjamin. 1984. "Fictionality and Fields of Reference: Remarks on a Theoretical Framework." *Poetics Today* 5, no. 2: 227–51.

Harvey, William R. 1969. "Charles Dickens and the Byronic Hero." *Nineteenth-Century Fiction* 24, no. 3: 305–16.

Herman, Ellen. 1996. *The Romance of American Psychology: Political Culture in the Age of Experts*. Berkeley: University of California Press.

Heyd, David. 1982. *Supererogation: Its Status in Ethical Theory.* Cambridge: Cambridge University Press.

Hitchens, Christopher. 2004. "Great Scot: Between Kipling and Fleming Stands John Buchan, the Father of the Modern Spy Thriller." *Atlantic Monthly*, March.

Housman, A.E. 1933. "The Name and Nature of Poetry." The Leslie Stephen Lecture, Cambridge, 9 May.

Howe, Irving. 1995. *The End of Jewish Secularism.* New York: Hunter College.

Howells, Coral Ann. 2004. *Where Are the Voices Coming From? Canadian Culture and the Legacies of History.* New York: Rodopi.

Howells, Coral Ann, and Eva-Marie Kröller, eds. 2009. *The Cambridge History of Canadian Literature.* New York: Cambridge University Press.

Hutcheon, Linda. 1988. *The Canadian Postmodern: A Study of Contemporary English-Canadian Fiction.* Toronto: Oxford University Press.

Hutcheon, Linda, and Marion Richmond, eds. 1990. *Other Solitudes: Canadian Multicultural Fictions.* Toronto: Oxford University Press.

Iannone, Carol. 1990. "The Adventures of Mordecai Richler." *Commentary* 80, no. 6: 51–3.

Kaplan, Lawrence. 2011. "Uncle Melech and Cousin Joey: The Search for the Absent Hero in A.M. Klein's *The Second Scroll* and Mordecai Richler's *St Urbain's Horseman.*" In *Failure's Opposite: Listening to A.M. Klein*, edited by Norman Ravvin and Sherry Simon, 179–90. Montreal and Kingston: McGill-Queens University Press.

Karmel, Pepe. 1999. *Jackson Pollock: Interviews, Articles, and Reviews.* New York: The Museum of Modern Art.

Kattan, Naim. 1965. "Mordecai Richler – Craftsman or Artist." *Congress Bulletin* (September/October): 46–51.

Kay, Barbara. 2011. "An Insult to Richler: Montreal Can Do Better." *National Post*, 24 June.

Kieval, Hillel J. 2000. *Languages of Community: The Jewish Experience in The Czech Lands.* Los Angeles and Berkeley: University of California Press.

Kincaid, James. 1969. "Symbol and Subversion in *David Copperfield.*" *Studies in the Novel* 1, no. 2: 196–206.

Klein, A.M. 1987. *The Second Scroll.* Toronto: McClelland and Stewart.

Korte, Barbara. 1994. "In Quest of an Arctic Past: Mordecai Richler's *Solomon Gursky Was Here.*" In *Historiographic Metafiction in Modern American and Canadian Literature*, edited by Bernd Engler and Kurt Müller, 493–505. Padeborn: Ferdinand Schöningh.

Kortenaar, Neil ten. 2004. "Multiculturalism and Globalization." In *The Cambridge History of Canadian Literature*, 556–79. Cambridge: Cambridge University Press.

Krafchik, Marcelline. 1988. *World without Heroes: The Brooklyn Novels of Daniel Fuchs*. London and Toronto: Associated University Presses.

Kramer. Reinhold. 2008. *Mordecai Richler: Leaving St Urbain*. Montreal and Kingston: McGill-Queens University Press.

– 2011. "Richler, Son of Klein." In *Failure's Opposite: Listening to A.M. Klein*, edited by Norman Ravvin and Sherry Simon, 169–78. Montreal and Kingston: McGill-Queens Univeristy Press.

Kreisel, Henry. 2004. *The Almost Meeting and Other Stories*. Edmonton: NeWest Press.

Lambert, Josh. 2005. "Canada's Mordecai Richler and Zionism: 'A Man without Land Is Nobody.'" *Midstream* 51, no. 4: 29–32.

Layton, Irving, with David O'Rourke. 2006. *Waiting for the Messiah*. Toronto: McClelland and Stewart.

Leiman, Shnayer Z. 2002. "The Adventures of the Maharal of Prague in London: Rabbi Yudel Rosenberg and the Golem of Prague." *Tradition* 36, no. 1: 26–58.

Lennox, John, and Ruth Panofsky, eds. 1997. *Selected Letters of Margaret Laurence and Adele Wiseman*. Toronto: University of Toronto Press.

Leonard, John. 1990. "Solomon Gursky Was Here." *The Nation*, 4 June. https://www.thefreelibrary.com/Solomon+Gursky+Was+Here.-a08481176.

LePan, Douglas. 2010. "A Country without a Mythology." In *Canadian Poetry 1920–1960*, edited by Brian Trehearne. Toronto: McClelland and Stewart.

Lewis, Richard J., dir. 2010. *Barney's Version*. 2010. Serendipity Point Films. 134 min.

Lewis, Wyndham. 1971. "The Greatest Satire Is Non-Moral." In *Satire: Modern Essays in Criticism*, edited by Ronald Paulson, 66–77. Hoboken, NJ: Prentice Hall.

Magder, Jason. 2016. "Richler Gazebo Vandalized: Mayor Says Police Presence Will Be Stepped Up." *Montreal Gazette*, 19 September.

Majer, Krzysztof. 2008. "The Picaro Messiah and the Unworthy Scribe: A Pattern of Obsession in Mordecai Richler's Late Fiction." PhD diss., Uniwersytet Lodzki.

– 2019. "From Painter to Schlockmeister: The Evolution of the 'Doubtful Artist' in Mordecai Richler's Fiction." In *Kanade, di Goldene Medine? Perspectives on Canadian-Jewish Literature and Culture/Perspectives sur la littérature et la culture juives canadiennes*, edited by Krzysztof Majer,

Justyna Fruzińska, Józef Kwaterko, and Norman Ravvin, 61–76. Leiden: Brill/Rodopi.

Maslow, Abraham H. 1970. *Motivation and Personality*. New York: Harper and Row.

– 1979. *The Journals of A.H. Maslow*. Monterey, CA: Brooks/Cole.

McElroy. Steven. 2010. "If It's So Easy, Why Don't You Try It." *New York Times*, 3 December.

McGrath, Charles. 2010. "Novelists Self-Portrait Distilled on Screen." *New York Times*, 24 November.

McSweeney, Kerry. 1979. "Revaluing Mordecai Richler." *Studies in Canadian Literature* 4, no. 2.

Moran, Maureen. 2006. *Victorian Literature and Culture*. London: Continuum.

Morra, Linda. 2001. "Playing the Fool: The Satire of Canadian Cultural Nationalism in Mordecai Richler's *The Incomparable Atuk*." *Studies in Canadian Literature/Études en littérature canadienne* 26, no. 1.

Myer, David. 1973. "Mordecai Richler as Satirist." *Ariel: A Review of International English Literature*.

Nabokov, Vladimir. 1959. "On a Book Entitled *Lolita*." *Encounter* (April): 73–6.

– 1990. *Strong Opinions*. New York: Vintage.

Nadel, Ira. 2011. Interview. Vancouver, 19 August.

Nadel, Robin. 2010. "Heroic Imaginings." *Canadian Literature* 207 (Winter): 90–102.

New, W.H., ed. 1990. *A Literary History of Canada: Canadian Literature in English*. Vol. 4. 2nd ed. Toronto: University of Toronto Press.

Newman, Peter C. 1978. *Bronfman Dynasty: The Rothschilds of the New World*. Toronto: McClelland and Stewart.

Nicholson, Ian A.M. 2001. "Giving Up Maleness: Abraham Maslow, Masculinity, and the Boundaries of Psychology." *History of Psychology* 4, no. 1: 79–91.

Nietzsche, Friedrich. 1955. *Beyond Good and Evil*. Translated by Marianne Cowan. Chicago: Henry Regnery Company.

Nischik, Reingard M., ed. 2008. *History of Literature in Canada*. Rochester: Camden.

Orwell, George. 1937. *The Road to Wigan Pier*. Published online June 2002. https://gutenberg.net.au/ebooks02/0200391.txt.

– 1946. "Why I Write." Published online August 2003. https://gutenberg. net.au/ebooks03/0300011h.html#part47.

– 1989. *Down and Out in Paris and London*. London: Penguin.

Osachoff, Margaret Gail. 1986. "Richler's Pastoral of the City Streets."
    In *Perspectives on Mordecai Richler*, edited by Michael Darling, 33–51.
    Toronto: ECW Press.

Ozick, Cynthia. 1988. *The Messiah of Stockholm*. New York: First Vintage
    Books Edition.

– 1994. "America toward Yavneh." In *What Is Jewish Literature?*, edited
    by Hana Wirth Nesher, 20–35. Philadelphia: Jewish Publication Society.

– 1997. *The Puttermesser Papers*. New York: A.A. Knopf.

Paley, Grace. 1987. "The Used-Boy Raisers." In *The Little Disturbances
    of Man*. New York: Penguin Books.

– 2005. "Clearing My Jewish Throat." In *Who We Are: On Being
    (and Not Being) a Jewish American Writer*, edited by Derek Rubin.
    New York: Schocken.

Panofsky, Ruth. 2020. E-mail exchange. 8 September.

Patai, Raphael. 1979. *The Messiah Texts*. Detroit: Wayne State University
    Press.

Perry, Ruth. 1992. "A Short History of the Term Politically Correct."
    In *Beyond PC: Toward A Politics of Understanding*, edited by Patricia
    Aufderheide, 71–9. St Paul: Graywolf Press.

Polk, James, ed. 1982. *Divisions on a Ground: Essays in Canadian
    Culture*. Toronto: Anansi.

Pollock, Zailig. 1986. "Duddy Kravitz and Betrayal." In *Perspectives on
    Mordecai Richler*, edited by Michael Darling, 123–37. Toronto:
    ECW Press.

– 1994. *A.M. Klein: The Story of the Poet*. Toronto: University of Toronto
    Press.

Posner, Michael. 2004. *The Last Honest Man: Mordecai Richler, an Oral
    Biography*. Toronto: McClelland and Stewart.

Prose, Francine. 1990. "Hopping Mad in Montreal." *New York Times*,
    8 April.

Ramraj, Victor J. 1983. *Mordecai Richler*. Boston: Twayne.

Ravvin, Norm. 1994. "Countering the Concentration Camp World:
    Ethical Response to the Holocaust in Canadian and American Fiction."
    PhD diss., National Library of Canada.

– ed. 2001. *Not Quite Mainstream: Canadian Jewish Short Stories*.
    Calgary: Red Deer Press.

– 2020. E-mail exchange. 8 September.

Redekop, Magdalene. 2004. "Canadian Literary Criticism and the Idea
    of a National Literature." In *The Cambridge Companion to Canadian
    Literature*, 263–75. Cambridge: Cambridge University Press.

Richler, Shmarya. 2010. Telephone interview. Efrat, Israel, April.

Rimmon-Kenan, Shlomith. 2002. *Narrative Fiction: Contemporary Poetics*. London: Routledge.

Robinson, Ira, Pierre Anctil, and Mervin Butovsky, eds. 1990. *An Everyday Miracle: Yiddish Culture in Montreal*. Montreal: Véhicule.

Rockaway, Robert. 2000. *But He Was Good to His Mother: The Lives and Crimes of Jewish Gangsters*. Jerusalem: Gefen.

Rorty, Richard. 1989. *Contingency, Irony and Solidarity*. Cambridge: Cambridge University Press.

Roth, Philip. 1979. *The Ghost Writer*. New York: Fawcett Crest.

– 1986. *The Counterlife*. New York: Vintage.

– 1989. *Goodbye, Columbus*. Boston: Houghton Mifflin.

– 1993. *Operation Shylock*. New York: Simon and Schuster.

– 2004. *The Plot against America*. New York: Vintage.

– 2005. "Writing about Jews." In *Who We Are: On Being (and Not Being) a Jewish American Writer*, edited by Derek Rubin, 42–63. New York: Schocken.

Rubin, Derek, ed. 2005. *Who We Are: On Being (and Not Being) a Jewish American Writer*. New York: Schocken.

Sacks, Sam. 2011. "Rich Man, Poor Man." *Commentary* (April).

Saperstein, Marc, ed. 1992. *Essential Papers on Messianic Movements and Personalities in Jewish History*. New York: New York University Press.

Sartre, Jean Paul. 1969. "Childhood of a Leader." In *The Wall*, translated by Lloyd Alexander. New York: New Directions.

Scholem, Gershon. 1971. *The Messianic Idea in Judaism*. London: George Allen and Unwin.

Schulberg, Budd. 1941. *What Makes Sammy Run?* New York: Penguin.

Schweid, Eliezer. 1992. "Jewish Messianism: Metamorphoses of an Idea." In *Essential Papers on Messianic Movement and Personalities in Jewish History*, edited by Marc Saperstein, 53–72. New York: New York University Press.

Seiler, Robert M. 2002. "Selling Patriotism/Selling Beer: The Case of the 'I Am Canadian Commercial.'" *American Review of Canadian Studies* 32 (Spring): 44–66.

Seltzer, Robert. 1980, *Jewish People, Jewish Thought*. New York: Macmillan.

Shapiro, James. 2010. "The Way He Was – Or Was He?" *New York Times*, 21 December.

Sheps, David, ed. 1971. *Mordecai Richler*. Toronto: Ryerson Press.

– 1974. "Waiting for Joey: The Theme of the Vicarious in *St. Urbain's Horseman*." *Journal of Canadian Fiction* 3 (Winter): 83–92.

Shklar, Judith N. 1984. *Ordinary Vices*. Cambridge, MA: Belknap Press.

Singer, Isaac Bashevis. 1955. *Satan in Goray*. New York: Noonday Press.

– 1966. *The Family Moskat*. London: Secker and Warburg.

Singer, Israel Joshua. 1985. *The Brothers Ashkenazi*. New York: Carroll and Graf.

Spacks, Patricia Meyer. 1971. "Some Reflections on Satire." In *Satire: Modern Essays in Criticism*, ed. Ronald Paulson, 360–78. New Jersey: Prentice Hall.

Stone, Harry. 1959. "Dickens and the Jews." *Victorian Studies* 2, no. 3: 223–53.

Tausky, Thomas E. 1986. "*St Urbain's Horseman*: The Novel as Witness." In *Perspectives on Mordecai Richler*, edited by Michael Darling, 75–91. Toronto: ECW Press.

Taylor, Charles. 1989. *Sources of Self*. Cambridge: Harvard University Press.

Toker, Leona. 2005. "Target Audience, Hurdle Audience, and the General Reader: Varlam Shalamov's Art of Testimony." *Poetics Today* 26, no. 2. https://web.archive.org/web/20190308124818id_/http://pdfs. semanticscholar.org/f330/95f62cab53247da8179537428ef5c775b6f4.pdf.

– 2011. "Syntactics – Semantics – Pragmatics (Still Having One's Cake?)." In *Teaching Theory*, edited by Richard Bradford, 63–77. Basingstoke: Palgrave Macmillan.

Trilling, Lionel. 1955. *Matthew Arnold*. New York: Meridian Books.

Troper, Harold. 2010. *The Defining Decade*. Toronto: University of Toronto Press.

Trubowitz, Lara. 2008. "Concealing Leonard's Nose: Virginia Woolf, Modernist Antisemitism, and 'The Duchess and the Jeweller.'" *Twentieth Century Literature* 54, no. 3: 273–306.

Trudeau, Pierre Elliott. 1969. "Speech to the Washington Press Club." 25 March. https://www.cbc.ca/player/play/1797537698.

Uris, Leon. 1986. *Exodus*. New York: Bantam Books.

Urmson, J.O. 1958. "Saints and Heroes." In *Essays in Moral Philosophy*, edited by A.I. Melden, 198–224. Seattle: University of Washington Press.

Van Toorn, Penny. 2004. "Aboriginal Writing." In *The Cambridge Companion to Canadian Literature*. Cambridge: Cambridge University Press.

Vassanji, M.G. 2009. *Mordecai Richler*. Toronto: Penguin.

Waddel, Nathan. 2009. *Modern John Buchan: A Critical Introduction*. Cambridge: Scholars Publishing.

Weintraub, William. 2001. *Getting Started: A Memoir of the 1950s.* Toronto: McClelland and Stewart.

Wiegand, Haike Beruriah. 2009. "Jewish Mysticism and Messianism in Isaac Bashevis Singer's Family Chronicle *Di Familye Mushkat* (*The Family Moskat*)." *European Judaism* 42, no. 2: 122–8.

Werblowsky, R.J. Zvi. 1992. "Messianism in Jewish History." In *Essential Papers on Messianic Movement and Personalities in Jewish History*, edited by Marc Saperstein, 35–52. New York: New York University Press.

Wilde, Oscar. 1992. *The Portrait of Dorian Gray.* Hertfordshire: Wordsworth Editions.

Wilson, Angus. 2006. "The Heroes and Heroines of Dickens." In *Blooms Modern Critical Views: Charles Dickens*, edited by Harold Bloom. New York: Chelsea House.

Wilson, J. Dover. 1966. "Introduction." In *Culture and Anarchy.* Cambridge: Cambridge University Press.

Wimsatt, W.K., and M.C. Beardsley. 1946. "The Intentional Fallacy." *Sewanee Review* 54, no. 3: 468–88. http://www.jstor.org/stable/27537676.

Wisse, Ruth. 1980. *The Schlemiel as Modern Hero.* Chicago: University of Chicago Press.

– 2000. *The Modern Jewish Canon.* Chicago: University of Chicago Press.

– 2001. "What's a Jewish Book?" *The Forward*, 26 October.

Wolobromsky, Rubie. 2019. Interview. Efrat, Israel, December.

Woodcock, George. 1970. *Mordecai Richler.* Toronto: McClelland and Stewart.

– 1990. *Introducing Mordecai Richler's* The Apprenticeship of Duddy Kravitz. Toronto: General Paperbacks.

Worcester, David. 1960. *The Art of Satire.* New York: Russell and Russell.

Wyman, Max. 2004. *The Defiant Imagination.* Vancouver: Douglas and McIntyre.

Yanofsky, Joel. 2003. *Mordecai and Me.* Calgary: Red Deer Press.

Index

Abe, Uncle (fictional character), 52, 57, 69, 70, 103
Aboriginal peoples, 146, 160. *See also* Inuit
abstract art, 166–7
Abu Issa al-Isfahani, 84
academia, 140, 168–70, 171
The Acrobats (Richler), 7, 23, 113, 136, 162
Adler, Melech (fictional character), 32, 37, 62, 77–8
Adler, Noah (fictional character): academia and, 168; Canadian culture and, 136; disillusionment with grandfather, 32, 78; encounter with beauty, 162; family loyalty, 32–3, 33–4; identification with Old World Jewish culture and values, 37; Jewish success validated by non-Jews and, 44–5; on nihilism, 95
Adler, Wolf (fictional character), 71, 117
Akiva, Rabbi, 17, 78, 83
Albert, Lionel, 115
Alfieri, Bruno, 167
Allan, Ted, 15
Allen, Woody, 170–1; *Zelig*, 56–7

Alroy, David, 84
Anderson, Patrick: "Poem on Canada," 199n2
anti-Americanism, 28–9, 149. *See also* United States of America
antinomianism, 84
anti-Semitism: accusations of against Richler's fiction, 4, 31, 68, 116, 184; authorial distance and, 119; comparison to Inuit's plight, 147; in Quebec and Montreal, 15, 28, 69–70; retaliatory provocations against, 58; in Richler's fiction, 75; Richler's response to, 74–5, 198n12; Roth on, 75
The Apprenticeship of Duddy Kravitz (Richler): anti-Americanism and, 28–9; anti-Semitism and, 28, 31; bar mitzvah film parody, 38, 166; comparison to *What Makes Sammy Run?* (Schulberg), 30–1; family loyalty, 26–7, 29–30, 31–2; gambling, 63; hero figure, 48–9; identification with Old World Jewish culture and values, 37–8; on Israel, 71; on Jewish success validated by non-Jews, 44–5;

Kotcheff's film adaptation, 15; liberal guilt, 121–2; on mediocre art, 163; on Quebec, 154; racism towards non-Jews, 117; significance of, 14, 23; on special treatment for people with physical handicaps, 100–1; student engagement with, 193n5. *See also specific characters*
Arnold, Matthew, 171, 172, 173, 179, 181
art. *See* culture, and moral values
Asch, Sholem, 92
Atuk (fictional character), 141–2, 143–4, 147, 167
Atwood, Margaret, 44, 138, 152; *The Blind Assassin*, 180
Auden, W.H., 163, 170
audiences: hurdle audience, 197n4; target audience, 100
Austen, Jane, 197n4
authorial distance, 119

Babel, Isaac, 17; *Sunset*, 52
Barber, John, 13, 193n3
Bar Kochba, 78, 83
Barney's Version (Richler): on abstract art, 166–7; on academia, 170, 171; on authentic art, 165–6; Boogie's death, 81, 201n6; Byronic hero and, 176–8; on Canada, 150, 152, 153; comparison to *Pale Fire* (Nabokov), 200n9; condemnation of Jewish nouveau riche, 45–6; conflation with Richler's views, 107; differences from previous novels, 186–7; discrediting culture's relationship with moral integrity, 11–12, 161, 174–6, 182, 186, 188–9; female characters, 35–7, 104, 106; on feminism, 107;

108–11; film adaptation, 13; first person narration in, 149–51, 187; flawed protégé/mentor relationship, 177–8, 179; French Canadians in, 156–7; homosexuality and, 114, 116, 157; identification with Old World Jewish culture and values, 39; on Israel, 73–4; on Jewish heroic values, 70; on liberalism and liberal guilt, 94–5, 121, 122; messianic allusions, 81, 96; narrative unreliability in, 151–2, 187; on nihilism, 96; popularity in Italy, 198n5; on Quebec and Montreal, 154–6; questioning "ordinary" values, 189–91; racism towards non-Jews, 118–19; repudiating resistance to social change, 187–8. *See also specific characters*
Bauer, Yehuda, 196n6
Baum Singer, Melina, 13, 158–9
Beardsley, Monroe C., 193n1
beauty, encounters with, 162
Beckett, Samuel, 7
Bélanger, Michel, 200n10
Bell, Marilyn, 142
Bellow, Saul, 22, 163, 170–1, 180–1, 201n4
Ben Canaan, Ari (fictional character), 50, 55
Benjy, Uncle (fictional character), 27, 37, 121–2
Bennet, André (fictional character), 136, 162
Berger, L.B. (fictional character), 17, 45, 95, 136, 164–5, 170, 180
Berger, Moses (fictional character): on abstract art, 166; and culture and moral integrity, 173–4; disillusionment with writers,

180; girlfriend of, 112–13; identification with Old World Jewish culture and values, 39; identification with underdogs, 41; on Israel, 72–3; literary biography and, 170; on mediocre writing, 164–5; messianic expectations for Solomon, 81; perception of Solomon, 57, 67, 70–1, 95, 190

Berman, Paul, 98

Bernstein, Richard, 98–9

Bezalel, Judah Loew ben (Maharal), 18, 196n2

Bezmozgis, David, 19

Bialik, Hayim Nahman, 54; "The City of Slaughter," 53

biography, literary, 170–1

Birenbaum, Molly (fictional character), 115

Birenbaum, Philip (fictional character), 115

Birenbaum, Sam (Sam Burns; fictional character), 72, 115, 164

Bishinsky, Leo (fictional character), 166–7, 175

Bishinsky, Shloime (fictional character), 63, 95, 180

Blake, Jason, 151

"Bond" (Richler), 119

Bonnycastle, Stephen, 12, 35, 43

Boréal Press: *Un certain sens du ridicule*, 14

Boudreau, Cathy, 194n2

Boy Wonder (Jerry Dingleman; fictional character), 48–9

Brand, Dionne, 134

Brauner, David, 157

Breines, Paul: *Tough Jews*, 54

Brenner, Rachel Feldhay, 51, 77, 81–2, 85, 86, 185; *Assimilation and Assertion*, 12

Brinker, Menachem, 99, 197n3

Britain. *See* England

Bronfman family, 20, 44, 62, 70, 194n8

Brontë, Charlotte: *Jane Eyre*, 178; *Villette*, 178–9

Brooke, Dorothea (fictional character), 179

Buchan, John: *The Thirty-Nine Steps*, 119

Buckley, Jerome Hamilton, 201n7

Burns, Sam (Sam Birenbaum; fictional character), 72, 115, 164

Bush, George H.W., 98

Butler, Samuel, 134

Byron, Lord, 201n6

Byronic hero, 176–8, 201n7

Cambridge History of Canadian Literature (Howells and Kröller), 137

Cameron, Donald, 127, 162

Camus, Albert, 7

Canada: about, 11, 131–2, 160, 185; Canadian identity, 138–9, 158–60, 199n5; Canadian Jewish literature, 17, 18–19, 72, 77; Canadian literature, 14, 23, 137–8, 158–60, 199n4; cultural inferiority complex, 133–5; Inuit, 79–80, 119–20, 143–8, 196n3, 199n6; Massey Commission and cultural protectionism, 132–3; over-valuing Canadian writers, 139; Richler on, 131, 132, 133, 138, 139, 152–3, 185; satire of, 11, 135–7, 139–43, 148–52. *See also* Quebec

Canada Council for the Arts, 133, 139

Canadian Jewish literature, 17, 18–19, 72, 77

Canadian literature, 14, 23, 137–8, 158–60, 199n4
Canadian Literature (journal), 13
Canadian Writing Today (Richler), 137
Captain Al Cohol Comics, 146
Carter, Adam, 138, 199n5
CBC (Canadian Broadcasting Corporation), 115
celebrity artists and writers, 166, 167–8, 186
Céline, Louis-Ferdinand: Voyage au bout de la nuit, 6, 193n2
Chabon, Michael: The Adventures of Kavalier and Clay, 18
Charnofsky, Clara (fictional character), 36–7, 108–9, 175, 194n2, 198n8
Charnofsky, Norman (fictional character), 39, 109–10
Charron, Claude, 153–4
Cheever, John, 152
A Choice of Enemies (Richler), 195n1
Christian messianism, 80–2, 83, 89
class, 9, 123–4, 125–6, 171, 173
Cluett, Robert, 12
Coates, Robert, 167
Cocksure (Richler), 20, 65–6, 80
Cohen, Leonard, 19, 77, 194n7
Cohen, Matt, 19
Cohen, Nathan, 12, 102, 113, 132, 186
Cole, Jonathan (Yosel Kugelman; fictional character), 45
Colucci, Sonny (fictional character), 41, 60
comedy. See satire
comic book heroes, 51, 52–3, 114
Conrad, Joseph, 120
Cooke, Nathalie, 13
Corbeil, Carole, 106

Costello, Frank, 59
Craig, Patricia, 106
Cude, Wilfred, 85, 185
culture, and moral values: about, 11–12, 161, 186; abstract art, 166–7; academia and, 140, 168–70, 171; appreciation for both high and low culture, 162–3, 181; authentic versus banal art, 165–6; celebrity artists and writers, 166, 167–8, 186; culture and moral integrity, 171, 172–4, 181; discrediting culture's relationship to morality, 174–6, 179–80, 182, 188–9; encounters with beauty, 162; flawed protégé/ mentor relationships, 177–9, 201n8; literary biography, 170–1; mediocrity, 163–5, 172, 200n1; protagonists and, 171–2; Richler's faith in writers and Western literary tradition, 179, 180–1

Darling, Michael, 50; Perspectives on Mordecai Richler, 12
Davey, Frank, 138
David Copperfield (Dickens), 177–8, 179, 201n7
Davidson, Arnold, 12
Davies, Robertson, 133, 134, 138; Fifth Business, 199n1; Voices from the Attic, 134, 199n2
Dawidowicz, Lucy, 53
Deer, Glenn, 195n1
Diaspora Jews, 54–6, 196n5
Dickens, Charles, 120; David Copperfield, 177–8, 179, 201n7; Oliver Twist, 112; Our Mutual Friend, 112
Dingleman, Jerry (Boy Wonder; fictional character), 48–9

disadvantaged, identification with, 41

Dolan, Bette (fictional character), 142–3

doubling, protagonist/hero figure, 7, 24, 193n2, 195n1

Douglas, Jeff, 199n3

Duceppe, Gilles, 200n10

Duplessis, Maurice, 28, 70

Durelle, Yvette (fictional character), 26, 27, 28, 29, 30, 154, 156

Einstein, Albert, 54

Eliot, George: *Middlemarch*, 178, 179

Elizabeth II, queen, 144, 199n7

Ellison, Ralph: *Invisible Man*, 64–5

empowerment, Jewish, 51–3, 56–8, 127

England, 124, 132, 173

Eskimos. *See* Inuit

false messianism, 83–4

family: loyalty to, 26–7, 29–30, 32–5, 45; protagonists as family men, 35, 36

female characters, 35–7, 102–3, 106, 109–10, 112–13, 186, 198n10. *See also* women and feminism

Fiedler, Leslie, 12, 171, 181, 197n1, 200n1

first person narration, 149–51, 187

Fleming, Ian, 119

Foran, Charles: *Mordecai*, 13

Forster, E.M., 120; *Howards End*, 121, 124

Frank, Jacob, 87–8, 93

Fraser, Colin (fictional character), 106–7

Fraser, Doug (fictional character), 148, 172

free indirect discourse, 148–9, 151

French Canadians, 156–7. *See also* Quebec

Friar, Peter John (fictional character), 38, 166

Friedan, Betty, 105

Frye, Northrop, 5, 100, 135, 137–8, 139, 199n4

Fuchs, Daniel, 62, 63

gambling, 63–4

gangsters, 59–63

Gaskell, Elizabeth, 120

gay characters. *See* homosexuality

Germans, 85–6

Gibson, Graeme, 9, 102

Gilbert, Sandra: *The Mad Women in the Attic* (with Gubar), 201n8

Gilman, Sander, 184

Glick, Sammy (fictional character), 30–1

"Going Home Again" (Richler), 116–17

Gold, Herbert, 133

Golem myth, 18, 77, 78–9, 86, 90–1, 185, 196n2

Gorky, Maxim, 50

Granatstein, Jack, 28–9

Great Britain. *See* England

"The Great Comic Book Heroes" (Richler), 51, 114

Greenberg, Miriam (fictional character), 35–6, 106, 112, 187–8

Greenstein, Michael, 77

Gretzky, Wayne, 143

"Gretzky in Eighty-Four" (Richler), 143

Griffin, Mortimer (fictional character), 65

Groulx, Lionel, 69–70

Gubar, Susan: *The Mad Women in the Attic* (with Gilbert), 201n8

Gursky, Aaron (fictional character), 56

Gursky, Bernard (fictional character), 57, 71, 80, 81, 95, 136–7, 166

Gursky, Ephraim (fictional character), 79–80, 84, 87–8, 89, 120, 197n5

Gursky, Henry (fictional character), 39, 72–3, 80, 88–9, 91–2

Gursky, Isaac (fictional character), 89

Gursky, Lionel (fictional character), 88

Gursky, Morrie (fictional character), 66, 104, 174

Gursky, Solomon (fictional character): appetites and lusts, 66, 104; on Canada, 131; and culture and moral integrity, 173–4; extravagance of, 67; gambling and, 63–4; ineffectiveness of, 129; Israel and, 58, 72–3, 91; Jewish empowerment and, 56–7, 127; Jewish triumphalism and, 117–18; literary biography and, 170; messianic allusions, 80–1, 91; perception of by Moses, 57, 67, 70–1, 95, 190; retaliatory provocations against anti-Semitism, 58

Ha'am, Ahad, 54

Habonim youth movement, 54, 71. See also Zionism

Hall, Theo (fictional character), 168

Hammel, Yan, 14

Hardy, Thomas: Jude the Obscure, 124

Harrison, Helen: The Jackson Pollock Box, 200n3

Harshav, Benjamin, 5–6

Hemingway, Ernest, 46, 104, 170–1

herd instinct, 88

hero figures: about, 7–8, 75–6, 183–4; appetites, lusts, and masculinity, 64, 65–8, 103–5; challenges identifying with, 129; concerns of, 97; and culture and moral integrity, 161, 172–4, 181; and discrediting culture's relationship to morality, 174–6, 179–80, 182, 188–9; disregard for political correctness, 97–8, 127; doubling of with protagonists, 7, 24, 193n2, 195n1; gambling and, 63–4; gangsterism and disregard for the law, 58–63; Golem myth and, 18, 78–9, 86, 90–1, 185; heroic Jewish values and, 24–5, 47–8; ineffectiveness of, 129–30; Jewish empowerment and, 51–3, 56–7, 127; as Jewish men, 23; moral complexity of, 50–1; physical absence of, 49–50; and resistance and self-defence, 53–4, 55; retaliatory provocations against anti-Semitism, 58; supererogation and, 24–5, 43, 47, 58–9. See also Dingleman, Jerry; Gursky, Solomon; Hersh, Joey; messianism; Moscovitch, Bernard "Boogie"; Spicehandler, Ziggy

Hersh, Jake (fictional character): Canada and, 136, 140; and culture and moral integrity, 172–3; on Diaspora Jews, 54–5; disappointment in literature and writers, 168, 180; family loyalty and, 34–5; as family man, 35; free indirect discourse and, 148; on Germans, 85–6; Golem myth and, 86; heroic versus ordinary values and, 48; homosexuality and, 115; identification with underdogs, 41; Jewish triumphalism and, 118; on Joey's opulence, 67–8; and Joey's self-defence against anti-Semitism, 69, 103; liberal guilt and, 123–5, 126, 128; liberalism and, 93–4, 121; mediocrity of, 163–4; perception of Joey, 51, 52, 79, 85, 86–7, 103, 173, 190; special pleading and, 101

Hersh, Jenny (fictional character), 103, 172–3

Hersh, Joey (fictional character): gambling and, 63; as Hemingway hero, 104; as hero figure, 51–3; ineffectiveness of, 129; Jewish empowerment and, 57, 127; masculinity of, 103–4; messianic presence of, 78, 79, 85, 86–7, 196n1; opulence of, 67–8; perception of by Jake, 51, 52, 79, 85, 86–7, 103, 173, 190; return to Israel, 90–1; self-defence against anti-Semitism undermined by Uncle Abe, 69, 103

Hersh, Nancy (fictional character), 35, 102, 112, 118, 163

Hitchens, Christopher, 119

Hoffenberg, Mason, 175

Hoffman, Abbie, 105

Holocaust, 51, 53–4, 56, 85, 184–5

homosexuality, 113–16, 157

hope, messianic, 79, 83, 86–7

Hopper, Blair (fictional character), 122, 187–8

Hornby, Stephen Andrew (fictional character), 60–2

Housman, A.E., 162

Howe, Gordie, 143

Howe, Irving, 25–6

Howells, Coral Ann, 158; Cambridge History of Canadian Literature (with Kröller), 137

Hughes, Ted, 108

humansexual, 114, 198n11

Hunt, Glen, 135

hurdle audience, 197n4

Hutcheon, Linda, 16, 138, 159–60, 199n5

"I Am Canadian" beer commercial, 135, 199n3

Iannone, Carol, 6, 43, 51, 78, 85, 183

identity, Canadian, 138–9, 158–60, 199n5

The Incomparable Atuk (Richler), 141–4, 147–8, 167, 199n6

Indigenous Peoples, 146, 160. See also Inuit

individual worth, 127–8

"Innocents Abroad" (Richler), 120

"Insight/Outside" (Richler), 153

Inuit, 79–80, 119–20, 143–8, 196n3, 199n6

Israel, 31, 53, 54–6, 71–5, 89–92, 196n5

Italy, 198n5

Ives, Suzanne, 12

Jane Eyre (Brontë), 178

The Jewish Community in Canada, volume 1, A History, 194n3

Jewish heroics, 24–5, 47–8. See also hero figures

Jews: Canadian Jewish literature, 17, 18–19, 72, 77; conspicuous displays of piety, 42; Diaspora Jews, 54–6, 196n5; empowerment of, 51–3, 56–8, 127; Jewish success validated by non-Jews, 44–5; Lubavitch, 3, 80, 89,

196n4; Richler's fiction and Jewish literary tradition, 17–18; Richler's protagonists and hero figures as, 23–4; "tough Jewish novels," 53; triumphalism of, 117–18; "whitening" of, 159, 198n9. *See also* anti-Semitism; Golem myth; Israel; messianism; ordinary Jewish values; Zionism

Johnson, Samuel, 134

Joshua Then and Now (Richler): on academia, 169–70; on Canada, 139–40, 148–9; critique as morally uncentred, 43; on culture and moral integrity, 175; female characters, 102, 112; on feminism, 106–7; free indirect discourse, 148–9; gangsterism and disregard for the law, 60–2; homosexuality and, 113, 114; identification with Old World Jewish culture and values, 40–1, 43; identification with underdogs, 41; on Jewish nouveau riche, 45; justice and communal hypocrisy, 41–2; liberal guilt and, 122–3, 128; political correctness and, 101; protagonist as family man, 35; on Quebec, 154; racism towards non-Jews, 118; and resistance and self-defence, 53–4. *See also specific characters*

Kafka, Franz, 7
Kaplan, Lawrence, 102
Katstein, Josef, 92
Kattan, Naim, 12
Kay, Barbara, 158
Keith, W.J., 4
"Kiss the Ump" (Richler), 111–12
Kitman, Kermit, 50

Klein, A.M., 17, 19, 77, 194n7; *The Second Scroll*, 17, 72, 92, 194n7
Kolber, Leo, 20
Korte, Barbara, 16
Kortenaar, Neil ten, 134
Kotcheff, Ted: *The Apprenticeship of Duddy Kravitz* film adaptation, 15
Kotler, Aharon, 196n4
Kovner, Abba, 53–4
Kramer, Reinhold, 17, 20, 37, 87, 106
Kravitz, Duddy (fictional character): anti-Americanism and, 28–9; anti-Semitism and, 28; comparison to *What Makes Sammy Run?* (Schulberg), 30–1; family loyalty, 26–7, 29–30, 31–2; hero figure and, 48–9; Jewish nouveau riche and, 44; on mediocre art, 163; racism towards non-Jews, 117
Kravitz, Lennie (fictional character), 27, 44–5, 71
Kravitz, Max (fictional character), 27, 48–9
Kreisel, Henry, 77, 194n7
Kroetsch, Robert, 138, 159, 199n5
Kröller, Eva-Marie: *Cambridge History of Canadian Literature* (with Howells), 137
Kugelman, Yosel (Jonathan Cole; fictional character), 45

Lacroix, Serge (fictional character), 156–7
Laferrière, Dany: *Comment faire l'amour avec un nègre sans se fatiguer*, 134
Lambert, Josh, 6, 7, 31
"Language (and Other) Problems" (Richler), 153–4

Lansky, Meyer, 59
"Lansky" (Richler), 59
Lantos, Robert, 133
Laurence, Margaret, 68, 75, 184
law, disregard for, 58–63
Layton, Irving, 19, 77, 194n7
Leivik, H.: *The Golem*, 18
Leonard, John, 56–7
LePan, Douglas: "A Country without a Mythology," 137
Levine, Norman, 19
Lewis, Wyndham, 134
LGBTQ+ characters. *See* homosexuality
liberal guilt: about, 128; in *The Apprenticeship of Duddy Kravitz* (Richler), 121–2, 128; in *Barney's Version* (Richler), 121, 122; class and, 125–6; discrediting of, 126–7; *Howards End* (Forster) and, 121; individual worth and, 127–8; in *Joshua Then and Now* (Richler), 122–3; Orwell and, 123, 125–6; special pleading and, 120, 121; in *St Urbain's Horseman* (Richler), 121, 123–5, 126, 128
liberalism, 9–10, 93–5, 98
Lies My Father Told Me (film), 15
literary biography, 170–1
"London Then and Now" (Richler), 167
loyalty, family, 26–7, 29–30, 32–5, 45
Lubavitch, 3, 80, 89, 196n4

MacLean's, 4, 19
Maharal (Judah Loew ben Bezalel), 18, 196n2
Mailer, Norman, 133, 167–8, 170–1, 201n5
Majer, Krysztof, 163, 171, 183, 187
Malamud, Bernard, 22

Mandel, Eli, 77
Mandelbaum, Doris (fictional character), 109–10, 198n10
Mann, Florence, 106
Marcenaro, Andrea, 198n5
masculinity, 103–5, 184. *See also* hero figures
Maslow, Abraham, 105–6, 112, 198n7
Massey Commission (Royal Commission on National Development in the Arts, Letters and Sciences), 132–3
McBride, Eve, 108
McCarthy, Mary, 201n5
McClure, Diana (fictional character), 66, 104, 112, 170, 174
McGill University: Richler Challenge Conference (2004), 13, 158
McGrath, Charles, 200n9
McIver, Terry (fictional character), 122, 150, 151, 176
McMaster, Stuart Donald (fictional character), 139–40
McSweeney, Kerry, 10, 34, 125, 183
mediocrity, 163–5, 172, 200n1
mentor/protégé relationships, 177–9, 201n8
messianism: about, 77, 96, 185; antinomianism and, 84; in *Barney's Version* (Richler), 81, 96; Christian messianism, 83; eclectic mixing of Christian and Jewish symbols, 80–2, 89; false messianism, 83–4; hope and, 79, 83, 86–7; Jewish messianism, 82–3; Lubavitch and, 80, 196n4; messianic charlatans, 87–9; return to Israel and, 89–92; Richler in conversation with other Jewish

writers, 92–3; in *Solomon
Gursky Was Here* (Richler),
79–80, 80–1, 87–9, 91, 95; in
Son of a Smaller Hero (Richler),
77–8, 95; in *St Urbain's
Horseman* (Richler), 78–9,
86–7, 90–1, 196n1; triumph
over nihilism, 95–6
Michaels, Anne, 19
Middlemarch (Eliot), 178, 179
misanthropy, 99, 141
misogyny. *See* women and
feminism
Molière, 99
Molson: "I Am Canadian" beer
commercial, 135, 199n3
Montreal, 14–15, 133, 154, 155,
158. *See also* Quebec
Moore, Brian, 15
moral vision, in Richler's fiction,
6–7, 10–11, 16–17, 24–5, 43,
161–2, 183. *See also* Canada;
culture, and moral values; hero
figures; messianism; ordinary
Jewish values; special pleading
Morra, Linda, 148
Moscovitch, Bernard "Boogie"
(fictional character): appetites
and lusts, 67, 104; as Byronic
hero, 176–8; as counterproof
to mythical hero figures, 190;
death, 81, 201n6; as discrediting
culture's relationship with moral
integrity, 11–12, 161, 174–6,
182, 186, 188–9; as empowered,
127; ineffectiveness of, 129; on
Israel, 73–4; on liberalism, 121;
messianic allusions, 81, 84, 96
Mowatt, Farley, 132, 185
Murdoch, Sidney (fictional character), 113, 169
"My Father's Life" (Richler), 33

Nabokov, Vladimir, 130, 170, 171,
201n4; *Pale Fire*, 200n9
Nadel, Ira, 193n5
Nadel, Robin, 8, 53
Nahman, Rabbi, of Bratslav, 96
narrative techniques: first person
narration, 149–51, 187; free
indirect discourse, 148–9, 151;
narrative unreliability, 151–2,
187
New, Bill, 4
New Criticism, 4, 193n1
Nietzsche, Friedrich, 88, 99, 197n5
nihilism, 7, 48, 93, 95–6, 99
Nischik, Reingard M.: *History of
Literature in Canada*, 137
"North of Sixty" (Richler), 146–7
nouveau riche, Jewish, 43–4, 45–6,
194n3
Nussbaum, Irv (fictional character),
74, 120

Oh Canada! Oh Quebec! (Richler),
157
"Oh Canada! Oh Quebec!"
(Richler), 20, 158
Orbach, Dr (fictional character),
41–2
ordinary Jewish values: about,
25–6, 46; calling into question,
189–91; condemnation of Jewish
nouveau riche, 43–4, 45–6,
194n3; family loyalty, 26–7,
29–30, 32–5, 45; identification
with Old World Jewish culture
and values, 37–43; protagonists
as family men, 35, 36
Orwell, George, 9, 11, 123, 125–6,
130, 161; *Down and Out in
Paris and London*, 123, 126;
The Road to Wigan Pier, 123
Osachoff, M.G., 6, 86

Ozick, Cynthia, 195n4; *The Messiah of Stockholm*, 96; *Puttermesser Papers*, 18

Paley, Grace, 22–3, 90
Panofsky, Barney (fictional character): on abstract art, 166–7; on academia, 170, 171; on authentic art, 165–6; on Boogie, 127; Boogie's death and, 81, 201n6; commitment to Boogie despite failings, 174–5, 179, 186, 190; conflation with Richler's views, 107; on feminism, 107, 108–9, 110–11; first person narration and, 149–51; homosexuality and, 114, 116; on ideal womanhood, 106; identification with under-dogs, 41; on liberalism and liberal guilt, 94–5, 122; marriage breakdown, 35, 187–8; messianic allusions and, 81; narrative unreliability and, 151–2, 187; on nihilism, 96; on Quebec, 154–5; racism towards non-Jews, 118–19
Panofsky, Michael (fictional character), 152, 155–6, 167
Panofsky, Ruth, 193n5
Parti Québécois (PQ), 200n11
Patmore, Coventry: "Angel in the House," 103
Perspectives on Mordecai Richler (Darling), 12
Peters, Jessica (fictional character), 109–10
philanthropy, 57, 101–2, 129, 198n5
piety, conspicuous displays of, 42
Pinsky, Irving (fictional character), 45

Plath, Sylvia, 108, 198n8
pleasure-seeking, 64, 65–8
Pocklington, Peter, 143
Podhoretz, Norman, 201n5
political correctness, 98. *See also* special pleading
Pollock, Jackson, 166, 167, 200nn2–3
Pollock, Zailig, 31
Pope, Alexander, 100
Postema, Pam, 111
post-humanism, 197n2
postmodernism, 16–17
Price, Norman (fictional character), 195n1
Prose, Francine, 7, 10
protagonists: challenges identifying with, 129; culture and, 171–2; doubling of with hero figures, 7, 24, 193n2, 195n1; heroic values and, 47–8; as Jewish men, 23–4; moral values of, 24, 25; as self-righteous misanthropes, 99. *See also* Adler, Noah; Atuk; Berger, Moses; Hersh, Jake; Kravitz, Duddy; ordinary Jewish values; Panofsky, Barney; Shapiro, Joshua
protégé/mentor relationships, 177–9, 201n8

Quebec: anti-Semitism in, 15, 28, 69–70; contentious relationship with Richler, 14, 153, 158, 200n10; negative depictions of Quebec and Montreal, 14–15, 133, 153–6; "Piss Quick" reference, 200n11; positive depictions of French Canadians, 156–7
queer characters. *See* homosexuality

race and racism, 116–20, 147. *See also* anti-Semitism

Ramraj, Victor J., 12, 43, 48, 70,
    86, 104, 106
Ravvin, Norm, 13, 19, 51, 193n5
Renault, Solange (fictional charac-
    ter), 122, 156
resistance and self-defence, 53–4,
    55, 56, 196n6
Richardson, Cedric (fictional char-
    acter), 36, 175
Richler, Daniel, 115
Richler, Martha, 168
Richler, Mordecai: approach to,
    3–4, 4–6, 21, 184; on authorial
    distance, 119; on Byron, 201n6;
    on Canada, 131, 132, 133, 138,
    139, 152–3, 185; Canadian
    Jewish literature and, 17, 18–19;
    Canadian literature and, 23, 137,
    158–60; comparison to Roth, 14,
    15–16; on conspicuous piety,
    42–3; critical interest in, 12–14,
    193n3; critiques and controver-
    sies over fiction of, 4, 6, 10,
    19–20, 132, 197n1; in England,
    132; family loyalty and breaking
    away from family, 33, 34, 194n1;
    feminism and, 106; fiction criti-
    cized for being anti-Semitic, 4,
    31, 68, 116, 184; on gangsters,
    59–60; on Germans, 85; on
    Gretzky, 143; on human foibles,
    50, 195n2; identification with
    Old World Jewish culture and
    values, 38–9, 40; on Israel and
    Diaspora Jews, 54–6, 71, 72,
    74–5; Jewish literary tradition
    and, 17–18; Judaism and, 3, 40;
    literary biography by, 170–1;
    moral vision of, 6–7, 10–11,
    16–17, 24–5, 43, 161–2, 183;
    popular interest in, 13, 198n5;
    post-humanism and, 197n2;

postmodernism and, 16–17;
    purpose for writing, 15, 161–2;
    on Quebec and French Canadians,
    14–15, 153–4, 157; resentment
    against American writers, 201n5;
    special pleading and, 97–8, 99,
    197n1, 198n12; in university
    curriculums, 13, 193nn4–5; on
    Western literary canon, 180–1;
    wives, 106, 194n2; on writers,
    179; Zionism and, 31, 54, 56, 71
Richler, Mordecai, writings: The
    Acrobats, 7, 23, 113, 136, 162;
    "Bond," 119; Canadian Writing
    Today, 137; A Choice of Enemies,
    195n1; Cocksure, 20, 65–6, 80;
    "Going Home Again," 116–17;
    "The Great Comic Book Heroes,"
    51, 114; "Gretzky in Eighty-Four,"
    143; The Incomparable Atuk,
    141–4, 147–8, 167, 199n6;
    "Innocents Abroad," 120;
    "Insight/Outside," 153; "Kiss
    the Ump," 111–12; "Language
    (and Other) Problems," 153–4;
    "Lansky," 59; "London Then and
    Now," 167; "My Father's Life,"
    33; "North of Sixty," 146–7;
    Oh Canada! Oh Quebec!, 157;
    "Oh Canada! Oh Quebec!," 20,
    158; "Sexual Harassment,"
    107–8; The Street, 6, 116–17;
    "The Street," 136; This Year in
    Jerusalem, 55–6, 71, 78; "Why
    I Write," 161–2, 168; Writers on
    World War II, 124. See also The
    Apprenticeship of Duddy Kravitz;
    Barney's Version; hero figures;
    Joshua Then and Now; protag-
    onists; satire; Solomon Gursky
    Was Here; Son of a Smaller
    Hero; St Urbain's Horseman

Richler, Nancy, 19
Richler, Shmarya, 40
Rimmon-Kenan, Shlomith, 26, 39,
    114, 148, 149, 151
Rockaway, Robert: *But He Was
    Good to His Mother*, 59
Room at the Top (film), 30
Rorty, Richard, 129–30
Roseboro, Virgil (fictional character),
    26, 27, 28, 29, 30, 100–1, 128
Rosenberg, Yudel, 18, 42, 77, 78–9,
    86
Rosenfarb, Chava, 19
Roth, Philip, 14, 15–16, 22, 73,
    75; *The Counterlife*, 16; *The
    Ghost Writer*, 16, 33; *Goodbye,
    Columbus*, 16; *Operation Shylock*,
    16, 73; *The Plot Against America*,
    15, 16, 75; "Writing about Jews,"
    75
Royal Commission on National
    Development in the Arts,
    Letters and Sciences (Massey
    Commission), 132–3

Sacher-Masoch, Leopold von, 92
Sacks, Sam, 13
Sartre, Jean Paul, 6; "The Childhood
    of a Leader," 99, 197n3
satire: of Canada, 11, 135–7,
    139–43, 148–9; of feminism,
    106–7, 108–11; ideological align-
    ment with audience, 100; of Inuit,
    79–80, 119–20, 143–6, 147–8;
    misanthropy and, 99; moral vision
    undermined by, 10–11; Richler's
    use of, 8–10. *See also* culture, and
    moral values; special pleading
schlemiel, 46
Scholem, Gershom, 87
Schubert, Irwin (fictional character),
    63

Schulberg, Budd: *What Makes
    Sammy Run?*, 30–1
Schwartz, Harvey (fictional charac-
    ter), 20, 43–4, 45, 136–7
Scott, Luke (fictional character),
    168
Second Mrs P. (fictional character),
    37, 45–6
Segal, J.I., 134
Seiler, Robert M., 199n3
self-actualization, 105–6, 112
self-defence and resistance, 53–4,
    55, 56, 196n6
self-righteousness, 43, 55, 127
Seligson, Eli (fictional character), 45
sexism. *See* women and feminism
"Sexual Harassment" (Richler),
    107–8
Shach, Elazar Menachem, 196n4
Shapiro, Esther (fictional character),
    114
Shapiro, James, 200n9
Shapiro, Joshua (fictional character):
    Canadian literary taste and,
    139–40; on culture and moral
    integrity, 175; as family man,
    35; free indirect discourse and,
    148–9; gangsterism and disregard
    for the law, 60–1; as Hemingway
    hero, 104; homosexuality and,
    113; liberal guilt and, 122–3,
    128; racism towards non-Jew,
    118
Shapiro, Pauline (fictional character),
    35, 112, 118
Shapiro, Reuben (fictional character),
    40–2, 43, 60–2
Shaw, Irwin: "The Girls in Their
    Summer Dresses," 108
Shelley, Percy Bysshe, 179
Sheps, G. David, 12, 162, 176–7,
    196n1

Shklar, Judith, 98, 99, 101, 126,
129, 145, 184
Singer, Isaac Bashevis (I.B.), 93;
The Family Moskat, 93; *The
Golem*, 18; *Satan in Goray*, 93;
The Sinful Messiah, 93
Singer, Israel Joshua (I.J.), 93;
The Brothers Ashkenazi, 93
Six Day War, 53
Snowe, Lucy (fictional character),
178–9
social change, 128–30
Solomon Gursky Was Here (Richler):
on abstract art, 166; Atwood on,
152; on Canada, 131, 136–7,
140–1, 152; controversy over,
20, 194n8; and culture and
moral integrity, 173–4; disillusionment with writers, 180;
extravagant tastes, 67; female
characters, 104, 112–13; Golem
myth and, 18; homosexuality
and, 113, 115; identification
with Old World Jewish culture
and values, 39; identification
with underdogs, 41; on Inuit,
79–80, 119–20, 144–6, 196n3;
on Israel, 58, 72–3, 91–2; Jewish
empowerment and triumphalism,
56–7, 58, 117–18; on Jewish
nouveau riche, 43–4, 45; Klein
and, 17; literary biography and,
170; on mediocrity, 164–5; messianic allusions, 79–80, 80–1,
87–9, 91, 95; moral vision undermined by satire, 10; on nihilism,
95; postmodern elements, 16;
Prose on, 7, 10; protagonist's
perception of hero figure, 57, 67,
70–1, 95, 190; on Quebec, 154;
racism against non-Jews, 119–20;
and resistance and self-defence,

53–4; retaliatory provocations
against anti-Semitism, 58;
Richler's insistence as fiction,
194n6. *See also specific
characters*
Son of a Smaller Hero (Richler): on
academia, 168; on Canada, 136;
controversy over, 4, 19–20, 33,
34; criticism of as anti-Semitic,
68; encounters with beauty, 162;
family loyalty and, 32–3, 33–4;
gambling and, 63; gangsterism
and, 62; identification with Old
World Jewish culture and values,
37; on Israel, 71; on Jewish nouveau riche, 45; on Jewish success
validated by non-Jews, 44–5;
messianic allusions, 77–8, 95;
on nihilism, 95; racism towards
non-Jews, 117. *See also specific
characters*
Sontag, Susan, 201n5
Spacks, Patricia, 9, 102, 144
special pleading (political correctness): about, 8–9, 97–8, 128–30,
185–6; feminism and, 106–12;
hero figures and, 127; history of
political correctness, 98; homosexuality and, 113–16; liberal
guilt and, 120–8; race and, 116–
20; Richler's dislike for, 97–8, 99,
197n1, 198n12; satire and, 100–
2; social change and, 128–30;
static posture towards, 99
Spicehandler, Ziggy (fictional character), 65–6, 80
Steerforth, James (fictional character), 177–8, 201n7
Stein, Harry (fictional character),
35, 123–4, 125, 126
Stein, Mickey (fictional character),
169

Steiner, George, 90
stereotypes, 64–5, 66, 144, 184
The Street (Richler), 6, 116–17
"The Street" (Richler), 136
St Urbain's Horseman (Richler):
anti-Semitism and, 15, 69–70;
on Canada, 136, 140, 148; on
celebrity writers, 168; and culture and moral integrity, 172–3;
on Diaspora Jews, 54–5; disillusionment with literature, 180;
family loyalty and, 27, 34–5;
female characters, 102, 112; free
indirect discourse, 148; Golem
myth and, 18, 86; hero figure,
51–3, 103–4; heroic versus
ordinary values, 48; on
homosexuality, 115; on Israel, 31,
55, 90–1; Jewish empowerment
and, 51–3, 57; Jewish nouveau
riche and, 44; Jewish triumphalism and, 118; liberal guilt and,
122, 123–5, 126, 128; liberalism
and, 93–4, 95, 121; on mediocrity, 163–4; messianic allusions,
78–9, 86–7, 90–1, 196n1,
196n1; narrative unreliability,
151; protagonist as family man,
35; protagonist's perception
of hero figure, 51, 52, 79, 85,
86–7, 103, 173, 190; on Quebec,
154; and resistance and self-
defence, 53–4; special pleading
and, 101. *See also specific
characters*
Styron, William, 133
supererogation, 24–5, 43, 47, 58–9

Tallman, Warren, 4
target audience, 100
Tausky, Thomas E., 51
Taylor, Charles, 188

Teitelbaum, Clara (fictional charac-
ter), 66, 104
This Year in Jerusalem (Richler),
55–6, 71, 78
Toker, Leona, 100, 197n4
Torah, honour of blessing, 42
"tough Jewish novels," 53
Trilling, Lionel, 171, 201n5
Trudeau, Pierre, 135, 146
Twentyman (fictional character),
142
Tzvi, Shabtai, 84, 87, 93

Un certain sens du ridicule (Boréal
Press), 14
underdogs, identification with, 41
United Kingdom. *See* England
United States of America, 28–9, 75,
135, 149
unreliability, narrative, 151–2, 187
Uris, Leon: *Exodus*, 50, 55
Urmson, James O., 24–5, 47, 57

Van Toorn, Penny, 146
Villette (Brontë), 178–9
Voltaire, 134; *L'Ingénu*, 141
Voyage au bout de la nuit (Céline),
6, 193n2

Wachtel, Eleanor, 102, 106, 186
Wade, Beatrice (fictional character),
112–13
Wade, Shirley (fictional character),
109–10
Wassermann, Jakob, 92
Weintraub, William, 19, 102
Wertham, Frederic, 114
"Why I Write" (Richler), 161–2,
168
Wiesel, Elie, 85
Wiesenthal, Simon, 51
Wilde, Oscar, 134

Wilson, Angus, 201n7
Wimsatt, W.K., 193n1
Wiseman, Adele, 19, 77
Wisse, Ruth, 16, 30, 31, 46, 75, 92, 184
women and feminism: hero figures and, 103–5; Maslow's self-actualization and, 105–6, 112; Richler on, 106, 107–8, 111–12; Richler's female characters, 35–7, 102–3, 106, 109–10, 112–13, 186, 198n10; satire of, 106–7, 108–11
Woodcock, George, 4, 23, 107, 141; *Mordecai Richler*, 12

Woolf, Virginia, 108, 198n8
worth, individual, 127–8
Writers on World War II (Richler), 124
Wyman, Max, 181

Yanofsky, Joel, 19–20, 50, 107, 180
Yehoshua, A.B., 196n5
Yiddish, 55–6

Zangwill, Israel, 92
Zelig (film), 56–7
Zionism, 31, 54, 56, 71, 90
Zucker, Benny (fictional character), 169–70